The Power User's Manual

Over 1,000 Hints & Tips for the Macintosh

The Power User's Manual

Over 1,000 Hints & Tips for the Macintosh

Randal L Kottwitz

Kottwitz & Associates

MacUser Publications, Inc., New York, New York USA

25 West 39th Street, New York, NY 10018
Compiled and packaged by Felden Holdings, Ltd.

Printed and bound in the United States of America

Cover by Martin Dixon
Production supervision by Alan Jeffries
Graphic design and production by the author using Aldus PageMaker™ page makeup software on an Apple® Macintosh Plus™ computer and an Apple® LaserWriter™ printer

Final camera-ready copy produced on a Lintronic 300P typesetter
courtesy of MacTypeNet, Livonia, Michigan

Trademark information is located at the back of the book

Disclaimer

"The Power User's Manual" is an independently produced product of MacUser Publications, Inc. Every effort has been made to supply complete and accurate information. However, neither the author nor MacUser Publications, Inc. shall be liable for any liability, loss or damage caused or alleged to be caused directly or indirectly by this book.

This book is dedicated to my parents,
Harriette and Cecil, and to "The Associates" —
Steve, Jan, Bill, Sherry, Kerry, Rick,
Ame, Tom, Peter, Spyder, Su, et al.,
for their incredible trust and support.

CONTENTS

PREFACE

HOW THIS BOOK WAS MADE

I feel an incredible sense of power right now. As I write this page, all the other pages of this book have been printed out on *MacTypeNet's* Linotronic 300P and most of the pages are at the printer's plant, being made into plates for the presses. You'll understand my sense of power when you hear how this book came into existence: The February, 1986 cover of *MacUser* featured a mockup of a fictitious book called "The Power User's Manual" to introduce the new "Tip Sheet" section of the magazine. When we handed out that issue at a trade show in San Francisco, the response from readers was enthusiastic, to say the least. *MacUser's* Publisher, Felix Dennis, decided the book should become a reality and gave my company the contract to create it.

I entered all of the hints into *Microsoft File* with carefully chosen categories, subjects and titles so that I could sort the database into the final order of the book at any time. This gave me the added advantage of having duplicate or similar hints show up near one another after the database was sorted, regardless of the order in which I'd entered them. A simple report showing the category, subject and title helped a great deal in preventing duplicate entries before they occurred. Steve Birchall edited the majority of the manuscript while it was still in the database manager. It wasn't as easy to edit in *File* as it would have been in a word processor, but by editing at that stage, we made sure that the database was usable for future editions of the book without repeating the editing process. We've been very careful to keep track of any changes that have been made since the text left the database and will now go back and enter those changes so no errors will creep back into the copy.

After the editing was complete, I dumped out a text-only report containing the complete text of the book. I opened the report in *MacWrite* and did some preliminary formatting before I submitted the manuscript to *MacUser* for approval. I used *Tempo* to create macros that formatted each category, subject and title. As a result, my formatting was absolutely uniform—no spurious spaces or lines that were accidentally one point size too large or small. In the meantime, I started collecting icons in another *Microsoft File* database. After *MacUser* approved the manuscript, I did a little more formatting in *MacWrite* (mainly adding the italics I couldn't use in *File*) to get the copy ready to lay out. At last, it all came together in *PageMaker*. I used a *Switcher* set of *PageMaker* and *File* to transfer the icons for each 16-page section onto the pasteboard and then dragged the icons into the text as they were needed. There was still quite a bit of formatting to fine-tune in *PageMaker*. Again, *Tempo* came to the rescue to implement some of my standard tricks for expanding and compressing copy to make the pages more attractive. After proofing the layout on the LaserWriter output, I shipped the disks to *MacTypeNet* for output of the final art. We weren't pleased with the large icons as they came out of the Linotronic, so in a bit of deference to the manual graphic arts, we cut the smoothed icons out of the LaserWriter output and pasted them onto the Linotronic pages.

The manuscript has grown substantially from the original version. The database is 546K. In *MacWrite*, it grew to 575K. The final *PageMaker* layout is 1,651K. The work has also survived some extreme changes in environment. When I started the manuscript, I was working on a 512K Mac with a 400K external drive and an ImageWriter. *File* was upgraded in the middle of the process, as were *Switcher* and *PageMaker*. As I write this, I'm working on a Mac Plus that's acting as the Server system on an AppleTalk/*MacServe* network connected to two other Mac Pluses, a LaserWriter, a Peripheral Land 20 megabyte SCSI hard disk, and a MACBACK streaming tape backup. The transition to the new hardware and software caused a delay in the preparation of the manuscript, but generated a lot of new hints at the same time. Eventually, it sped the process enough to make up for the delay.

So there you have it—how to produce a book in a database manager and end up with camera-ready copy for the printers. As the author and graphic artist, I've had nearly total control of the project—thus, my sense of power. I hope you find the book useful. My electronic blood is on every page. After going through every step of the process, I have a lot of comments about the stress and responsibility that falls on the author in a complete desktop publishing environment. But, that's another book…

Randal L Kottwitz
July, 1986 – Merrimack, New Hampshire

ACKNOWLEDGMENTS

You hold in front of you the last five months of my life. However, there are a great many people who contributed to the finished product. I especially want to thank Dr. Steve Birchall, my editor and dear friend who managed to make my bleary-eyed hacking into readable English. Also, my thanks to Felix Dennis, my publisher, for his patience and support, to Steve Bobker for his help in gathering as many icons as we could, and to the staffs of both the US and UK versions of *MacUser*, for all their many kinds of help. Frank Lee at *MacTypeNet* deserves a halo for coming in at the last minute to typeset the final copy when we weren't satisfied with the LaserWriter output, and for his patience as I rushed disks off to him in Michigan. My clients and associates have also been very patient as their projects have been rescheduled and rearranged to allow for my completion of the manuscript and layout. Finally, to all of the people listed below who contributed material through letters to *MacUser*, conversations at trade shows, telephone calls, articles, E-Mail, and by many other means, my heartfelt thanks:

Caroline Arms, Paul Balyoz, Hazel Bennington, David Biedny, Nerys Breville, Dennis Brothers, Joshua Samuel Brown, Dawn R. Browning, Patrick Buckland, Bill Bunting, Andy Campbell, Simon Chamberlain, Jerry Chapman, Doug Clapp, Dan Cochran, Russ Coffman, David Nicholson Cole, John Conquest, Linda Custer, Marty Czachor, Jr., Brian Davis, Craig Dewey, John Dvorak, Mike Eisenstein, Chris Espinosa, Peter Favaro, Stephanie Ferm, Carl Firman, Peter Fleischhacker, Ame Choate Flynn, Tom Flynn, Daisy Genovese, Glenn Goodrich, Roy Hampshire, Liz Heaney, Andy Hertzfeld, John Hill, Dr. C. Hiller, Tracie Forman Hines, Bob Hines, Allison Hjul, Shelley Hoffman, Charlie Jackson, David Jackson, Peter Jackson, Dawn L. Johnson, Ellen Joseph, Andy Katz, Guy Kewney, Gregory King, Tom Kingsland, Gilbert Kohl, Bill Velle Koop, Bill Kubeck, Richard Kutner, Tykeia Leigh, Tony Lewis, Kevin Long, Melia Maldenado, Steve Maller, Jason Mart, Neville Maxwell, Tysin McDaniel, Robert McDowell, Ian McKinnell, Forrest Milkowski, Cliff Morrison, Roger Munford, Tammy Ng, Gregory O'Neill, Timothy Onosko, Joel S. Peskoff, Max Phillips, Mark Raymonds, Sarah Ritblatt, Amanda Roland, Don Rose, Maggie Runcorn, Phillip Russell, Jerry Sanders, Karen Schaejer, Joe Sharra, C. J. Sherwin, Arnie Slapin, Sam Solon, Anthony Taylor, David Teitelbaum, Darren Tomerfield, Larry Tompkins, Peter Trinder, George Tseng, Tony Tyler, Bill Wagstaff, S. Wathanasin, Spyder Webb, Jack Weber, Mike Wesley, Caesrae West, Max Whitby, Theodore H. Xaviera, and Larry D. York

I'd like to give special credit to all of the user group newsletters published in the Mac community. They, more than any other medium, have been responsible for disseminating quickly the kind of valuable information you'll find in this book. Many of them were very generous in supplying their back issues for my research. Keep up the good work!

In the process of assembling this book, I've learned that there is no such thing as an original hint. I was thoroughly convinced after reading the tenth version of how to do almost anything in *MacPaint*. So, for every hint you read here that you thought was your original idea, thanks! I probably got it from the next person you told it to. And so it goes…

Randal L Kottwitz
July, 1986
Merrimack, New Hampshire

INTRODUCTION

HIDDEN GEMS

When Apple introduced the Macintosh, one of the first applications we had to run on our new friendly machines was Bill Atkinson's *MacPaint*. Bill filled *MacPaint* with all sorts of hidden features that were activated by various special key and mouse combinations. I watched Bill play with his program at the Mac's first public showing at the Boston Computer Society. He did some amazing things! A couple of months later a 128K Mac took its "small" footprint on my desk and I brought out *MacPaint* to do my own amazing things. But—how did he do that again? Well, let's look in the manual—yeah—all 32 pages of it. Sure, it told me how to do all the things I already remembered how to do, but not how to recreate those amazing things Bill did in Boston.

It was inevitable. Almost from the beginning, magazines, newsletters and user group meetings were filled with little gems on how to uncover the features the *MacPaint* manual didn't address. Soon, there was *Multiplan*, and some of us wanted to know how to change the fonts to get more columns on the printed page. I think I read at least three different solutions to that problem before I found one that worked. There were silly ones, too. I remember my delight the day I found out how to get bold italic sheep in Geneva with OPTION-~. I've still not found a use for bold italic sheep, but when you had to deal with all the limitations of the 128K Mac, it felt good to know you could at least get cute animals on the screen by just typing—and print them out, too!

Many developers in the Mac market have followed *MacPaint's* lead and introduced powerful programs with minimal documentation. It's a good philosophy, this idea of intuitive programs that need no documentation, but I've yet to find a program that can't profit from a little explanation, and most need more than a little! That's what this book is all about.

Many of the hints I've read in the magazines and newsletters are insufficiently explained or are just plain wrong. In some cases, the hint will work, but for reasons other than those given in the printed explanation. What I've attempted to accomplish in this book is to gather all of the hints together in one place, organized for easy reference, and written in plain English. When possible, I've tested each of the hints to make sure it works. Also when possible, I've included a clear and complete explanation of why it works in order to eliminate some of the wives' tales that have sprung up around the Mac.

The more you know about how your Mac and its software work, the more efficient you'll be in operating it and the more you'll try to do with it. The Mac is still a relatively young computer, and these hints will help you explore dialog boxes your mouse has never clicked before.

HOW TO USE THIS BOOK

This book is designed for you to keep next to your Mac and use as a reference manual on a daily basis. General material that applies to almost every reader is at the front of the book in the sections called "General Information," "The Finder," and "Macintosh;" immediately followed by the section for Macintosh Plus and upgrade owners. The rest of the book is in alphabetical order by major category. (Most categories refer to specific software or hardware.)

If this is your first time reading the book, read through the general sections at the beginning first, and then through the sections for the specific software and hardware that you own. If you have time, read the sections for software that is similar to what you own. For example, you may find a hint under *Microsoft File* that will trigger a new idea about how you might use *OverVUE*. After you've read all of the information that applies to your situation once, I've provided a couple of tools to help you find it again. The Table of Contents gives the starting page number for each major category. The Major Category Index in the back is in the same order as the book, but will be more convenient than paging through the book if you want to scan a large number of hint titles. The Subject Index is arranged by the subheadings used in the book to subdivide the major categories.

For example, suppose you want to find a hint you've read concerning the number of fonts in *MacDraw* and you can't remember if it was in the "MacDraw" or the more general "Fonts" section. There are three different ways you could find the hint. You could scan both the "MacDraw" and "Fonts" sections of the text until you found it. Or, you could go to the Major Category Index in the back of the book and scan the MacDraw and Fonts sections of the index until you find the title of the hint you want. Or, you could look in the Subject Index under Fonts and find that there's a hint in the MacDraw category that specifically refers to fonts. The last is actually the most efficient, but any of the methods will work. It sounds more confusing than it is, and you'll find the organization is intuitive after you've utilized it a couple of times.

I hope this book saves you some valuable time. It's nearly inevitable that there will be future editions as the Mac changes and new software comes to market. In the meantime, check the "Tip Sheet" section every month in *MacUser* for the latest hints and tips. If you discover a new hint that's not in the book, send it to me care of MacUser Publications, Inc., 25 West 39th Street, New York, NY 10018. It may get published in the monthly "Tip Sheet," and I'll include it in the next edition of this book. If I do, your name will appear in the acknowledgments. Happy hinting!

General Information

BACKUPS

Protect Your Time Investment

If you're the type of person who doesn't backup your files because you're worried about the disk expense, be sure to weigh the value of your time invested in creating your files. Even if you paid yourself minimum wage, the time you would need to re-create your files probably would cost you more than the extra backup diskettes. At 400K or 800K, a data disk can hold a lot of archive backup files and one of those could save you thousands of dollars in time investment when you need the information again. Don't forget the option of using an old spreadsheet, layout, graphic, letter, etc. as a jumping off point for a new project. The hours your old backups save may be your own.

BAD DISKS

Forcing Disk To Eject

In dire cases, eject a disk by pushing a straightened paper clip into the small hole just to the right of the disk drive slot. This doesn't work very well (if at all) on the newer 800K disk drives.

Try Reinserting A Rejected Noisy Disk

Sometimes, the disk inside the hard plastic case doesn't get aligned properly when you insert it in the drive. When this happens, you'll hear the disk brushing against the sides of the plastic case as it spins and the Mac may reject it as a bad disk. If this happens and you hear the disk scraping against the shell, eject it immediately and try reinserting it, even if the Mac has accepted the disk. If you don't have immediate problems with such a disk, some are likely to develop as you try to use it further and you may risk losing some data.

BOOTING

Disk Won't Boot, But Doesn't Bomb

If your disk doesn't show a Bomb icon, but gets ejected, it isn't damaged. It only lacks a *System* file.

Fooling the Disk Drive

If your 400K disk drive won't accept a badly damaged disk for erasure or re-initialization, you can fool it into thinking it is reading a blank disk. First, use the *Finder* to eject any disks in the drives. Then look carefully at the right-hand side of the disk drive slot, where you'll find a small black lug next to a metal pin. Carefully press this down and the Mac thinks you just inserted a blank disk. A dialog box asks if you want to initialize it. Insert the bad disk into the slot and click the Initialize box. Needless to say, all files on the disk will be lost — but this is only a way to reclaim the disk, not the data. If you are using 800K drives and *Finder 5.0* or later, you can make the Mac accept the disk for reinitialization by holding down COMMAND-SHIFT-TAB when you insert it.

Jammed Programmer's Switch

Are you getting a "Sad Mac" icon at startup time, and don't know why? Look for the error code `0F000D`, with the "Grumpy Mac." If you have installed the Programmer's Switch, this error message usually indicates that the switch is jammed, or in the wrong slots.

Missing *System* File

When the "Sad Mac" icon, with the code `0F0064` appears on the screen when you startup the Mac, it means the *System* file is missing. You may have inserted a data disk first, instead of an application disk. If you want to use this particular disk as a startup disk, just put a *System* folder on it. If you think the disk you inserted was a startup disk, you may have to replace the *System* file.

Programmers' Switch Doesn't Clear All Memory

Don't use the Programmers' Switch on the side of the Mac to reset the system, because it deliberately doesn't clear all memory and invoke the ROM's self-diagnostic procedure. The only way to start with a completely clean slate is to turn off the power for a few seconds, then switch the Mac back on. The Shut Down option on the Special menu does almost the same thing, but without actually turning the power off. However, some applications leave certain bookkeeping information in RAM and Shut Down won't clear this data.

Reconstructing A Bombed Disk

If your disk Bombs when inserted, you might be able to get around this by holding down the COMMAND and OPTION keys while the Mac tries to boot the disk. The Mac will reconstruct the disk's desktop file and if that was your only problem, the disk should be fine. Only use this procedure in emergencies, since you'll lose folder titles and window sizes—though not folder contents.

Repairing A Bombed Disk

If your startup disk bombs, insert another startup disk and wait until the Mac finishes constructing the desktop. Eject the second disk and reinsert the damaged one. If the data hasn't been totally fried, the Mac should ask if you want it to repair the disk.

Second Drive Won't Always Boot

Some disks, especially games and other commercially produced software, can only boot from the internal drive. So, don't get too upset if the machine claims that a heavily copy-protected disk in the external drive is "unreadable." Try it in the internal drive before tearing your hair out.

CLIPBOARD

Clipboard Undo

The Clipboard holds only one item of information at a time. When you CUT or COPY something new, it replaces the Clipboard contents. Sometimes the former contents of the Clipboard are gone forever. However, in many applications, choosing UNDO (COMMAND-Z) will not only take the new selection off the Clipboard, but replace its former contents, as well.

The Clipboard Can Be As Large As Remaining Memory

The only limitation on the size of the Clipboard is that it must be able to fit in the available memory. If the application program you're using needs some of the memory being occupied by the Clipboard, it will save it to one of your disks (which one varies according to the application, although most store it on the startup disk). The application you're using usually warns you if the information you're trying to cut or copy is too large for the Clipboard. If it doesn't, the Mac will beep to let you know that it can't do the operation you're requesting.

You Can Append To the Clipboard In Some Applications

When the first developer's guidelines for the Mac were released by Apple, they included no provision for a program that wanted to be able to add to the current contents of the Clipboard instead of replacing them. However, a new edition of the guidelines has gone out and it includes an "append" function for the Clipboard. The guidelines state that SHIFT-COPY, or SHIFT-COMMAND-C should let the user add the current selection to the end of the current Clipboard contents.

This does not mean that most programmers have chosen to implement this feature. It definitely is not available in *MacPaint 1.5, MacWrite 4.5*, or *MacDraw 1.7*. The only current Mac application we know of that uses this feature is *Laserbase 1.2*.

Unfortunately, SHIFT-COPY is only likely to work in new and upgraded versions of existing packages, and in completely new packages coming to the market. The only way to find out if the software you have bought supports this feature is to try it with some unimportant data. If it's a feature you want to see implemented in a future version of one of your favorite applications, write to the publishers and let them know your opinion!

COMMAND KEYS

Eject A Disk At Any Time

To eject a disk from the internal drive, press COMMAND-SHIFT-1. To eject from the external drive, press COMMAND-SHIFT-2.

Eject Both Disks Quickly

You can use SHIFT-COMMAND-E to eject the diskettes in both floppy drives. This command is supported by the *Finder* and by some applications. Notably, Microsoft applications do not support it.

MacPaint Screen Dump

COMMAND, SHIFT and 3, pressed together, take a *MacPaint* "picture" of what's currently on the screen, if the disk has enough space to store it. If not, a beep lets you know it can't be done. You can take as many as ten "pictures" after system startup (within the limits of disk space). *MacPaint* stores the files on the disk and names them sequentially from "Screen 0" to "Screen 9." Later, you can use *MacPaint* to customize these graphics for your own use.

Mouse Button Will Delay Screen Dumps

If you hold down the mouse button when you press the command key sequence for screen or printer dumps, the dump will delay until you release the mouse button. This can be especially handy if you want to freeze some action on the screen for your dump and you have to catch the action "on the fly" without pausing your application.

Printer Dump of Active Window

Dump an image of the active window to the ImageWriter by pressing COMMAND, SHIFT and 4.

Printer Dump of Whole Screen

Dump the entire Mac screen to the ImageWriter, menu bar and all, by pressing COMMAND, SHIFT, CAPS LOCK, and 4.

Undo

If you inadvertently cut or backspace over important information, remember that COMMAND-Z (UNDO on the EDIT menu) usually restores the last action taken, up to the last mouse click.

CONSORTIUM SOFTWARE

Get University Consortium Software from Kinko Graphics

You can get some of the software developed by the Apple University Consortium schools through Kinko Graphics shops in some college towns. If there's not a Kinko Graphics shop near you, you can order the software by mail or via a toll-free number (800-235-6919) or in California 800-292-6640. Call them for more details on the software that's available. Some of it is quite amazing.

COPYING

Transferring Tabular Data From Database Managers or Spreadsheets

Many applications store their data as tables. Most database managers and spreadsheets store their data with Tab characters between the fields or cells, and Return characters between records. Many others offer you the option of storing their data in that format so you can transfer data to other programs. When you transfer tabular data into another type of application, such as a word processor, the columns won't appear until you set the Tab stops (moving the Tab pointers on the ruler in *MacWrite*). You may have to make some changes to your margins, fonts, and text sizes to get the data to appear exactly in the columnar format you desire. This also helps when transferring data from one database manager to another. Just set up the fields with the same names and in the same order and send it to the new database manager.

Transferring Text Files Into Database Managers or Spreadsheets

To transfer tables from text files into most database managers and spreadsheets, you must use a Tab character to separate each column, and a Return character to separate each line of the text file's table. Each column will become a successive field or cell, and each line of the table will become a database record

Suggestions For Custom COMMAND Keys (Macros)

Now that a number of programs that allow you to add COMMAND key sequences to any menu option are on the market, here's a list of suggested shortcuts for some of the Mac's more popular applications:

APPLICATION	MENU	COMMAND	MACRO	REMARKS
MacWrite	File	P	Print	Disable P for Plain text
MacWrite	File	Q	Quit	
MacWrite	Format	H	Show/Hide Rulers	
MacWrite	Style	1,2,3, etc.	Font sizes	
MacPaint	File	Q	Quit	
Finder	Edit	K	Show Clipboard	K for Klip — get it?
Finder	Special	T	Clean Up	Change menu to "Tidy Up"
Finder	Special	W	Erase Disk	Change menu to "Wipe Disk"
Finder	Special	G	Shut Down	Change menu to "Goodbye"

or a spreadsheet row. Some applications (such as stock quotes downloaded from Dow Jones via *Straight Talk*) use hard spaces instead of Tab characters to separate the columns. You'll have to replace each group of spaces with a Tab character. In most word processors, you can use the search and replace function to simplify this process. (See "Search and Replace Tabs Using Note Pad" for information on how to use Tab characters in the Find and Change dialog boxes of *MacWrite*.)

CUT & PASTE

Use Cut Command, Not BACKSPACE

If you want to cut part of a document to reposition it elsewhere, make sure to use the CUT command (EDIT menu or COMMAND-X) once you've highlighted what you want to move. Pressing the backspace, instead, loses the information permanently if you don't UNDO immediately. When you edit with the CUT command, the data remains on the Clipboard until you cut something else. To avoid losing any work, paste the cut data where you'll want it to be immediately after cutting it.

DEFAULT DISK

Choose Default Disk For Storage of Screen Snapshots

When you take a *MacPaint* snapshot of a Mac screen with SHIFT-COMMAND-3, it is stored on the current default system disk. If you want to redirect your screen shots to a different disk or volume, use a disk utility desk accessory (like *DiskInfo* or *DiskTools*) to make your desired destination disk the default disk before you take your snapshots.

DELETING FILES

Confidential Data

Deleting a file is easy — just toss it in the trashcan, right? No! The problem is that the actual data is still on the disk. What the Mac does is to change the file's block markers so the disk drive can re-use that portion of the disk again. The Erase Disk option will do a better job as it writes zeros on the entire surface of the disk and then creates a new directory. Some other utilities are available (like *TheCleaners* from Bear River Associates) which will remove confidential data and all references to it on the disk. But, short of incineration, the only sure way to get rid of a file completely is to use the most powerful bulk eraser you can find (copy the files you want to keep onto another disk first!). Even after using any of those three methods, law enforcement labs have the means to read the faint traces of magnetism remaining. They can determine the particular disk drives used on that disk because of the magnetic signature each head leaves on the disk—that's how Nixon got caught on the Watergate tapes.

When Your Disk Is Full, Use Save As... To Replace Old Files

When you're working within an application, and try to save a document, but get a disk full message, the easiest solution is to use another storage disk. Also, you can use one of the desk accessories that can delete files to make space for your document. But what do you do if you're out of disks and/or don't have that desk accessory? Simply use the Save As... option from the File menu and use the name of an old file that you don't need anymore. When the Mac asks you if it should replace the existing file of that name, click the Yes button. If your new file isn't substantially larger than the one you're replacing, this should allow you to save your new work.

DIALOG BOXES

Use TAB Key To Move from Field to Field

You can keep your hands on the keyboard and move from field to field in all Macintosh dialog boxes. Simply hit the TAB key to move to the next field. For example, in the Page Range boxes of a print dialog box, you can enter the beginning page number in the first box and then hit TAB to move the insertion point to the ending page number box.

DISK CONFIGURATION

Some Applications Require Printing Resource On Their Disks

Remember that some applications (including *MacDraw*) require that a copy of the printing resource (a file in the *System* folder with the same name as your printer, such as ImageWriter or LaserWriter) be on the same disk as the application. This is especially important when configuring a two-disk combination for use with *Switcher*.

DISK MENU

Express Alphabetic Scrolling

When scrolling through a list of files in the "Open" dialog box from within an application, press the first letter or two of the file's name to "express" straight to the section you want.

Delay Until Repeat Determines Fast Search Criteria on Mac Plus

If you use the fast search to jump to a specific place on a disk menu (see Express Alphabetic Scrolling), and get strange results, the reason could be that the Delay Until Repeat setting doesn't fit your typing speed. On the Control Panel in *Finder 5.0* and later, the Delay Until Repeat setting not only determines how long you must hold a key down to make it repeat, but also determines how long you can pause between characters when jumping around in a disk menu. When you type in the first two letters of a file name and pause too long between keystrokes, the Mac will find the first one, then assume that the second letter is for a new search. For example, if you type in "UR" it should jump to the first file starting with those two letters. But, if you type too slowly, it will jump to the first file beginning with letter U, then jump to the first file starting with R. If this becomes an inconvenience, just change the setting on the Control Panel.

Double-Click As "Open" Button Alternative

When you've found the file you want in the "Open" dialog box from within an application, just double-click on its name to open the file.

RETURN and ENTER Keys As "Open" Button Alternative

When you've highlighted the file you want in the "Open" dialog box from within an application, you don't have to mouse over to the OPEN button. Just press RETURN or ENTER to open the file.

Save Files with Numbers Before Their Names for Quick Selection

The shortcut method of jumping to a filename in a disk menu by typing the first few letters of its name is handy–especially in MFS. But, when you have a lot of files with similar names in your disk or folder, it becomes less useful because you have to type quite a few letters of a file's name to get to the exact one you want. If you're careful to remember your system, you can speed this process by placing a number in front of each of your filenames. The menu will sort the numbers before the alphabetic filenames and you can simply hit one or two number keys to speed to the file you want.

Type A Few Characters Of A Folder's Name To Find It

The express scrolling technique (used to find files in the disk menu) works with HFS to find and open Folders through several levels of nesting, too. If you have a file nested inside several folders, you can shuffle through them quickly by typing enough of the outermost folder's name for it to appear highlighted, hitting RETURN, typing enough of the next folder's name, and so on until your file's name is highlighted. Hit RETURN again and your file will open.

Use A One or Two Letter Code To Designate Subdirectories

With the MFS (as opposed to HFS) filing system, the scroll window in the disk directory window can be made to scroll to a file beginning with the letter or two you type from the keyboard. (See "Express Alphabetic Scrolling"). You can use this feature to create subdirectories, storing all your files that pertain to a particular topic under names that begin with the same one or two letter code. For example, if you were a consultant working for a number of clients, including *MacUser* Magazine, and stored files for several clients on one disk, you could use MU at the beginning of each file that pertains to MacUser and have all of those files located in one section of the disk directory, accessible by hitting MU on the keyboard when the disk menu comes up.

Use TAB Key As Drive Button Alternative On A Mac Plus

When you are in the disk menu of an application on the Mac Plus, you can hit the TAB key instead of clicking on the button for the disk drive.

DISKETTES

Don't Leave Disks In Your Drives With the Power Off

Most likely, leaving a disk in your drive when your Mac is turned off won't hurt the disk. However, when you leave a disk in the drive, the read/write head is directly over the disk, ready to go. A small burst of static electricity through it could accidentally erase a small amount of information on the disk. While the damaged area might be tiny in terms of actual number of bits erased, the missing data could disable a whole program.

Apple's technicians have calculated the odds on this happening. A disk left in the drive has a 0.02% chance of being damaged. If the disk were removed, its chances of being damaged in the average disk storage environment are half that, or 0.01%. So, on the whole, removing all disks from the Mac when you shut it off is a safer practice.

Magnetic Fields

Keep all disks away from magnets. Information is stored magnetically, so exposure to a strong magnetic force will scramble data permanently.

Remove Plastic Hook from HP Diskettes Before Using with Mac

Hewlett-Packard diskettes have a little plastic hook on the surface of the case to hold the metal shutter back. This hook sometimes becomes lodged in a Mac's disk drive, preventing you from removing the diskette. If you want to use HP diskettes in your Mac, use a knife or other tool to remove the hook cleanly from them. If you succeed, they should work just fine.

Use View by Name To Create Disk Labels

You can use the Mac's built-in printer dump facilities to make disk labels from your desktop. First, open the window for the disk you want to label. Then, choose By Name from the View menu to display the filenames. Now, use the size box to shrink the window to the approximate size of a disk label. Type COMMAND-SHIFT-CAPS LOCK-4 to dump the window to your printer. You can print out on regular paper and use tape to attach the labels, or you can print out on a page size label (available at most stationery stores) and simply trim the edges. If you want, you can use COMMAND-SHIFT-3 to create a *MacPaint* document from your desktop and further edit or enhance your labels in *MacPaint* before printing.

Write Protect Switch Sometimes Doesn't

The write-protect tab on Mac diskettes is not completely fail-safe. The tab is not a mechanical lock that prevents saving data to that disk, but is just a slot for a sensing finger to fall into, thus tripping a switch. The Mac always checks to see if the switch is on or off before writing onto that disk. But, if you have a bug-ridden application, font, or desk accessory, and it crashes, it could, on rare occasions, bypass the tab's setting and write all kinds of random garbage as it goes down. Public domain, homebrew, and pre-release software are particularly susceptible to this problem.

You Can Use Rubber Cement Thinner To Remove Label Adhesive

If you change labels on your disks fairly frequently, you'll often see a build-up of the sticky residue left over from the old labels. The easiest way to remove it is by dabbing it with a little rubber cement thinner on a Q-tip. This cleans the disk without damaging its plastic casing. Just be very careful not to get any thinner in any of the openings. If you do, it will destroy the disk. If it contains valuable data, be sure to back it up before you use this technique–just to be sure.

FILE CONVERSION

Converting Databases That Don't Use Tabs As Field Delineators

Most Macintosh Database Managers use Tab characters to delineate the fields, and Return characters at the end of each record. However, database managers on other machines (such as *DataStar* on the IBM-PC) often use special characters for this function. Converting their files for use on the Mac is difficult, even after getting them into the Mac with *PC-To-Mac-And-Back*, or a similar utility.

A few file conversion programs (like *1st Port*) are available to do the job for you. However, you can do it without such a utility. First, transfer your database from the alien computer into the Mac as a text file using the appropriate utility. Then, open the file with *MacWrite* and change all the field separation characters to Tabs and all the end-of-record characters to Returns

FILE FLAGS

Definitions of File Flags

You can use *Fedit* or a similar utility to look at the files on your disk and the status of their file flags. The definitions of the various file flags are as follows:

Protected	This file can't be duplicated by the *Finder* or be moved to another disk, folder, or to the trash.
Locked	You can't use the *Finder* to trash, replace or rename this file.
Invisible	The icon for this file is not displayed on the desktop.
Bundle	This file contains all the data the *Finder* needs to display a file's icons and make all of the necessary cross-references between an application and its documents and resources.
System	If this flag is used, the file is a *System* file.
Bozo	This flag is left over from an old copy protection system that's ignored by recent *Finders*.
Busy	The file is open on your Mac or on one of the systems on your network.
Changed	Usually only active with a Busy file, this means that the file has been changed since it was last saved. Be sure to save it before quitting the application or closing the file.
Inited	The icon for this file has been assigned a position on the desktop.

or Enters. Then, open up the Mac database of your choice, and create an entry form that suits the data. Re-open the *MacWrite* file, copy a lump of data into the Clipboard, re-open the database, and paste. If your Tabs and Returns are in the right places, your data should go automatically into the right places in the Mac database's entry forms—allowing you to analyze data in the usual way.

GRAPHICS

Poor Man's Tracing Stylus

You can make your mouse into a poor man's tracing stylus by wedging a section of a toothpick into one of the grooves in the cable connector on the mouse. Simply wedge it into one of the spaces so that the point of the toothpick is just a little off the surface of the desktop. Then, turn on the freehand drawing tool in your graphics program and use the point of the toothpick to trace the image you want to transfer to your screen.

Save Money On Electronic Clip Art

You don't have to spend a lot of money on disks of electronic clip art. There are many public domain printed clip art books available in book stores and through the mail. Dover Books is an especially good source. You can transfer the printed clip art onto your own disks by digitizing it or tracing it with the mouse or a graphics tablet.

HARD DISKS

Dummy Files Can Buffer *System* File Spread

To avoid having the Mac spread your *System* file all over the hard disk as you add and delete fonts and desk accessories, create some small dummy files or a dummy volume right after you first create your *System* file. Give them names that show the order of their creation (Dummy #1, Dummy #2, etc.). Then, when you want to make modifications to the *System*, delete some of your dummy files (in the same order you created them) or the dummy volume to make room for the modifications. This technique will keep your *System* file in a contiguous section of your hard disk and keep your Mac running at optimum speed.

Hard Disk's *System* File Will Spread Out If You Modify It A Lot

If you frequently modify the *System* file on your hard disk drive, it can get spread all over the disk, linked by many pointers, so the Mac can retrieve all the pieces. When this situation gets out of hand, your operations will slow down and you're tempting fate for a crash. If you think this might be the case, back up your whole hard disk to floppies and reinitialize it. Now, restore your files one by one, *System* files and applications first. This will solve the problem with your *System* file and will "de-fragment" all the rest of the files on your disk, too. Simply restoring your hard disk from a streaming tape backup won't solve this problem, as the tape will simply restore the *System* files in their fragmented form.

Use Extension Cable and Sound Shield Noisy Disks

If your hard disk makes enough noise to bother you when it's running, get an extension cable and move it further away from you or behind something that will help block the noise. If you have an older hard disk, you can use a joystick extension cable from Radio Shack. If you have a SCSI hard disk, your extension cable won't be that simple to find, nor will it be inexpensive. You could also try putting your hard disk inside a sound absorbing cabinet intended for a printer.

Use Shut Down Option Before Powering Off Hard Disks

If you use the Shut Down option from the Special menu before you power off your hard disk, your startup time will be substantially shorter the next time you start up from the hard disk.

MEMORY SPACE

Shrinking the Clipboard

Are you about to run out of memory in an application? Reduce the size of the Clipboard to minimum by copying a single character into it by selecting the character and cutting or copying. Do this procedure twice to ensure that you have removed the original Clipboard contents.

MENUS

Ellipsis After A Menu Entry Means There's More

The Mac's menus tell you whether it will execute a selected action immediately, or if selecting it leads to another dialog box before the Mac will act. An ellipsis (…) after a menu item means that it leads to a dialog box before executing any action. For example,"Save As…" leads you to a dialog box to enter a filename before saving whereas Save executes directly with no dialog box (unless it's a new file that needs a title before the Mac can save it for the first time).

Use *Resource Editor* To Customize Menus & COMMAND Keys

You can use the *Resource Editor* to add or change COMMAND key equivalents for any menu item in most Macintosh applications. After you've opened the application with the *Resource Editor*, find the MENU resource and open it. There, you'll see each of the menu items, listed by their MENU ID numbers. You'll probably have to open several before you find the item you want to work with. Once you find it and have its window open on the desktop, you'll see a field labeled "keyBoard equiv." If a COMMAND key equivalent for the item already exists, you'll see a character in the box. If not, it will be blank. Simply add a new character, or change the one in the box (remember that capitalization makes a difference), and close all of the windows. When the *Resource Editor* asks if you want to save your changes, click the Yes button. WARNING: Be sure you don't enter a COMMAND key equivalent that's already used by another menu item. The results when you run your application are quite unpredictable. Always be sure that you're working on a backup disk to avoid serious problems and loss of data or applications.

MIMEOGRAPH

Use Geneva 10-pt. with Tall Adjusted for Mimeo Masters

The combination of the Mac and the ImageWriter makes a great tool for creating mimeograph masters. The Geneva font will make the clearest stencil, but the 10-pt. size will break down on the stencil and the 12-pt. size will not allow you to get very much text on the page. However, if you print out a Geneva 10-pt. document using the Tall Adjusted option in the Page Setup dialog box, the Mac will add just enough space between the letters when it prints out to keep the characters from breaking down on the stencil.

Use the Mac To Make Clearer Mimeograph Stencils

The Mac and the ImageWriter work together to make great mimeograph stencils. In fact, you can do a better job of including halftones on the ImageWriter than you can on expensive stencil cutting machinery. You can digitize photos with a digitizer and then screen them with *MacPaint* before cutting your stencil. When your document is complete, remove the ribbon from your ImageWriter and set the paper thickness to four sheets. You may want to experiment with screening your digitized images with different patterns to get the effect you want on the final mimeo output.

NAMES

Don't Use A Colon In A Filename

The Mac won't let you use a colon in any filename. The reason is that the system uses a colon in the way it remembers where a file is located. For example, if you save a file named "Profits" on a disk named "Multiplan Work," the Mac actually stores the file under the name "Multiplan Work: Profits" so it remembers not only the name of the file, but where it's stored as well. If you try to use a colon in the filename, it will cause confusion.

File Names Similar To System Names

Don't name files with any words that the Mac might think are part of its operating system, like "Minifinder." It confuses the machine and often results in the file being permanently lost.

Keep Disk Names Distinct

Make sure your disks have different, meaningful names, and are clearly marked. That way you won't have to insert your entire disk collection when the Mac asks for a particular disk. Also take care to label the disk with exactly the same name as the one that appears on the desktop. If it's a data disk only, put the name of the application it relates to on the label, and in the comments box in the Get Info dialog.

Keep Document Titles Short

The Mac will allow you to create a document title of up to 63 characters. However, short names are much more convenient. Who wants to drag icons around with 63-character names hanging onto them? Bear in mind, too, that the disk menu displays only the first 20 characters. Abbrevs are grt!

OTHER COMPUTERS

Use ImageWriter Cable to Interface Radio Shack Model 100 with Mac 512

You can use an ImageWriter cable attached to the modem port on a Mac 512 (with the older port configuration) to interface your Mac and Radio Shack Model 100. First, attach the cable to the Mac's modem port and to the Model 100's RS-232 port. Make sure that the terminal program on each computer can support XON/XOFF protocol. The only special modification you'll have to make is on the Model 100. Use BASIC to `POKE 63066,255`. This adds linefeeds to the carriage returns on the Model 100 so the Mac can interpret the paragraph formatting correctly. To "undo" the `POKE`, just reboot the Model 100 when you're finished with the transfer.

PARAMETER RAM

How To Reset

The Mac's battery maintains 20 bytes of RAM, called the "Parameter RAM" in an EEPROM (Electrically Erasable Programmable ROM). This data set remains intact even with the Mac's plug pulled out, but if the battery goes dead, or if you disconnect it, then the Parameter RAM is lost. Then you have to go back, open the Control Panel, and reset all its items. Some peripherals (such as the early versions of ThunderScan) clobber this data accidentally because of the way they use the ports. Certain processes in assembly language will wipe out the Parameter RAM too. If that happens, turn the Mac off, disconnect the battery for about 30 seconds. Reconnect the battery and turn the Mac back on, and use the Control Panel to reset the Parameter RAM (don't forget to reset the clock too). Parameter RAM maintains the following parameters in those 20 bytes:

Validity status
Mode-port configuration
Printer-port configuration
Alarm setting
Default application font
Auto-key threshold
Menu blink
Printer connection
Speaker volume
Double-click time
Caret-blink time
Mouse scaling
Preferred system start-up disk

PUBLICATIONS

Wheels for the Mind Subscription Info

Wheels for the Mind is a quarterly publication from Apple computer, aimed at Mac users in the Apple University Consortium. It contains a lot of good introductory information on using the Mac, many hints and tips for experienced users, and news of happenings in the Consortium Schools. The first year's subscription is $12.00. For more information, contact Beth Moore at Apple Computer, Inc., 10201 North DeAnza Blvd., MS23D, Cupertino, CA 95041. (408) 973-5040.

RECOVERING FILES

Try Loading Bad Files from Within Applications

If you can't get a data file to run from the desktop, don't panic (at least not immediately). First, start the application you used to create the data file. Then, close any current documents in the application, choose Open, and see if you can get the damaged file to load from the disk menu. If it will load, immediately save it under another name on another disk. If this won't work, it's time to get out *MacZap* or another disk fixing utility and see if you can fix the file with it.

SCROLLING

Clicking In the Gray Scroll Area Will Scroll One Screen

In most applications and in the *Finder*, you can scroll one screenful at a time by clicking in the gray area on either side of the scroll elevator. If the file doesn't have another screenful to show, the screen usually will scroll as far as it can. Notable exceptions to this are most database managers. Some of them don't recognize the click at all and others interpret it to mean scroll one record (or some other increment).

SELECTING

Double-Click, Then Drag To Select Text Word By Word

Normally, when you click and drag the cursor over text, the Mac selects text character by character horizontally, and line by line vertically. If you double-click (to select a word), hold down the mouse button after the second click, and then drag, the Mac selects text word by word horizontally, and line by line vertically.

Scrolling Doesn't Affect Selections

In the *Finder* and in most applications, you can use the scroll bars without affecting your current text, object, or icon selection. This is especially helpful if you have selected icons from several sections of a window and want to scroll around to find others for selection with SHIFT-CLICK or if you want to look over a large section of text you've selected in a word processor before you cut or copy it.

Selecting Large Blocks of Text

If you want to select a large part of your document, in most applications you don't have to spend time dragging the cursor across the text. Instead, click at one end of the text, then use the scroll bar to get to the other end of the section you want. Hold the SHIFT key down while clicking the mouse. The Mac instantly highlights all text between the two clicked points.

Selecting Whole Words

Double-click on a word to highlight it without having to drag the cursor all the way across it. Whatever you type in next will replace the highlighted word.

SHUTTING DOWN

Close All Applications and DAs Before Flipping Switch

In many cases, applications and desk accessories are designed to recover properly if you turn off the Mac's power switch without closing them. However, that may damage some applications and desk accessories permanently if you do so. To be safe, always make sure that you've closed all documents, applications, and desk accessories before you flip the switch.

Eject All Disks Before Flipping Power Switch

Never shut the Mac off without first ejecting all disks. This protects against accidentally damaging disk files.

STARTUP

Changing the Welcome Message

Many Mac users are probably aware that you can make your own startup screens for your Mac with a public domain program called *Screenmaker*. However, special startup screens can take as much as 20K of your valuable disk space. However, you can alter the

Possible Version Numbers for System Software

When you do an ASCII search on a system file with a disk editor, you can find the version number for the system software you're looking at. Open the *System* file with *Fedit* and do an ASCII Search from the Options menu. Look for the string "Version" and you should see which version of the system software you have. The possible versions are:

Versions 3.0, 3.1, 3.1.1b and 3.2	04-Jan-86 and later (Versions released with or shortly after the Mac Plus that support HFS)
Version 2.1	01-Sept-85 (Second major system update that came with *Finder 4.1*)
Version 2.0	08-Apr-84 (Released with *Finder 1.1g*)
Version 1.1	24-Apr-84 (Released with *Finder 1.0*)
Version .097	12-Jan-84 (Still occasionally found!)

"Welcome to Macintosh" message in the Mac's own startup screen without taking more disk space. Use a utility that allows you to alter hex/ASCII code on a disk, such as *Fedit*, *MacTools* or *ExamineFile*. In the middle of sector 6 on any disk containing a system file, you will find the words "Welcome to Macintosh." Write the message you want over the words. Your message can be no longer than "Welcome to Macintosh," but it can be shorter—just substitute space characters for the extra letters. Save the sector and the next time you boot the altered disk, your new message will appear in the startup screen.

SYSTEM

Modify Startup Disks To Make Other Systems Ignore Them

Normally, when you launch a new application on a startup disk which isn't the current startup disk, the Mac switches over to use the *System* software on the new application's disk. That has the effect of making the new disk the startup disk. You can modify the new application disk's *System* (with *ResEdit* or *Fedit*) so this switch doesn't occur. First use a disk utility to remove the invisible *MultiFinder* application. Then, use *ResEdit* or *Fedit* to make the *Finder* on the

Common System Error IDs

System errors cause a dialog box to appear on-screen with the words, "Sorry, a system error has occurred," next to the Burning Bomb icon. The two buttons in the dialog box are labelled Restart and Resume. Normally, the Resume button is dimmed and pressing Restart merely resets the system, losing all the data still in the machine, but not saved to disk at the time of the crash. The box always shows an error ID number to help software developers figure out what's wrong. Over 50 different ID numbers are in use, but the most common are:

- 2 Address error—This means that the program contains an error.
- 3 Illegal Instruction—This is another program error.
- 13 Uninstalled interrupt—You'll get this if you press the rear button of the programmer's switch without the correct software running.
- 25 Out of memory—"Good" programs should warn you well in advance to prevent this occurrence, but some don't — so, watch out for it.
- 26 Can't launch program—This means that the Mac can't find the program you wanted to run. (For example, if you've designated a startup application and thrown away the *Finder*, when you quit the application, the *System* will look for the *Finder*. If it's not there, you'll get an ID 26 error message.

application's disk invisible. Now, if you launch the application while running under another disk's system, the Mac won't switch to the new application's system.

System 3.1 Can Create MFS Disks Unreadable By Older Macs

Some users have reported problems when using disks created with a particular *Finder* and ROM combination on a different system. In particular, older Macs with 64K ROMs can't read some 400K MFS disks that have been initialized under *System* 3.1 on a machine with the 128K ROMS. Be very careful if you're going to swap diskettes among machines with a mixture of old and new ROMs.

SYSTEM CRASHES

What To Do With A Sad Mac

If you get a sad Mac on the screen, the Macintosh manual simply says "go and see your dealer." But, this is a drastic solution to what is usually a very simple problem. The only time you can get a sad Mac icon on-screen is immediately after you put a disk in after switching on the machine. Underneath the icon, you'll see a six-digit code, with some flickering pixels underneath. The code is intended to help the software or hardware manufacturer to locate the fault. If the six-digit code begins with the letters 0F, it means the *System* file has been damaged. The cure is to start up with a working disk and copy its *System* file over to the damaged disk. If the first pair of digits you get is not 0F, then your Macintosh may well be faulty and you should take it to your dealer immediately.

TEXT FILES

Saving Primary File Doesn't Update Text Only Copy

Remember that in most applications, when you save a "Text Only" copy of a file using Save As..., the file that remains active is the original formatted file, not the new text only copy. If you use Save to save the active file after making changes, the Mac updates only the formatted file on the disk, but the text only copy remains unchanged. To make sure that a text only copy of your file is the latest version, always update it immediately after saving the formatted file.

UPDATES

Be Careful Putting Updated *System* and *Finder* on Copy-Protected Disks

The best rule of thumb to use when deciding whether or not to update the *System* files and *Finder* on an older copy-protected application disk is "Don't." Copy protection tends to make disks rather fragile, so updating with a new *System* or *Finder* may render your application unusable. In the case of the game *Airborne!*, the game file is actually called "Finder." Updating the *Finder* on this disk will destroy the game. If you must try updating a copy-protected application, use a copy utility like *Copy II Mac* or *MacZap* to make a backup of the application and work on that disk. Then, work with the updated disk with unimportant data, trying most of the options (printing, sorting, etc.) before you work with any data you care whether you lose or not.

Make Sure You Always Use the Latest Printer Drivers

Apple is constantly working to improve the Mac's system software – the *System*, *Finder*, and the various printer drivers. Always make sure, when you update your *System* and *Finder*, that you check to make sure you have the latest versions of the printer drivers as well. *MacUser* publishes a list of the latest versions of most major software in each issue.

VERSION NUMBERS

Definition Of Version Number Arrangement

With the release of the Mac Plus, Apple started a new system to define the format of version numbers of its software. The format is N.NXM, where N.N is the intended release version number. X is a letter designation for the development level of the software: D means it's in development; A means it's an alpha test version; and B means it's a beta test version. The M is a number sub-designation for the X. For example, *Finder 5.1B17* was beta release 17 of *Finder 5.1*.

Where To Find A Program's Version Number

To find out which version of a program you're running, go the the Apple menu and select the

About... item. You'll then get a dialog box on-screen that will give you all the relevant details. Sometimes other relevant information such as the names of the programmers, address and phone number of the publisher, and/or help menus are also located in this box. Usually, the way to get rid of the box is by clicking anywhere outside its borders.

WINDOWS

Resizing Default Window Sizes with *ResEd*

You can use *ResEd* (version 1.0D5 or later) or any other resource editor to change the default sizes of the windows in any Mac application. Here is a method for making *MacWrite's* document, header and footer windows open to their maximum width on the screen if you frequently work with wide margins. First, open the WIND resource and you'll see *MacWrite's* four window resources. The document, header and footer windows are 301, 302 and 303, respectively. Open each one separately and change the "boundsRect." For the document window, change them to 38, –58, 337 and 550. For the header and footer windows, change the boundsRect figures to 45, –58, 205 and 550 in each. You may want to use other numbers—these will make the windows open so the 8-inch mark on the ruler is visible and you'll have to do some shifting and resizing to bring the scroll bar into view.

This technique will work on any other Mac application, but be sure you know what window you're changing or you could end up with some very strange displays.

Six Types of Windows And Their procIDs

The Mac uses six types of windows, each with a different "procID" number. You can change the procID of a window by opening an application's WIND resource and then opening the particular window's resource window. A standard document window (like you see in *MacWrite*) is procID Type 0. Type 1 is a dialog box with a double border. Types 2 and 3 are message boxes—Type 2 has a single line border and Type 3 has a drop shadow. Type 4 is a document window like Type 0, but without a resizing box in the lower right corner, and Type 16 is a window like the Apple *Calculator* desk accessory window.

WORKING SPEED

You Can Stay Several Key Strokes Ahead

The Macintosh keeps track of the keystrokes you make while it's off doing something, even though it may not indicate so on its screen. You can stay several key strokes ahead on dialog boxes IF YOU KNOW WHAT YOU'RE DOING! For instance, you can hit the ENTER key to select the highlighted button in a dialog box before the Mac can draw the box on the screen. The Mac remembers your choice and responds as soon as it's fininshed drawing the box. However, make sure you know what the next dialog is going to be before you try to respond to it in advance.

The Finder

ABORTING

Finder 5.1 Can Be Stopped with COMMAND-PERIOD

How many times have you mistakenly double-clicked an application that you didn't really want to launch? You had to wait for it to launch, quit and wait for the desktop to reappear. Luckily, *Finders 5.1* and later support an abort option that's already supported in many applications. If you want to stop what the *Finder* is doing (copying files, launching a program, etc.), hold down the COMMAND key and type a period (.). You may have to do it a couple of times to get the Mac's attention, but it should work.

APPLICATIONS

Application Can't Be Found To Open...

When you double-click on a data file's icon, the Mac first must Open the application you used to create that data file. It looks on all the available disks and/or volumes to find the application before Opening the data file. If the Mac can't find the necessary application on one of the disks, it will tell you that it can't find the application to Open the file. Sometimes (as with text only files), you may be able to Open the file from within an application even if double-clicking on the data file won't launch that application. To find out which applications will Open a data file, select its icon and Get Info from the File menu. The file's type should give you a clue as to what applications will Open the data file.

Trashing An Application

When deleting an application from the desktop, press the OPTION key while dragging the application's icon to the trashcan. This automatically trashes the application without confirming it through a dialog box.

BAD DISKS

Ejecting A Bad Disk

If the sad Mac face comes up, making it impossible to eject the disk from the *Finder*, reset the Mac while holding down the mouse button. (To reset, depress the front button on the programmer's switch on the left side of your Mac or, if you've not installed the programmers' switch, flip the Mac's power switch off and back on again.) The disk should pop right out of the internal drive.

Reconstructing the Desktop On A Damaged Disk

Once in a while, the *Finder* on a disk will get confused because of damage to a disk and will not boot. This doesn't mean the data on that disk is necessarily destroyed. Try booting the disk while holding down the COMMAND and OPTION keys. The Mac will attempt to reconstruct the desktop. (However, your folders will lose their names and become "Untitled #1, Untitled #2," etc.). If this technique doesn't work, you'll need to use a disk utility such as MacZap.

BUGS

Finders 5.1 & *5.2* Don't Close DAs or Send Goodbye Kiss

During a Shut Down, both *Finders 5.1* and *5.2* fail to Close desk accessories and don't send a Goodbye Kiss. This will cause accessories with open files to have serious problems. When using these *Finders*, be sure to Close all DAs before shutting down.

Losing Files With New Folder Command on an Ejected Disk

Finder version 4.1 contains a potentially dangerous bug: If you select New Folder on a disk that's already been ejected (but still has its image on the desktop), the folder appears in white. If you then return the disk to the drive, the other files turn from their dimmed image back to black and white, but the new folder becomes dimmed. If you move files to this new folder, they may get lost forever.

Trashing Icon of Disk Not Inserted May Crash System

Boot your Mac with a disk that has *Finder 4.1* on it. You can boot using either the internal or external drive. Insert any other formatted disk in the other drive (call that Disk B). Now, eject Disk B by pressing COMMAND-E or by selecting the eject command on the File menu. (Don't drag the disk icon into the trash can just yet.) Now, insert yet another disk (not the original Startup disk or Disk B) in the vacant drive. As soon as the drive starts to spin, immediately drag the icon of Disk B into the trash. Bang! ID=02. Needless to say, avoid this procedure!

COMMAND KEYS

Bringing A Buried Window To the Front

If you have a lot of windows open on your desktop, you may sometimes bury a window you want so deep that it seems impossible to find, no matter how much window shuffling you try. To bring the window you want back to the front and make it active, double-click on its hollow icon (disk or folder) on the desktop or in a window. The icon's window will jump immediately back to the front and become the active window.

COMMAND Turns On Clean Up Grid when Dragging

If you hold down the COMMAND key while you drag an icon with the mouse, the Clean Up grid will be turned on as long as you hold down the key. As you drag the icon, it will jump from grid position to grid position. If you normally keep your windows aligned with the Clean Up menu option, this is a quick way to keep your new changes neat. This technique works with *Finder 5.1* and later.

Express Window Closing

To close all of the open windows on the desktop, hold down the OPTION key and click on the Close button of any window. All of the open windows on the desktop will close at the same time. This technique works with *Finder 5.1* and later.

OPTION-Double Click Temporarily Opens Windows

If you hold down the OPTION key when you double-click on a disk or folder icon, the window for that icon will open, as usual. However, if you Open a document or application, the windows you Opened this way will be closed when you return to the desktop. This technique works with *Finder 5.1* and later.

COPYING FILES

Don't Copy Too Many "by Name" Files At A Time

Finder 4.1 has a tendency to crash if you try to copy too many files at a time by dragging them while displayed "by Name." Choose another View menu option or drag only a few files at a time.

Drag Folders & Documents, Not Disk Icon, onto Hard Disks

When you are copying a large number of files to your hard disk, select all of the files and drag them. Don't drag the disk icon onto the hard disk icon. When you drag the disk icon, the Mac copies the disk's directory along with the files, and the extra directory may cause some problems.

Drag the Icon

To copy a file onto another disk, just drag the file icon over to the recipient disk. This retains the old file name, and avoids new file names like "Copy of (old filename)." For a group of files, just select them while holding down the SHIFT key, and move the entire group to the other disk.

Put Multiple Files In Single Folder To Speed Copying

If you want to copy a group of documents from one disk to another, you can speed the process by placing all the files you want to transfer in a single folder and then dragging the folder to the new disk. This saves you time if you're using a single-drive Mac because it minimizes the number of disk swaps.

Replacing A Folder Replaces All Of Its Contents

When you drag a folder to another disk, the *Finder* places a copy of that folder's contents on the new disk. If that disk already contains a folder of the same name, the *Finder* will ask if you want to replace items with the same names with the selected items. The *Finder* considers a folder as an item, regardless of its contents. Therefore, if you click the Yes button, the copy operation will replace the contents of the old folder with the contents of the new one. If the old folder contained files that aren't in the new one, those files will be deleted. To be sure you're not replacing valuable files, check the contents of a folder before replacing it.

Some Files Couldn't Be Read and Were Skipped

If you get this message when you're trying to copy files with *Finder 4.1*, the two most likely causes are that the files you are trying to copy have some form of copy protection implemented, or the disk is defective. This alert box shouldn't appear unless one of these conditions exists.

DELETING FILES

Saving Files from the Trashcan

Files thrown into the trashcan are not actually removed until you specifically issue the Empty Trash command, Quit the current application, launch another application, or take any action that takes you off the desktop. To see if a file is still in the trashcan, Open the trashcan (by choosing Open from the Edit menu or by double-clicking on its icon) and look at its contents. If the file you want to retrieve from the trash is in the window, just drag it to the desktop, or to another disk or folder.

DESKTOP NEATNESS

Empty Folder In Old *Finders*

If you use an older *System* (previous to release 4.1 of the *Finder*), store the Empty Folder in the System Folder to reduce desktop clutter.

Express CLEAN UP

If you use *Finder* version 4.1 or higher, you can perform super clean-up operations by holding down the OPTION key while selecting the CLEAN UP option. This method shuffles the icons into place much faster, and puts them into locations near the top of the window.

DISK SPACE

Clean Up Desktop File On Frequently Used Startup Disks

As the *Finder* works with you and performs all of the file manipulations you require, it stores a little bit of information about every file you've ever copied, trashed, saved, etc. As a result, it slowly accumulates a desktop file full of information—most of which you'll never need again. If you are working with near-full disks, clean up this file occasionally. You can use a disk utility to throw away the desktop file, or you can hold down the OPTION and COMMAND keys while you boot the Mac with the disk you want to clean up. You'll have to rename your folders (they now have names like "Untitled #1, #2," etc.), but the regained disk space (which could be 15K or more) will be worth the effort. Your files and their names are not affected.

EJECTING DISKS

Express Shut Down with Older *Finders*

If your *Finder* doesn't include a Shut Down command, a quick way to eject all disks is to Close all windows, then press COMMAND-A (to select all the disk icons on the desktop). Press COMMAND-E to eject all the disks, and turn off the power switch.

Fast Disk Eject

To eject a disk quickly from the desktop, drag the disk icon to the trash can. This works only with *Finder* version 4.1 or higher, and does not work with the startup disk. With *Finders* version 5.1 and higher, you can do this with the startup disk, as well. However, its icon will remain on the desktop, dimmed.

ERASE DISK

Erasing A System Disk

If you try to choose Erase Disk from the Special menu when the current startup/system disk is selected, you'll find the command dimmed. To erase a system disk, you have to start up the Mac with a system disk other than the one you want to erase. Then, insert the other system disk in the external drive, make sure it's selected, and you'll be able to use the Erase Disk command.

GET INFO

Comments Sometimes Appear for More Than One File

Some versions of the *Finder* have a rather elusive bug in the way they use the Get Info comments box. If two files have names that are too short and/or too much alike, comments written in the Get Info box for one file may show up in the other's Get Info box. This is another reason to keep your file names distinct.

Larger Comments Box On Mac Plus

The Comments box in the Get Info dialog box with *Finder 5.1* and later on the Mac Plus has a larger capacity than in earlier *Finders*. You can type in many more lines than you can see in the box and scroll through them with the Mac Plus' cursor keys.

Memory Size In Get Info Doesn't Account For Invisible Files

The memory size that you see in the Get Info box for some applications is not accurate for the amount of space the application takes on the disk. The reason is that some applications work with related invisible files. Although these files take up space on the disk for the applications, the Get Info box can't report their size as included with the application.

Use Comments Box to Distinguish Among Files

You can keep a brief description of a file and/or instructions for using it in the Get Info box. This can make browsing through files a lot quicker because you don't have to open each one to see what's in it. When you choose Get Info from the *Finder*, you'll see a dialog box giving some vital data on the file you selected. Type in a brief description in the comments box.

HFS

HFS Won't Display Folder Size Unless It's Open

Finder 5.0 and later uses the Hierarchical File System. Although HFS is faster and more efficient, it can't display a folder's size in its window. If you choose display by size in a folder or disk window, the folder sizes won't be shown. To find out the size of a folder, you'll have to select it's icon and choose Get Info from the File menu.

ICONS

Don't Panic If a Document Doesn't Display Correct Icon

Sometimes, when you copy a document from one disk to another, the correct icon to display it doesn't go along. Don't panic. Simply Open the document (requiring the presence of the appropriate application). When you next return to the desktop, the *Finder* should have gotten the correct icon information from the application. If the icon still is not right, you may have other problems with the document, application or *Finder*.

How To Alphabetize Icons

You can make the icons in a window rearrange alphabetically, but the procedure is a little strange. First, make the window you want to alphabetize the active window. Then, select "by Name" from the View menu. Now, select all the the icons in the window, pick them up and drop them en masse back on the icon for the window they came from (file folder or disk). Select "by Icon" from the View menu and all of the icons should be rearranged in alphabetical order. You can use the same procedure to organize the icons according to the other view options. Just be sure that you choose the organization you want (date, size, etc.) before dragging all of the icons to the folder or disk.

Icons Are Bundled With The Files They Represent

When you copy a program from one disk to another, a number of *Finder*-related resources need to accompany it. These *Finder*-related resources include the program's icon, and icons for documents the program created. Each program has an on-off flag called a bundle bit that tells the *Finder* whether any such resources are present and need to be copied. If the bundle bit is set, the *Finder* will copy the program's bundle resource to the new disk and bring along the appropriate icons. If the bundle bit isn't set, that program's icons will get left at home on the original disk and won't be copied. Either set the bundle bit before copying the program, or, since some terminal programs such as *MacTerminal* don't transmit that information, set it using a *Set-FileInfo*-type program or *Fedit*.

INITIALIZING DISKS

COMMAND Key Combo To Initialize Disk on *Finder 5.0* and Later

You can get *Finders 5.0* and later to initialize a disk by holding down the OPTION-COMMAND-TAB keys when you insert it. You'll be offered the familiar options of Cancel, Single-Sided, and Double-Sided.

LOCKED FILES

How To Lock A File

Important applications or files that shouldn't be tampered with should always be Locked. Choose Get Info from the File menu and click on the Locked box. An X in the box means that the file can't be thrown away, copied or have its name changed. Click on the box again to unlock.

Trashing A Locked File

When deleting files from the desktop, press the OPTION key while dragging a locked file to the trashcan. This automatically unlocks the file without having to go to the Get Info dialog box.

Use Cursor To Find Out If A File Is Locked

An easy way to tell if a file is locked is to select the file on the desktop and move the cursor over the filename. If the file is not locked, the cursor changes shape to an I-beam (so you can change the name if necessary); if it is locked, the cursor remains an arrow. This is usually simpler than choosing Get Info.

MEMORY SIZE

Mac Calculates Its Ks with 1000s, Not 1024s

When the *Finder* (versions 4.1 and earlier) reports the size of a file, folder or disk in Kilobytes (Ks), it doesn't use the computer standard of 1024 Bytes per K. Instead, it uses 1000. Although this doesn't make much difference to the user, it can cause major confusion for programmers. *Finders* version 5.0 and later use the correct number of Bytes for these calculations.

NAMES

Renaming On the Desktop

Rename a disk, file or folder by clicking once to highlight it, then typing the new name. Click anywhere else on the screen to save the new name.

Undoing Accidental Name Changes

Did you ever accidentally erase or type over the name of a file or disk? You don't have to re-enter it from scratch. Just hit BACKSPACE until what you typed is gone and then hit RETURN (or click the mouse—the cursor can be anywhere). The original file or disk name will reappear.

Use "By Name" from View Menu To Alphabetize Lists

Although the method is a little awkward, you can alphabetize lists with the "By Name" option from the *Finder's* View menu. First, use the New Folder command to create the window in which your list will be displayed and give it a name. Then, with the window active, select New Folder again and rename the resulting icon with the first item in your list. Continue choosing New Folder and assign one item name to each folder. When you have entered your complete list, choose "By Name" from the View menu and your list should appear in the window—alphabetized. You can print out the list with COMMAND-SHIFT-4 , or just use it from the screen. Theoretically, you could alphabetize as many items as you can fit empty folders into the remaining disk space. However, if you need to alphabetize lists often, or have long lists, a database manager (even a low-end "cheapie") is a better tool for this purpose.

OPENING FILES

Open A Document with An Application Other Than Its Creator

Some combinations of documents and applications will work together, even if there's no obvious way to get the application to open the document. Normally, a document retains the name of the application that created it. Thus, if you double click on its icon, it will Open its creator application and load the document. However, sometimes you can make a document and a different application work together. On the desktop, use the SHIFT-Click combination to select the document and the application you want to use it with. Then, with both selected, choose the Open option from the File menu. This doesn't work with all combinations and may cause serious problems with some. Always experiment on backups so you don't lose any valuable data or programs.

PRINTING

Printing A Group of Files

Print several files in a row by selecting them from the desktop with the selection rectangle, then choosing Print from the File menu. The Mac will print them according to the arrangement of the icons, from top to bottom and left to right.

Printing Files In A Specific Order

To print several files in a specific order, go to the *Finder* and SHIFT-CLICK to select the documents. After you select Print..., the Mac will print the files in the same order as you selected them.

SCROLLING

Use Scroll Bars To Move Around Inside Windows

You don't have to expand the size of windows to see other sections of them. You can use the scroll bars on the window to move around and see more icons without making the window any larger. With *Finders* version 5.0 and later, you can click on the small box on the right end of a window's grab bar to make it expand to the size of the screen.

SET STARTUP

Using the Set Startup Command

You can make the Mac automatically run any application on the startup disk when you start up your system. To make an application "auto-run," select its icon on the desktop so it's highlighted and choose Set Startup from the Special menu. This command will work on any startup disk you insert, whether it's the current startup disk or not. This fact is important if you want to set an application as the startup program on a *MiniFinder* disk that doesn't contain a *Finder*. The only way to make an application "auto-run" on such a disk is while you're operating your system from a startup disk that contains a full *Finder* so you can get at the Set Startup command. Only applications can be made startup applications, not documents. However, some applications (like *Switcher*) allow you to designate a document with a special name that the application will load whenever you start up the applications, whether from the desktop or when the application "auto-runs."

Changing or Turning Off Set Startup

Once you have made an application the startup program for a disk with the Set Startup command, it's not very obvious how you can change or turn off the command. If you want to make another application on the same disk the new startup application, simply select the new application's icon and choose Set Startup from the Special menu. If you want the system to start up with the *Finder* or *MiniFinder*, follow the same procedure. Select the *Finder* or *MiniFinder* icon and invoke the Set Startup command.

SMALL ICONS

Using Small Icons

Finders versions 5.0 and later display a mini-icon with the file name if you choose any display option other than "by Icon." These icons behave just like the large ones and you can move, Copy, Open, and otherwise manipulate them in generally the same manner as the large icons.

Using Small Icons Dangerous with Older *Finders* and *Finder 5.0*

Finder 5.0 exhibits a nasty bug when you use a *Finder 5.0* folder with older *Finders*. The problem is that older *Finders* can't understand certain parts of HFS. If you create a folder under *Finder 5.0* and display it with Small Icons (which are not a part of the old MFS), you may run into the problem. When you are running under an old *Finder*, don't try to use a disk containing an HFS folder displayed with Small Icons. If you replace a file in that folder with a new file of the same name, the Mac will trash the entire contents of the folder and only the new file will remain.

STARTUP DISK

Change Startup Disks Without Re-Booting

Make a newly inserted disk the startup disk by Opening the new disk on the desktop. Then Open its System folder and, while holding down the COMMAND and OPTION keys, double-click on the *Finder* icon. The *Finder* will open (like an application) and the new *Finder's* desktop will appear with its startup disk's icon in the upper right hand corner of the screen.

Making *Finder* An Application

Here's another simple way to change startup disks without rebooting. If you need to change startup disks frequently, use the *Fedit* utility to make the *Finder's* "type" an Application (APPL) on each disk that you use. To change the startup disk, insert the new one, and just double-click on the new disk's *Finder*.

Use *Fedit* To Prevent *Finder 4.1* from Switching *Systems*

You can prevent *Finders 4.1* and later from switching startup disks when you Open an application on a startup disk other than the current one. First, do this only on a copy of your disk—*Fedit* can be dangerous! Open the *Finder* in *Fedit*. Find `B678 0210 6738` and substitute `B678 0210 6038`.

TRASH

Dragging File from the Trash To Different Volume Destroys It

In any of the 5.x series *Finders*, dragging a file out of the Trash onto a different volume than the one you threw it away from removes the file, permanently, from both the Trash can and the destination volume (and it's already gone from the original volume). Remember, in HFS, each folder is a separate volume. Therefore, be sure to put things back into their original folders immediately if you remove them from the Trash. Then, you can move them in the usual ways.

Duplicating A File In the Trash will Crash *Finders 5.1* & *5.2*

If you're using *Finder 5.1* or *5.2*, trying to Duplicate a file in the Trash window will crash the System. Why anyone would want to do this is beyond your humble author's imagination.

VERSION 5.0

Intermittent "File Not Found" Error with Hard Disks

Finder 5.0 occasionally generates an "Application Can't Be Found" error when running with a hard disk, even when the application is present and the creator and file type are correct for the document you're trying to Open. To fix the problem, simply replace the application on the hard disk.

WINDOWS

Finding Hidden Icons

You can accidentally lose an icon by placing another icon directly on top of it. The effect of this is to hide the bottom icon completely when you're viewing files by icon. If you've hunted and hunted through the window and can't find a file, try viewing the files by any of the other options under View. The Mac will sort the files into a list according to your choice. Any previously hidden files will be easy to find.

Moving A Background Window

Move a background window without making it active by pressing the COMMAND key while dragging the window by its title bar.

Macintosh

AUDIO

Adjusting Volume On Mac and Amplifier

When you have connected the Mac to your audio amplifier (with both volumes turned down first), follow this procedure to set the volume to the level you want. First, set the amplifier's volume to a safe, low level. Then, increase the volume on the Mac's Control Panel desk accessory until you have a strong signal, but not so strong as to cause any distortion. If you have a tape deck, use its meters to get a reading of 0 VU. Otherwise, you'll have to use your ears. Then, use the amplifier's volume control to adjust the volume to a comfortable listening level.

Connecting the Mac Directly To A Tape Deck

You can connect the Mac's audio output directly to a tape deck to make recordings. Be sure you check the signal on the tape deck's VU meters before you start recording. If your tape deck is stereo, you'll have to use a mono-to-stereo converter cable to put the Mac's signal into both channels.

Control Panel & Amp Volume Should Be Turned Down Before Connecting

Before you connect your Mac and amplifier with an audio cable, use the *Control Panel* desk accessory to turn the Mac's volume way down before you turn it off to connect the cable. Also, turn the volume on your amplifier down before you turn it on after making the connection. If you don't follow this procedure, you could damage your speakers.

Make Sure Amp and Mac Are Turned Off Before Connecting

Be sure that you turn off the power to both your Mac and amplifier before you connect them with an audio cable. You risk damage to both your Mac and stereo system if you don't.

Never Plug Mac Into Amplifier's Phono Input

You can plug the audio cable from the Mac into the AUX, Tape In, Tuner, CD or almost any other component input jack. However, NEVER plug the Mac's cable into the Phono input jack.

Turn Down Volume Before Using Headphones

You can use "Walkman" style headphones plugged directly into the audio output jack on the Mac. However, be sure to turn down the volume on the *Control Panel* desk accessory before you do so or you could permanently damage your headphones, or worse, your hearing! Since the Mac has a mono output, you may want to use a mono adaptor plug to put the signal into both earphones, but of course, it still won't be stereo.

Use A Tape Deck's VU Meters To Set Levels

If your audio system has a tape deck with VU meters, you can use it to adjust the appropriate levels from the Mac. First, make sure the tape deck is turned on and set to monitor the sounds coming in from the Mac. Then, set the Mac's volume with the *Control Panel* desk accessory to a point where the loudest sound registers 0 VU on the tape deck's meters. The meters should never go into the red zone. This procedure will ensure that you get the strongest possible signal into your audio system without overloading the inputs.

Use Amplifier's Infrasonic Filter To Eliminate Clicks & Pops

If your amplifier is so equipped, use its infrasonic filter when running the Mac's sound through your audio system. The filter will eliminate most of the unpleasant effects of the clicks and pops from the Mac's switching. Besides giving a more pleasing sound, this will eliminate wear and tear on your speakers.

Watch Out for Static when Connecting

Be very careful that you and the cable have discharged any static electrical charge you might be carrying before you connect your Mac and amplifier. The static could discharge through the audio port on the Mac and cause serious internal damage.

BATTERY

Battery Life and Type

When the time comes to replace the battery (used to maintain the correct time and the Parameter RAM when the Mac's power is off), you may find yourself mystified trying to find a replacement at the local drugstore. It's not one of the more common types, and usually is available in camera stores. Use an Everready #523-BP, 4.5 volt or equivalent (such as Ray-O-Vac #RPX-21, Duracell #PX-21 and Panasonic #PX-21). How do you know when to replace it? In normal usage, it should last about two years. When the time and date become erratic and inaccurate, it's nearly dead.

Resetting the Clock May Take A Couple of Tries

Some Macs try harder than others when remembering the information stored in the battery-supported Parameter RAM (clock setting, speaker volume, etc.). If your clock does not reset when you remove the battery and replace it, try the procedure again. Be sure to leave the battery out for 30 seconds or more.

CABLES

Be Very Careful of Static When Connecting or Disconnecting

Static electricity is one of the worst enemies of computers. Most of your Mac's circuitry is designed to handle a maximum of 15 volts. Your body can carry a charge of as much as 4,000 volts. Because of this, be sure to discharge yourself (touch something that's grounded) before touching any of the cable connectors on your Mac. Then, to be doubly safe, handle the cables only by their plastic casings. NEVER touch any of the pins in the connectors. If you touch one of the metal casings or pins while carrying a static charge, the discharge pulse could easily damage the chips on your Mac's logic board.

Don't Use Standard Telephone Handset Cord with Keyboard

Although it looks the same, the cable the Mac uses for its keyboard is not a standard telephone handset cable. In the phone cable, some of the wires cross between the plugs whereas in the Mac's cable they are straight plug-to-plug connections. Some telephone systems also require this kind of cable, so you might be able to find replacements or extension cords in phone specialty catalogs (professional equipment). At least one mail order company offers these specially configured cables: Your Affordable Software Co., 1525 N. Elston Ave., Chicago, IL 60622. Phone: (312) 235-9412.

Sound Cable

A proper cable to connect the Mac's audio output to a stereo system is hard to find. Usually, you have to kludge it up with adaptors. But, Radio Shack has just the right cable (part # 42-2153). It has a mono, mini phone plug at the Mac end, and a pair of RCA phono plugs at the audio system end. If necessary, you can extend it with adaptors and another audio cable.

DISKETTES

Tie Disks To Mac with Fishline To Prevent Disappearance

If you work in an educational setting, you know how easily diskettes that have been checked out seem to walk away. You can use monofilament fishline to attach disks to the Mac so they'll stay with the machine. First, drill a small hole in the upper corner of your diskettes, opposite the write-protect slider. ONLY WORK WITH A BACKUP OF YOUR DISK AND BE SURE THAT YOU CAREFULLY REMOVE ANY DUST GENERATED BY THE DRILLING. THIS TECHNIQUE CAN TRASH DISKS!!! Now, tie a piece of fishline through the hole in the diskette and the other end through the chain slot on the back of the Mac. This is great if you're working with a small number of applications at most of your workstations.

KEYBOARD

Avoid Pushing Keyboard Up Against Mac

The Mac gets a great deal of the fresh air it uses to cool itself through the front panel vents above the plug for the keyboard. Although this looks like a good place to store the keyboard while you're not using the Mac, it blocks the vents under the front panel and may lead to overheating. Leave some extra space, or find a better place to put the keyboard on your desk.

The CAPS LOCK Key Can Confuse *System* On Startup

Have you ever noticed that, at the beginning of each session, your Macintosh keyboard doesn't always work as it should? Well, the first thing to check is the CAPS LOCK key. A small bug in the ROM (pre-128K ROM) ignores the CAPS LOCK key if it's locked down while the machine is going through its initial set-up procedure. But, after booting with CAPS LOCK down, the Mac defiantly displays everything in lower case. The cure is to press the CAPS LOCK key once to release it, and then press it again. The Macintosh will respond by finally working as it should.

MEMORY SIZE

Checking Memory Size Without A *Finder* on an Unfamiliar Mac

A sexy programmer's trick for checking the memory size of a Mac is to hold down the rearmost programmers' switch and turn the power on. If you have a 512K Mac, an angry Mac face with `0F00D` as the message should appear. This is a good trick when you have to deal with a Mac you don't know, as is the case in schools and large companies.

MOUSE

Performing a "Mousewash"

After many months of operation, especially in a dusty or lint ridden environment, cleaning the mouse according to the instructions in the Mac manual may not do a thorough enough job to improve mouse performance. Taking the mouse apart is fairly simple. First, remove the ball according to the directions in the Mac's manual. Then, remove the two Phillips-head screws on the base of the mouse near the cord. With the base down, gently remove the top half of the mouse case, pushing the cord gently down out of its socket in the upper case. You can now see three rollers (two black and one silver) that roll against the mouse and transmit instructions to the Mac. They retain dirt and grime that normal cleaning doesn't remove. Clean them with a cotton swab and denatured alcohol. DO NOT TRY TO REMOVE THE CYLINDERS; THE SHAFTS ARE DELICATE AND WILL BREAK! Use the tip of a toothpick to remove strands of hair or lint that have become wrapped around the shafts supporting the cylinders. DO NOT USE METAL TOOLS OF ANY KIND WHEN WORKING INSIDE THE MOUSE! Clean the rubber ball with a soft, clean, dry cloth. To reassemble the mouse, make sure the mouse button and spring are properly seated, carefully reinsert the cord into the upper half of the case, and replace the two screws. Then, replace the ball and its mounting ring. BE VERY CAREFUL WHEN PERFORMING THIS OPERATION. AN OUNCE OF PARANOIA MAY BE WORTH MANY REPAIR DOLLARS!

Use Peel & Stick Felt Pads To Smooth Mouse Movement

The two plastic "feet" under your mouse can become worn after a lot of use on a hard surface. To prevent this wear and make the movement of your mouse smoother, purchase four small peel & stick felt pads from your local hardware store and attach them to the four corners of the underside of your mouse. They'll wear out and need occasional replacement, but they're cheaper than another mouse and can act as a "poor man's mousepad." Another good solution is to use circles cut from the fuzzy side of peel and stick velcro.

PLACEMENT

Don't Block Vents

Never block the vents on the front, top and sides of the Mac. The cooling system depends on cool air flowing in through the bottom vents and rising to the top as it gets heated. This sets up a convection current that keeps the Mac cool. Without air circulating through it at all times, the Mac can overheat and/or crash. Serious damage to chips can result from overheating, too. Common ways of blocking the vents without being aware of the problem are putting disk drives or other desk objects too close, or sticking loose papers between the Mac and one of those items. Never leave a file folder or stack of papers on the top of the Mac.

PORTS

Pin-Out Information for Mac's Serial Port

The following is the pin-out information for the signals the Macintosh (not the Mac Plus or port-updated Macs) sends and receives through its modem and printer ports:

PIN	OFFICIAL NAME	DESCRIPTION
1	Cold ground	Ground connection
2	+5V	Power supply output (low current) (not present at all on newer ports)
3	Cold ground	Another ground connection
4	TXD+	Transmitted data (high)
5	TXD-	Transmitted data (low)
6	Filtered +12V	Another power supply output
7	Handshake	Control signal (DTR, for example)
8	RXD+	Received data (high)
9	RXD-	Received data (low)

POWER

Operating A Mac On Foreign Power Systems

Macs and other Apple computer equipment sold in the U.S. are designed to work on 107 to 132 volts, 50 to 60 Hertz Alternating Current. If you are going to take your Mac to another country, check on the rating of their power "mains." Most other countries have 220 to 240 volts, 50 Hertz Direct Current. To use your Mac on one of these systems, you'll have to use a stepdown transformer rated at 60 Watts for the Mac or one rated at 240 Watts for a Mac/ImageWriter combination. If you're in doubt, call Apple before you leave and get the necessary converters before you even think about plugging it in to unknown power outlets.

PROGRAMMERS' SWITCH

What's the Extra Plastic Piece In the Mac's Accessory Box?

Apple calls this the "Programmers' Switch," implying that ordinary mortals shouldn't need it. But, programmer or not, you'll find this a handy attachment for the Mac if you're not the type who bumps around in the back of the Mac and may press it accidentally. The switch snaps in between the air vent bars on the side of the Mac away from the internal floppy drive, so that the two spines on the switch touch two buttons on the Mac's circuit board. One of these buttons resets the computer, and the other interrupts it.

If you press the front part of the switch, the Mac will reset itself—a tone sounds and the screen displays the familiar floppy disk icon, complete with flashing question mark. It's almost like turning the Mac off and on, but without switching the power off. (See "Programmers' Switch Doesn't Clear All Memory.")

Pressing the rear part of the switch produces an interrupt—it stops the currently running program and puts up one of the dreaded Bomb error messages. This facility enables programmers to interrupt their own programs just as soon as a bug appears. However, any Mac owner may find this useful—if only to escape from any bugs you find in commercial or public domain software.

You can't harm the Mac by hitting the programmers' switch. Indeed, it's a good idea to avoid turning the power off and on when you're dealing with such delicate electronics.

Shave Molding Flash Off Sticky Programmers' Switches

If you're having problems with your Programmers' Switch getting jammed when you press one of the buttons, remove it and check around the mold marks for excess plastic that didn't get cleaned off. You can use a razor blade or X-acto knife to remove the excess plastic molding flash and you'll probably solve your sticky switch problem.

SCREEN

Shimmering Screen May Mean Loose CRT Ground Wire

If your Mac's screen jiggles every once in a while and acts as though it's about to collapse from overwork, don't panic. It may be a simple problem with one of the ground wires on the CRT. Don't try to fix this yourself unless you REALLY know what you're doing. The voltages around a CRT are extremely dangerous (even after you turn the computer off or disconnect it from the wall current), because the capacitors can hold a high charge for a long time. However, a friendly technician should be willing to take a look at it for you without emptying your wallet.

Some Fans May Cause the Mac's Screen To Waver

If you have a fan installed to cool your Mac and the screen starts to shimmer and waver, remove the fan and see if the problem continues. Some owners of Fanny Mac have reported that it's especially likely to produce some problems with the screen.

SPEAKER

Turning Off the Speaker

Here's a simple way to get rid of the chime that sounds each time the Macintosh wants to attract your attention—and without altering the *Control Panel* settings from the Apple menu. All you have to do is put a Walkman-style mini phone plug into the rear external audio jack at the back of the Macintosh. Once done, the menu bar flashes each time the chime would normally have sounded.

TROUBLE SHOOTING

Overheating With Analog Board Rev. B

Some users who upgraded their 128K Macs to 512K have reported overheating analog boards. (The analog board is the circuit board containing the sound and power supply circuits and is mounted on the left side of the Mac.)

The first 72,000 or so Macs (all 128s, obviously) used Rev. B of the analog board. All later Macs (both 128 and 512s) have Rev. C. Component for component, they are identical, although the layouts differ slightly. Rev. B has one extra part, the analog fence. The analog fence is a metal strip that sticks up from the board. It is supposed to act as a heat sink to radiate the power supply's heat into the air. The problem is that it also blocks the air flow sufficiently to cause a slightly greater problem. The heat problem does not affect 128K Macs, but 512s have more heat-producing memory chips. Most 512K Macs with the analog fence have no heat problems. However, if you have heat problems, a technician can easily remove the fence. But if it ain't broke, don't fix it! On the Mac Plus, the memory chips are in the low current drain CMOS form, so they produce less heat than the 512K's chips.

Macintosh Plus

CABLES

You Can Use Some Apple //e Cables with Mac Plus

If you're having a hard time getting the right cables for your Mac Plus, try asking your dealer for the following substitutes: To connect the Mac Plus to an ImageWriter I, a //e modem cable (A2C0311) will work. To connect the Mac Plus to a Hayes-type modem, you can use a //e printer cable (A9C0313).

DEBUGGER

Available Commands

The 128K ROMs shipped with the Mac Plus and included in upgrades to older Macs have a built-in debugger. The commands it supports are MacBugs commands DM, SM, G and register commands.

Debugger Is Quirky within *Microsoft Word*

You'll be better off to not try to use the 128K ROMs' built-in debugger within *Microsoft Word.* It will exhibit quirky behavior and may crash your system.

Don't Run Built-In Debugger when Modem Port Is Occupied

Don't try to run the 128K ROMs' built-in debugger when you have a modem or other device connected to the Mac's modem port. When you try to use the interrupt switch, your system will freeze up.

How To Quit the Debugger and Return To the Desktop

You can quit to the desktop from the debugger by issuing the command `G 40F6D8` to exit-to-shell.

DISK CACHE

Be Sure To Choose Shut Down Before Powering Off

If you use the disk cache from the *Control Panel* on the Mac Plus, be sure that you choose Shut Down from the Special menu before you turn off the power switch on your Mac. The disk cache doesn't write changes back to the disk immediately after you make them. If you power off without triggering the cache to save the most recent changes (by using the Shut Down command), you may lose some of the changes you've made from the *Finder*.

Disk Cache May Prevent Some Programs from Running

The disk cache on the Mac Plus (controlled from the *Control Panel* desk accessory), may prevent some older programs from running. Games are particularly susceptible, but watch out for others, such as *HFS Backup* and *TML Pascal*.

DISK MENU

Use Arrow Keys To Get Around Disk Menu

You can use the arrow keys on the Mac Plus keyboard to maneuver around the disk menu under HFS. If you hit the down arrow once, it selects the first available folder in the menu. Hitting it again will scroll down to the next available folder. If you hit the up arrow once, the last available folder will be selected and subsequent presses will scroll up the menu. COMMAND-Up Arrow moves you up one level in the disk hierarchy and COMMAND-Down Arrow moves you down one level in the hierarchy.

Use Up and Down Arrow Keys to Scroll Directory

When you are looking at the disk menu within an application, you can use the Mac Plus' Up and Down Arrow keys to scroll through the menu of files, either in a folder or on the root level of the disk.

GAMES

Suggested Modifications for Incompatible Games

Games seem especially prone to problems on the Macintosh Plus. Here are some modifications that may make your favorite game compatible. First, work ONLY on a backup of the disk. (Of course, if you don't have a copy utility that will bit copy the disk or if it's protected with a scheme that prevents bit copying, you'll not be able to do this.) Then, use *Fedit* to change the primary screen addresses to `$3FA700` from `$7A700`, the secondary screen buffer addresses to `$3F2700` from `$72700`, and the primary sound buffer from `$7FD00` to `$1FFD00`.

Turn Off the Disk Cache When Running Games

Some games have many problems with the Mac Plus, but some can be made compatible simply by turning off the Mac Plus' disk cache from the *Control Panel*.

KEYBOARD

Plus and Minus Keys Reversed On Some Early Keyboards

And the beat goes on. Apple proved yet again that man is not perfect. Some of the early versions of the Mac Plus keyboards have the plus and minus keys reversed. The plus key subtracts and the minus key adds...Sigh...Talk to your dealer.

RECOVERY

Fedit Version 3.7 and Later Will Recover Data from 800K Floppies

As of this writing, only one utility exists for recovering data from bad files on 800K floppies. The program is *Fedit* version 3.7 from John Mitchell. This program is distributed as shareware on many online services and user group disks. It is a godsend to the Mac community and we've been told that very few people have sent in the shareware fee. If you use the program, please send the shareware fee to Mr. Mitchell. It's the only way to encourage more people to publish their programs via this method.

SCREEN DUMPS

Use *Camera* Desk Accessory To Take Screen Shots with Menus

On the old Macintosh, taking a screen snapshot of whatever was on the screen (with COMMAND-SHIFT-3) was easy. With the new 128K ROMs on the Mac Plus and 512K Enhanced, you'll have problems if you try to take a screen snapshot when you have a menu pulled down or if a dialog box is showing. However, you can use the *Camera* desk accessory (available on *CompuServe* or from many user groups) to take a time-delay snapshot. You can set the amount of time you want *Camera* to wait before taking the snapshot so you can get to the dialog box you want or pull down the appropriate menu (very handy in writing documentation). *Camera* will also let you hide the cursor and choose whether to save the snapshot as a *MacPaint* file or send it to the ImageWriter.

SCSI DEVICES

Make Sure One SCSI Device Is Switched On Before Starting Mac Plus

Some early Mac Pluses have a bug in the ROM which requires you to start up any SCSI devices you have connected before you start up the Mac Plus. Otherwise, the Mac won't start up properly. There were only a few of the machines produced with this problem and the only way to tell if yours is one of them is to try it.

SCSI PORT

Use the SCSI Port ONLY for SCSI Devices

The DB-25 connector used for the Mac Plus' SCSI port is used by a number of peripherals, both SCSI and other. Never connect a non-SCSI device to the Mac's SCSI port! You may do permanent damage to your Mac.

SERIAL PORTS

Serial Ports Don't Supply Power On Mac Plus

When Apple changed the port configuration for the Mac Plus, they made one seemingly minor change to the serial ports—they no longer supply low voltage power on one of the pins. As a result, some of the peripherals that required power from the Mac (like *ThunderScan*) will not run on the Mac Plus. You'll have to get a special adaptor from the manufacturer (if it makes one) that will supply power from an external source to the peripheral.

Radio Shack Power Supply for Peripherals

If you know how to do the necessary wiring, you can get a power supply from Radio Shack for peripherals that need, but can't get, power from the Mac Plus serial ports (such as *ThunderScan*). Radio Shack's unit can supply both 5V and 12V, and the part number is: #277-1022. BE SURE THAT YOU KNOW WHAT YOU'RE DOING!

STARTING UP

Hold Down the Mouse Button To Skip Memory Test

You can skip the memory test the Mac Plus runs every time you start it up by holding down the mouse button until just after the beep. Don't hold it down any longer, or you'll eject any disks in the drives. Don't use this technique every time. Memory's not infallible and you should let the Mac Plus check it occasionally.

STARTUP DISK

Disk Drive Priority for Startup Disk

When you start the Mac Plus, it first looks in the internal floppy drive for a startup disk. If it finds none there, it looks in the external floppy drive and, finally, to the SCSI port. The first startup disk it finds becomes the current startup disk and the default drive.

Switching Startup Disks with a Hard Drive

On a floppy disk-based Mac, you can switch startup disks by Opening an application on a startup disk other than the current one. However, if you're working on a hard disk, this doesn't switch startup disks. With a hard drive, hold down the OPTION key when you Open the application on another startup disk (hard or floppy) and the *System* will automatically make that disk the current startup disk.

SYSTEM CLOCK

Resetting the System Clock

The new *Control Panel* for the Mac Plus doesn't have a place where you can set the system clock. To set the clock, you must have the *Alarm Clock* desk accessory installed in the *System* on your startup disk. Just click on the flag icon on the right side of the clock display to show the icons you need to reset the clock.

SYSTEM TOOLS

Check the Version Numbers of the Printer Drivers

The *System Tools* disk shipped with the Mac Plus and Mac Plus Upgrades did not contain the latest version of the printer drivers as of 4/3/86 (*ImageWriter 2.1*, *AppleTalk ImageWriter 2.1* and *LaserWriter 1.1*). However, the latest versions of the *ImageWriter* (2.2), *AppleTalk ImageWriter* (2.2), and *LaserWriter* (3.0) were available as of that date on the Printer Installation disk shipped with the LaserWriter and LaserWriter Plus. Since then, *ImageWriter 2.3*, *AppleTalk ImageWriter 2.3*, and *LaserWriter 3.1* have been released—along with *System 3.2* and *Finder 5.3*. Check with your dealer to get the latest versions of all three drivers. They have been substantially improved.

Saving Time with a 400K External Drive

The *System Tools* disk shipped with the Mac Plus and Mac Plus Upgrades is a double-sided disk. If you try to use the *Installer* program on that disk on a system with an 800K internal and 400K external drive, you'll only be able to use the internal drive to update double-sided disks and you'll swap disks forever. To simplify the process, copy the contents of the *System Tools* disk to a formatted single-sided disk (it will fit) and use the *Installer* from that disk in the external drive.

UPGRADES

Old External Keypad Has Problems with New ROMs

If you hook up an old external keypad to a machine that's been upgraded with the new ROMs, the first character you type on the keyboard won't appear on the Mac. If, instead, you type the first character on the keypad, it repeats until you stop it by striking another key. You'll either have to get the Mac Plus keyboard with its own keypad or put up with the idiosyncrasies.

Power Supply Sturdier On Mac Plus Than On Upgrades

The power supply in the Mac Plus has some components that are sturdier than in 512K Macs. When you upgrade a 512K Mac, you don't get the new power supply.

Airborne!

SPECIAL

Cactus Changes To Christmas Tree On Christmas Day

It's nice of programmers to include little "plums" that make their programs more interesting and can unexpectedly bring a smile to your face. The cactus on the *Airborne!* game screen changes to a Christmas tree on Christmas day. All together now...awwww! (You can see the effect by changing the Mac's system calendar to December 25 with the *Alarm Clock*.)

AppleTalk

CHOOSE PRINTER

Choose Printer May Freeze System from Within Applications

Beware of the difference between the old *Choose Printer* desk accessory and the new replacement, called *Chooser*. If you run the old *Choose Printer* desk accessory while in an application on an AppleTalk network, your system may freeze. Update to HFS and the new *Chooser* desk accessory, or always remember to run the old *Choose Printer* desk accessory from the *Finder*. See the hint, "My Network Doesn't Work," for ideas on how to recover from a frozen network.

IMAGEWRITER

Confusing A Non-AppleTalk ImageWriter

Always turn off AppleTalk on the *Control Panel* after you physically disconnect your Mac from AppleTalk.

If you try to print on a non-AppleTalk ImageWriter connected directly to your Mac, the printer will get very confused unless you change the setting on the *Control Panel* (*Finder 5.0* and later). Simply selecting Shut Down and changing startup disks won't help, but you can reset it by turning off the Mac's power. Conversely, remember to use the *Control Panel* to turn AppleTalk back on when you physically reconnect to AppleTalk.

PRINTING

Don't Print *MacWrite* and *MacDraw* Documents At the Same Time

Don't try to print a *MacWrite* document from one Mac and a *MacDraw* document from another on an AppleTalk network and a LaserWriter. The *MacWrite* document will print, but the *MacDraw* document won't be completed.

RAM DISKS

Many RAM Disks Are Incompatible with AppleTalk

Be careful when running RAM disk programs on an AppleTalk network. You may experience some problems, especially when printing.

RESET BUTTON

Reset Button Doesn't Break AppleTalk Connection

When you turn off the Mac, it breaks its connection with AppleTalk. However, pressing the Reset Button on the Programmer's Switch does not break the AppleTalk connection.

SYSTEM SOFTWARE

Make Sure All Macs On the Network Are Using the Same *System*

Make sure that all of the Macs connected to an AppleTalk network are using the same version of the *System* software, printer drivers, and *Finder*. If you have a Mac Plus on the network with a Mac 512 or 128, you must update the system disks for the Mac 512 and/or 128 with the *Installer* utility on the Mac Plus' *System Tools* disk. The "non-plused" Macs won't be able to save to folders from within applications, but other than that, they will work very well with the Hierarchical File System.

TROUBLE SHOOTING

AppleTalk Crashes When I Launch A Program

Some programs, games in particular, initialize the printer port when they start up. This will crash AppleTalk. The way around this is either to disconnect AppleTalk before booting the disk, or just don't boot it on that machine. Here's how to recover from the crash: After ejecting the disk, shut all the nodes in the system off for about 30 seconds. When you power back up, everything should work just fine.

My Network Doesn't Work

If your network doesn't seem to be working and you can't figure out why, the first thing to do is to shut off everything connected to AppleTalk, and check all the connections. Then restart the system. If the gremlin was caused by a loose connection, this whole-hog approach should take care of it.

If you still have a problem, turn off and disconnect each unit again. Now start connecting Macs back up to the network, one at a time, starting from the machine closest on the network to the LaserWriter. The gremlin could be anywhere, from a faulty port on the Mac itself, to a bad wire, to a piece of hardware or software that mysteriously jams up the works. Usually, it's caused by a loose connection. Once the network has been disconnected, your disks will usually have to be told the LaserWriter is connected again. (See "The LaserWriter's Not On the *Choose Printer* Menu.")

The LaserWriter's Not On the *Choose Printer* Menu

Sometimes, for a number of different reasons, your disks will "forget" that the LaserWriter is connected to your network. To remedy the problem, go to *Choose Printer*, select the printer port, choose APPLETALK CONNECTED from the buttons at the bottom of the dialog box, and wait to see if the LaserWriter appears in the scroll box. If it doesn't, select APPLETALK DISCONNECTED and hit OK. Then select *Choose Printer* again and go through the whole process until the LaserWriter decides to put in a grand reappearance. If you're operating on a Mac Plus or an upgraded Mac 512K, you probably won't have this problem. If you do, you can use the *Chooser* in a similar manner to get back in touch with your LaserWriter.

Assembly Language

A-TRAPS

Make A Program Stop At Its Beginning with An A-Trap

All programs must initialize QuickDraw when they start. However, you can get a program to stop as soon as it finishes initializing QuickDraw by setting an A-Trap at `_InitGraf (A86E)`.

COPYING FILES

Copy Original Dates With A File

If you want the process of copying files to work the same way as the *Finder* handles it, be sure to copy the file's creation and modification dates from the original directory entry. Otherwise, the operating system will assign new dates to the copy by default.

FILE FLAGS

The Inited Bit

Don't set the "Inited" bit. In the file flags, the "Inited" bit specifies that the file's icon has a place on the screen and it is controlled by the *System*.

OPERATING SYSTEM CALLS

Application Must Perform Call To `_TEInit`

If an application doesn't make a call to `_TEInit`, none of the desk accessories will work. This is not documented, but your application must perform this call in order for the user to be able to access desk accessories while it's running.

`_PBDelete` Will Delete A Locked File

Although undocumented, the `_PBDelete` call to the Mac's operating system will delete a locked file. Be careful.

The Launch Mac Call

You will see a description of the file-information parameters when you make a Launch Mac operating system call. You must ask your program to allocate them. Allocate a handle and point the low-memory location to the parameters you set up. The volume-reference-number field of the parameters is also important. Some applications don't handle files with volume prefixes properly.

Volume Names with `_PBSetVol`

If you want to supply a volume name when making a `_PBSetVol` call to the Mac's operating system, a colon must follow the volume name. This is not documented. However, don't apply this to all calls. For example, `_PBEject` won't allow you to use a colon.

TRANSFER MENU

Use Resource Editor To Modify Transfer Menu

When you are Opening an application, the Transfer Menu tells the application which files it can access. The Mac stores the Transfer Menu as a resource and you can modify it with a resource editor. With such an editor, you can add and modify entries to the Transfer Menu resource (prefixed by the volume name, if necessary), so you can make files accessible to an application and speed up transfers. This is great if you want to be able to Open a macro file from within an application.

Color Print

RIBBONS

Avoiding Problems With the ImageWriter

Using the *Color Print* ribbons with the ImageWriter creates many problems not present with ordinary black ribbons. If you haven't paid much attention to the ImageWriter manual before, you certainly will. In particular, be sure to keep the printhead spotlessly clean, especially with the yellow ribbon. Also, monitor the distance of the printhead from the paper carefully.

Concertware

HFS

Keep All Your Instrument and Player Files In Same Folder

Concertware will tell you it can't find an Instrument if it's not in the same folder as the Player. To solve the problem, keep all of your player and instrument files in the same folder.

Copy II Hard Disk

800K FLOPPIES

Use To Copy Protected Applications from 400K to 800K Floppies

Copy II Mac is not capable of moving copy protected applications from 400K to 800K floppy disks. It will only make another 400K copy. To move your applications to 800K HFS disks, pre-format an 800K disk with a *System* folder containing any *System* files, *Finder*, printer drivers, and desk accessories you want to have on your finished disk. Then, treat the external drive like a hard disk and use *Copy II Hard Disk* version 5.2 or later (shipped with *Copy II Mac*) to "install" your copy protected application on your pre-formatted 800K HFS disk. We've tried this with most of the Microsoft applications with great success and it should work fine with any of the applications listed in *Copy II Hard Disk's* listing of supported applications.

RAM DISKS

Use *Copy II Hard Disk* to "Install" Copy-Protected Programs

You can use the *Copy II Hard Disk* utility to install copy-protected applications to your RAM disk. This will prevent you from having to deal with a key-disk routine when you run some applications and will allow others to run from the RAM disk that otherwise would not run.

Courier 2400 Modem

PLACEMENT

Don't Put Your Phone On Top of the Courier 2400

The Courier 2400 looks like it was designed so you can put your phone on top of it. However, some users have reported problems with overheating when their phones block the cooling vents. For best results, keep your phone on the side of your Courier.

UPGRADES

Early Versions Have A Defective ROM

Some of the very early versions of the Courier 2400 modem were shipped with ROMs that display some subtle problems. To check the version of the ROM in your Courier 2400, issue the `ATI0` command. The ROM version number will appear. The correct version is 243. If yours is version 241 or 242, call USRobotics at 1-800-DIAL-USR to arrange for a free replacement.

Crunch

MEMORY SPACE

Cells Aren't Given Space Until Used Once

As with most spreadsheets, *Crunch* doesn't allot space to cells in memory until you enter a value. Once a cell has contained a value, however, it occupies memory even if you remove the value later. For example, if you Open and fill a work area of 7000 cells and later delete those values, the program indicates that the entire area is in use, and less than half the normal amount of memory remains for work. Thus, avoid Opening cells unless you intend to use them. Also, try to organize and limit the shape of your work area before entering values.

Deja Vu

HINTS

Killed In the Detective's Office

You probably won't walk in so hastily next time!

Locked Door

It probably needs a key. Check your inventory, including all wallets, envelopes, and boxes, to find one that might work. (To use the key, click on it, then select Operate, then click on the door or the lock.) If the key doesn't work, try shooting the lock. If it doesn't work on the first try, it won't work at all, so start checking every area for the key that will work.

Locked Safe

This needs a combination, which you can find by carefully examining everything in a particular location.

Need Addresses

You will find a total of five addresses in the game. Four are relatively easy to find—just examine every item you come across. Open desks—and even dead bodies—to get them. The fifth address is only available if you can manage to get the kidnap victim to talk. If all else fails, try Operating items on each other, or on the person in question…

Out of Bullets

My, but you're a violent soul! You can get more bullets in two different ways: Buy them, or find a new gun somewhere. If you buy bullets, don't forget to Open the gun and reload it.

Stuck In A Cab

You didn't conserve money carefully enough, or forgot to bring another address along. Let's hope you saved the game before you made this fatal mistake, because there's no way to rectify the situation now.

You Have All the Evidence But Are Still Under Arrest

You must have forgotten to do something. Try Operating all your objects on each other. Then, examine those objects. One combination produces the right result. If you still get arrested, you probably don't have all the evidence.

Deluxe Music Construction Set

AUDIO

Hooking Up To An External Audio System

Try running *Deluxe Music Construction Set* (*DMCS*), *MusicWorks*, *Concertware* or *SmoothTalker* on your Mac and the resulting sound is far from impressive. But connect the Macintosh up to your stereo system… and experience a revelation! You'll hear the full range and subtleties of the sound chip for the first time.

All you need—apart from a stereo system—is a cable with a mini phone plug at one end and a pair of phono plugs at the other. Fit the phono plugs into the equivalent AUX jacks on your stereo and the mini phone plug into the back of the Macintosh (near the modem port). Now, go to the *Control Panel* desk accessory and turn the volume slider all the way down. If you don't do this, you will get a good deal of distortion as the sound is amplified to an unacceptable level. (On *MusicWorks*, which sports no volume control slider on its own *Control Panel* desk accessory, turn down the volume control on-screen before playing the music.) Adjust stereo controls to your taste (or use headphones) and revel!

The Macintosh produces a mono signal, so it is advisable to select a MONO setting on your amplifier panel—otherwise, the sound may all come through one speaker (or one earphone).

BUGS

Copy Protection Bombs on a Hard Disk

If your try to run *DMCS* from a hard disk, the copy protection bombs, rather than asking for a key disk.

Don't Remove the Special Fonts

DMCS requires special musical notation fonts present in its *System* file, so don't remove those in an attempt to save disk space or add other fonts.

Don't Save to a Full Disk

Don't try to save a file to a full disk. The program reportedly will destroy your file in the process.

EXTERNAL SPEAKER

Use External Speaker Option If Using An Audio System

If you're running the sound from the Mac through your audio system, make sure you select the External Speaker option in *Deluxe Music Construction Set.* This will remove the software "filter" that equalizes the sound for the one-inch speaker on the Mac. If you don't make this adjustment, the sound going to your hi-fi speakers will have extremely boomy bass.

Demonstration Software

GETTING OUT

Last Ditch Solution

If you can't find any other way to quit a looping demonstration program (e.g. early *SmoothTalker* demos), reset the Mac while holding down the mouse button. The disks should pop right out of the drives.

GUIDED TOURS

Don't Try To Run From Another Startup Disk

Most Guided Tour disks from Apple and other software publishers make some special modifications to the *Finder* and *System* files. In many cases, these changes make the guided tour programs incompatible with regular *Finders* and *Systems.* To make sure you don't have any problems, always be sure to shut down your Mac before inserting the guided tour disk. When finished, shut down again before inserting a disk with normal *System* and *Finder* files.

MAC GUIDED TOUR

Making *AMAZing* A Stand-Alone Game

You can take the *AMAZing* game from your *Mac Guided Tour* disk and make it a stand-alone video game. First, format a blank disk using a startup disk running *Finder* version 1.1 and copy the *System* and *Finder* files onto it. Then, insert your guided tour disk and copy the *AMAZing* file to your new disk. Select the *AMAZing* icon and choose Set Startup from the Special menu. Shut down and start up again using your new disk. *AMAZing* will run automatically.

Use *AMAZing* To Generate Mazes for Other Purposes

AMAZing is a very good maze generating program. You can use the Mac's built-in ability to take a snapshot of the screen to move *AMAZing's* mazes to other files. When you see a maze you like, use SHIFT-COMMAND-3 to take a *MacPaint* snapshot of it. You can then use the resulting "Screen 0" file in *MacPaint* or move the maze from there to other programs.

Desk Accessories

ALARM CLOCK

Phantom Blinking Apple

Ever notice the desk accessory menu's apple flashing away wildly while you work? It's the silent alarm on the *Alarm Clock.* You may have forgotten that you had set the alarm, or you may have set it inadvertently the last time you looked at the clock. Just select *Alarm Clock* from the apple menu and click on the key symbol at the far right to turn off the alarm.

You Can Set the *Alarm Clock* By Typing

You can set any section of the *Alarm Clock* by typing. Just select the element you want to change and type the setting you want. Move from element to element by hitting the TAB key. You cannot change the AM/PM setting by typing, so be sure to type the time in 24-hour format. For example, enter 5:22 PM as 17:22:00.

APPLICATIONS

Always Close Desk Accessories Before Quitting or Shutting Down

Be sure to Close any desk accessories you may have open before you quit an application or shut down from the *Finder.* If you don't, you can damage your *System* file, the desk accessories' data files, or the application you were working in when you caused the problem.

Desk Accessories In Applications

You can attach Desk Accessories directly to the applications in which you want to use them, instead of to the *System* file (see "Use *Font/DA Mover* To Attach Fonts & DAs To Applications"). By doing so, you can exceed the maximum of fifteen DAs Apple recommends for the *System* file (see "Maximum Desk Accessories In the Apple Menu"). When you run the application, the DAs attached to it will appear in their usual places on the apple menu just below the "About..." selection. The Mac will fill up the remaining DA slots with those attached to the *System* File, up to the maximum combined number. This feature is especially handy if you are running a set of applications with *Switcher*. You can have your favorite DAs available for each application, even though the total for all applications exceeds fifteen. See the following hint for the Mac Plus modifications to this procedure.

Desk Accessories In Mac Plus Applications

The procedure described in the previous hint will work fine with the old 64K ROMs. However, the new 128K ROMs automatically sort the desk accessories on the Apple menu in alphabetical order. To make the desk accessories attached to your application appear on the first part of the Apple menu for that application, you'll have to "trick" the *System* into thinking they come first alphabetically. To do so, use a resource editor after you've installed the DAs you want in your application. Open the name resource for each of the DAs in your application (be sure you don't change the DAs installed in your *System* file) and precede its first letter with a blank space. The Mac's sort routine will "see" the blank spaces as coming before any character in alphabetical order and place your DAs at the top of the Apple menu.

CALCULATOR

Calculator Will Solve Equations

Do you do a lot of mathematical calculations? Let the Mac's Cut and Paste function speed up the process of entering the numbers into the *Calculator*. If you've typed a mathematical formula into a document (x = 2*a + b), and then show it with the numerical values substituted for the algebraic symbols (x = 2*14 + 7), just select the numerical portion after the "=" sign. Then choose the Copy option from the Edit menu. Paste it into the *Calculator* and it will automatically press the right keys and arrive at the answer. Now, Copy and Paste the *Calaculator's* results back into your document. The font used for the result is always Geneva, so you may want to leave it selected to reformat it. The *Calculator* will ignore any text, except the letters "c" or "e" between the numbers of your equation. With the exception of those two letters, the *Calculator* disregards all text, Carriage Returns, and Tab characters, between the parts of an equation.

CAMERA

Don't Use *Camera* DA with the HyperDrive 20

The *Camera* desk accessory doesn't run properly on the HyperDrive 20. If you you really need it, see the hints on Incompatibilities in the HyperDrive section of this book for an installation procedure that may work.

CHOOSER

Chooser Requires Later Versions of Printer Drivers

The *Chooser* desk accessory requires the *ImageWriter* driver version 2.1 or higher and the *LaserWriter* driver version 1.1 or higher in order to work properly. Get the latest versions from your dealer. If you find yourself stuck using an old *System* and printer driver for some reason, use the *Choose Printer* desk accessory instead of the *Chooser*.

Use *Control Panel* To Record *Chooser* Changes In Parameter RAM

At startup, the Mac loads the contents of the battery supported Parameter RAM (PRAM) into a low memory portion of RAM. When you use *Chooser* to make changes to your printer and AppleTalk settings (normally stored in PRAM), the changes are only made to the copy of PRAM in the regular RAM. The Mac will not alter the PRAM settings when you turn it off. To "trick" the Mac into changing the PRAM settings, make the changes you want on *Chooser*, and Close it. Then select the *Control Panel* and make any change on any control. You can leave it, or return it to the original setting. Now, Close the *Control Panel*, and the Mac will alter the PRAM settings for both the *Control Panel* and the *Chooser*, and retain them in the battery supported PRAM.

CONTROL PANEL

Changing *Control Panel* Applies To All Disks

When you change the settings on the *Control Panel*, the changes are recorded in battery-maintained Parameter RAM, not on the disk containing the *Control Panel* desk accessory. Don't bother to go from disk to disk, changing the *Control Panel* settings on each. Once is enough. Unless you need to change the settings often, remove the *Control Panel* from your startup disks. You'll regain almost 8K on each one. Of course you'll want to keep one disk with the *Control Panel* on it so you can readjust the settings when you desire, or after the battery goes dead. The only *Control Panel* setting that's an exception to this rule is the desktop pattern setting. That setting is stored only on the startup disk the pattern is assigned to. If you want to change the desktop pattern for a startup disk, you must install *Control Panel* in its *System* file.

Don't Try To Use Disk Cache with Old ROMs

The new *Control Panel* desk accessory shipped with *Finders 5.0* and later includes a panel to set an automatic disk cache for your Mac. However, this will work ONLY with the new 128K ROMs. If you try to use it with the old ROMs, it will have no effect.

Never Set Key-Repeat To Zero

The Mac's start-up ROM has a bug that misinterprets a Key-Repeat setting of zero on the *Control Panel* desk accessory. The setting should turn off the key repeat function completely. Instead, the Mac interprets it as "repeat as fast as your little circuitry can." Never set the key-repeat to zero! This problem has been fixed in the new 128K ROMs.

DELETING

Always Leave One DA in a *System* File

Always leave at least one desk accessory in each *System* file. Removing the last desk accessory destroys the *System* file on that disk. The Mac will not be able to read it again until you replace the *System* file (not folder) with one from another disk.

DISK UTILITIES

Make Sure They Work with HFS

If you're working with HFS, be extremely careful about using Disk Utility desk accessories. Some (like *DiskInfo* and *DiskTools*) have been released in versions which are compatible with HFS, but others may do strange things to your disk and folder directories. To be sure, check the manual or contact the publisher of the utility to find out if it's completely compatible with HFS. Always make a backup copy before experimenting.

KEY CAPS

Leave *Key Caps* On the Screen While Writing

When typing text into *MacWrite*, or most other applications, selecting the *Key Caps* DA every time you need to find a special character can be a real nuisance. To get around this, you can leave the *Key Caps* in the background and shrink your document window down so you can see the keyboard display below it. Then, when you press the OPTION key, you can see at a glance where all those symbols are.

LABEL 1.0

Label 1.0 will Crash a Mac Plus

Do not try to use the freeware desk accessory *Label 1.0* on a Mac Plus. The system crash will amaze you!

MEMORY SIZE

Maximum Memory Allocation for Open Desk Accessories

If you are using a 128K Macintosh, you may experience memory problems if you try to Open too many desk accessories at once. Try to keep the total for all DAs under 18K—for 512K owners, a top limit of 32K is best. You won't have as much trouble with the Mac Plus and its one megabyte of memory, but you should still Close desk accessories you're not using. Few desk accessories carry out full memory checking, and if you Open too many of them at once on-screen you may find that you get a Serious System Error dialog box before you know anything is wrong. Desk Accessories also take up useful memory when in the "background," so be careful.

Memory Sizes of Apple Desk Accessories

The following chart shows the memory size (disk space required) for the standard issue Apple desk accessories:

ACCESSORY	BYTES
Alarm Clock	4069
Calculator	2505
Choose Printer	5802
Chooser	8311
Control Panel	7457
Key Caps (Old)	1645
KeyCaps (New)	2641
Note Pad	2595
Puzzle	963
Scrapbook	3256

MOCK SERIES

Use *Mock Terminal* & *Mockwrite* To Cut & Paste Messages

When you're using *Mock Terminal*, you can Cut and Paste from *Mockwrite* to send text. With all the messages you wish to send stored in *Mockwrite*, and displayed on one side of the screen, you can Cut each one at the time you want to send it and Paste it into the *Mock Terminal* window at the appropriate time.

NOTE PAD

Keep Multiple *Note Pads* On One Disk

You can keep multiple *Note Pads* on one disk by renaming the *Note Pad* data file in the *System* folder. This is especially handy if you've filled a *Note Pad* with information you want to keep, but still want to put additional information in your *Note Pad*. Simply rename the *Note Pad* data file from the *Finder*. Then, when you next ask for the *Note Pad* from the Apple menu, a new *System* file called "Note Pad" will be created. You can get your old *Note Pad* back by renaming the new *Note Pad* data file and changing the old file's name back to "Note Pad."

Pasted Text Retains Formatting Information

The *Note Pad* will display text only in 12-point Geneva. However, when you Paste in formatted text from a document, it doesn't lose the formatting information it had before it was Pasted. When you "re-Paste" it into another document which supports formatting, all of the orignal fonts, sizes and styles will reappear.

NUMBER

Maximum Desk Accessories In the Apple Menu

Apple Computer recommends that you install no more than fifteen desk accessories in your *System* file. Eighteen Desk Accessory names will fit in the Apple menu when Chicago is being used as your system font. However, you may run into some confusion if you exceed the recommended fifteen. To make more desk accessories available, use Apple's *Font/DA Mover* to install them directly into the application in which you intend to use them (see "Use *Font/DA Mover* To Attach Fonts & DAs To Applications"). *Word Count*, for example, is only useful in *MacWrite* or *Microsoft Word*, so you can install it directly into one of those applications and it will not appear on the Apple menu unless you are running the program in which you installed it. (See "Desk Accessories In Applications.")

ORDER

Placing DAs In Custom Order On the Apple Menu

The Mac Plus automatically alphabetizes the desk accessories on the Apple menu. With older systems, however, you'll have to alphabetize them yourself or place them in any other custom order you like. Use the Font D/A Mover to Open the *System* file on the disk you want to modify. Remove all the desk accessories, one by one, to a dummy file. Then, copy them back into your *System* file, starting with the DA you want to be at the bottom. When you return to the desktop, the Apple menu will be in the order you desire.

SCRAPBOOK

Each Page of Scrapbook Usually Shows File Type & Creator

Since the Scrapbook always shows text in 12-pt. Geneva, you can't tell if it has font, size and style designations that will appear when you Paste it into a document in an application. If you need to know, look in the lower right corner of the Scrapbook. Most pages have two four-letter codes to indicate the name of the file's creator and its file type (TEXT or PICT). The first code tells you whether a TEXT file contains formatting information or not. If MWRT precedes the code TEXT, the text on that page of the Scrapbook was created in *MacWrite*. When you Paste it into a *MacWrite* document, it will appear with all its formatting information.

Leave Scrapbook Open On Desktop If You Use It Frequently

If you do a lot of work with the Scrapbook, transferring many items back and forth between it and your document, you can save time by leaving a small portion of it visible outside the border of your document. For example, in *MacWrite*, resize your document window so you have a sliver of space showing outside its window on the desktop. Now, Open the Scrapbook and move it so part of it covers the sliver of space you left. When you click on your document window, you'll still be able to see a little bit of the Scrapbook showing off to the side. To make it active again, simply click on the visible sliver.

Make An Index

Reserve the first page or two of large Scrapbooks for an index. Otherwise, you'll have to move through them page by page. Keep your index entries short and you can move the Scrapbook page back and forth from the *Note Pad* to add, modify or delete entries. For a larger index, create it in *MacWrite*. Doing it in *MacPaint* takes up more disk space.

Multiple Scrapbooks On the Same Disk

You can work with several Scrapbooks on the same disk. After you fill your first Scrapbook while you're in your application, quit to the desktop, and rename the Scrapbook File so that the Scrapbook can't access it. Adding a single character (i.e. Scrapbook File1) is sufficient. Back in your application, you'll have an empty Scrapbook that you can fill with more words or pictures. When you need the pictures in a specific Scrapbook, just rename it "Scrapbook File." You can copy the various Scrapbooks to another disk to store them until needed. You can also keep libraries of specialized Scrapbook files for various projects.

Desktop Publishing

CAPTIONS

Use Larger Sans-Serif Fonts for Captions

For captions in your publication, use a sans-serif face (like Helvetica) that's a point size or two larger than your body copy. That's right—larger. Many times, captions are the only things people read in a publication, so use complete sentences, and get your article's main points across in the captions. Avoid using *italic* fonts for the text of a caption—those typefaces are more difficult to read.

CONTENT

ALWAYS Use A Disinterested Proofreader

One often overlooked part of the process in desktop publishing is proofreading. How often have you seen an otherwise professional looking publication that is riddled with misspellings, grammatical errors, and missing words or sentences. Don't try to proofread your own work and don't trust an article's author as the final proofreader. You're both too close to the material and can easily "read in" missing words and overlook grammatical errors that you've seen repeatedly in the process of laying out the pages.

FONTS

Don't Go "Font Happy"

A good rule of thumb is to use only two or (at most) three fonts in a single publication. The reader's eye will get confused trying to sort out words in too many different typefaces. Use larger sans-serif fonts (like Helvetica) for your headlines and subheads, and serif fonts (like Times) for your body copy.

LAYOUT

Don't Feel You Have To Compose Pages Sequentially

With a paste-up program, you don't have to layout your pages sequentially. If you're waiting for a late article for the first page of your newsletter, just leave some space for it and continue it on an inside page when it comes in. You might need to edit the late article to fit the reserved space, or find a short fill item, but it could make the difference in getting your publication out on time.

Keep "Continued On..." Lines As Separate Items

Inserting a "continued on page..." in a word processor can be maddening—it creates a ripple effect on everything following. In your pasteup program, it's easy—just make it a separate item from the article. That way, if you make any changes to the article that disturb the lines, your continuation notice will stay put. Use the same technique for "continued from..." lines.

MEMORY MANAGEMENT

Avoid *Switcher* and Use Large RAM Cache If Possible

If you do all of your text and graphics ahead of time and store them in the Scrapbook, you shouldn't have to keep graphics and text editing programs in *Switcher* or a RAM disk. Instead, use the extra RAM for a disk cache—it speeds things up dramatically. Don't necessarily use the largest size cache (start at 256K on a Mac 512, 384K on a Mac Plus), since some DAs and the Clipboard use big chunks of memory.

NEWSLETTERS

Keep A "Junk" Page To Store Frequently Used Items

If you lay out a newsletter or other publication often, keep a dummy junk page in your publication to store frequently used graphics, headers and other elements. It's a handy place to store elements that float from one place to another from issue to issue. When you want to use an element, just drag it to the Pasteboard, click on the target page where you want to place it, and drag the element into position. Just before you print your final copy, delete the junk page. This technique is faster than scrolling through pages of the Scrapbook and one page should give you plenty of space if you're a little neat and overlap items.

Keep A "Shell" of Your Newsletter To Use for the Next Issue

Here's a big time-saver. After completing your first newsletter with a new pasteup program, go back and delete everything but the parts that will be common to future issues. Leave everything you think you might want for the next issue—column headings, membership information, masthead, and the basic page structure. Rename this shell version of your newsletter and when you start the next issue, drag the shell to your work disk, rename it for the current issue, and Open it. Paste in your new copy and graphics and half the work's been done already. Be sure to update your shell with each issue so you don't lose track of new elements you've added since you created the last shell.

TRAINING

Don't Ignore the Basics!

Just because you have a wonderful computer like the Mac, an amazing printer like the LaserWriter, and a snazzy new page layout program, don't think that pages are going to lay themselves out. Go to the library and get some basic books on graphic arts and typography. (An old favorite of mine is *Arnold's Ancient Axioms: Typography for Publications Editors* by Edmund C. Arnold from Ragan Report Press, 407 South Dearborn Street, Chicago, IL 60605. It's a little dated, but full of rules of thumb that will steer you away from disasters.) Beginners really need to know about the ways to produce a readable publication. These books will get you started with things like preferred line length for a given point size, indentation, minimum type size, etc.

Dinner at Eight

MENUS

Take A Screen Snapshot Of Menus To Modify In *MacPaint*

Dinner At Eight is very limited in the way it handles the printing of its menus. It has only one pattern and layout. If you want to enhance the printed menu with other graphics (or dishes whose recipes you didn't get from *Dinner At Eight's* database), use COMMAND-SHIFT-3 with the menu showing on the screen to create a *MacPaint* file. Now you can Open the file (Screen 0) with *MacPaint* and enhance it as much as you want.

SILVER PALATE EDITION

Be Sure To Clear Category Selection Before Browsing Another

Rubicon has put so many categories in the *Silver Palate Edition* that cross referencing among categories is not possible. As a result, you have to be sure to click on the Clear button before selecting a different category on another browse screen.

Disk Drives

EXTERNAL DRIVES

Running an 800K External Drive with Old ROMs

You can use an 800K external drive with a 512K Mac that hasn't had the new ROMs installed. To do so, however, you MUST have *Finder 5.1* or later, *System 3.1.1* or later, and the *Hard Disk 20* system file present in the System folder on your startup disk in the INTERNAL drive. With this arrangement, you can use the extra data storage capabilities of the 800K drive, but you cannot use it as the startup drive. Remember, the *Hard Disk 20* system file must be on the disk so the old ROMs can recognize a disk of more than 400K capacity. Ignore the "disassembler installed" message if it appears when you boot.

PLACEMENT

Placement Near Macintosh

Don't put an external drive on the left side of the Mac. The magnetic field from the machine's power supply can cause interference with disk reads and writes.

Dollars & $ense

MAC PLUS

Printout All Files Before Upgrading to Mac Plus

If you have been using *Dollars & Sense* on an older Mac, and want to upgrade to a Mac Plus, beware that *Dollars & Sense* will not work on the Mac Plus. Monogram has promised a fix for several months, but has not shipped it. Because of the incompatibility between *Dollars & Sense* and the new 128K ROMS, opening your files under the old version of the program can introduce serious errors. Be sure to make a complete printout of all your data before you take your Mac to the shop for its brain transplant.

PRINTING

Limited Screen Dumps

In *Dollars & Sense*, the only way to create screen dumps is to use COMMAND-SHIFT-CAPS LOCK-4. As well as sending a screen dump to the ImageWriter, it will create a *MacPaint* file on your disk. Note that only one file may be saved to the disk at a time. If you want to make more files (i.e. do more screen dumps), you must move the existing file to another disk first.

Edit

BUGS

Backspaced or Inserted Characters May Not Redraw Properly

The Apple *MDS 68000* assembler, *Consulair C*, *TML Pascal*, and *MacAdvantage Pascal* all use the same *Edit* program from Apple. The following hints refer to that *Edit* program. When you backspace or insert characters in *Edit*, the Mac might not initially redraw the letters correctly. If you scroll the faulty text off the screen and back again, everything should be fine.

Be Careful About Volume Name Lengths with Version 2

Version 2 of Apple's *Edit* program has a lot of bugs. For instance, if the volume name of your system disk is longer than the volume name of your data disk, *Edit* will crash.

ENTER Key Creates Invalid Character

If you use the ENTER key in *Edit*, it doesn't act like ENTER in *MacWrite*. Instead, it inserts an invalid ASCII 03. See "Make ENTER Characters Visible for Programming" for a solution to this problem.

Paste Function Doesn't Always Paste At Insertion Point

When you Paste something in *Edit*, it doesn't always appear at the insertion point. It may show up somewhere else in the document. Be careful.

Tabs Are Preset At Eight Spaces For Monaco 9-Pt.

The tabs in *Edit* are preset at eight spaces for 9-pt. Monaco text. If you change fonts, the tabs will not readjust.

FINDING

Use A Select Range To Select Text You Want Used In A Find Operation

If you have a select range in *Edit*, a find operation will use that range as the "compare" entry.

OPENING FILES

COMMAND-K Will Allow You To Open File Without Dialog Box

When in *Edit*, if you type COMMAND-K, you can Open a file by typing its filename and bypass the Open dialog box.

Select the Filename You Want To Open To Activate COMMAND-D

Edit has a menu option to Open a file by name. However, it remains dimmed until you've selected the text that comprises the name of the file you want to Open. After you've selected the file name with the mouse, the option is available from the menu and can also be invoked with COMMAND-D.

Excel

APPLICATIONS

Create Form Letters with Data Inserts and "&" Function

You can use *Excel* to create form letters. First, create the list of data you want to merge into your letter with the database function. Then, create a macro that will develop the data inserts from that list. Now, use the "&" Function in a loop to link the data inserts and the context of the letter to surround them. Turn off the gridlines and the record numbers and you'll be able to print your letters. You'll need a little practice to develop the letter format you want to use, but if this is your only need for a database manager, *Excel* will do the job admirably.

DATABASES

Don't Forget That You Can Create A Separate Data Entry Form

Entering the information for a database directly onto a spreadsheet in *Excel* can be a frustrating experience. You might prefer to enter the data in a different order than you want it on the spreadsheet, or you may have so many fields that you're constantly scrolling the screen back and forth to look at a single record of your database. *Excel* has an easy way around this problem. Create a separate *Excel* document as your data entry form. Then create a macro to extract the data from the form and Paste it into the database cells on your spreadsheet. Now you can simply fill out the data entry form and invoke your macro to Paste it into the next row on your spreadsheet database. It's a little more complicated than we can describe here, but with a little experimentation, *Excel* should provide some powerful database management capabilities for you.

Leave A Sliver of Space On Screen Below Data Entry Form

When you are designing a form for data entry into a database section of your spreadsheet (see "Don't Forget That You Can Create A Separate Data Entry Form"), leave a sliver of space at the bottom of your screen. Make it large enough to show a couple of lines from your spreadsheet. Now, you can Open the destination spreadsheet's window to see the lines where your macro will Paste the information from your data entry form. This isn't necessary, but the feedback helps to reassure you that your macro is working properly and Pasting your data in the correct place.

Preselect Entry Field Sequence In Data Entry Forms

You can preselect the order in which the ENTER key selects fields. First, hold down the COMMAND key and select the fields in your form in the order you want to use them for data entry. Now, define the whole selection with a single name. During data entry, the cursor will jump from field to field in the order you selected each time you hit the ENTER key.

DATES

Use Series Feature To Create Column Header Dates

Here's a method to make *Excel* automatically fill in the dates at the heads of your columns. Our example here is for months (January, February, etc.) to keep it simple, but you should be able to expand this example to increment by almost any amount of time you want. First, select (highlight) the cells you want filled with the months (12, in this case). Then, select Number from the Format menu. Type "mmm" into the dialog box if you want the months abbreviated, or "mmmm" if you want them spelled out. Without deselecting the cells, enter 1 in the first cell and hit ENTER. Go to the data window and select Series. In the dialog box, select Series in Row, Type Date, Month Date Unit, and increment of one with no stopping point. Now, go back to the spreadsheet, type 2 in the second cell, and hit ENTER. Your dates should appear. Experiment with this until you can do it for whatever time increment is appropriate for your work.

Use the NOW() Function To Enter Current Date or Time

You can use the NOW() function to enter the current date or time into a cell. Use one of the following functions with it to define which part of the information should be displayed: DAY(), HOUR(), MINUTE(), MONTH(), WEEKDAY(), or YEAR(). For example, the formula to enter the current month in a cell would be =MONTH(NOW()).

FILES

Pre-release File Compatibility

If you are having difficulty getting *Excel* to read files, they may have been created by someone using the pre-release version. The file format for the old 6-6 pre-release version of *Excel* is not the same as the released version. However, you can convert files very easily via the SYLK format.

HEADERS & FOOTERS

Editing Header or Footer Text Longer Than the Entry Box

In a header or footer entry box (in the Page Setup dialog box), you can enter text that is longer than the box can display. If you need to edit this text later, you can view it by placing the cursor in the visible text near the right end of the entry box and dragging off the end. The text will scroll to the left and the extra text will appear, already selected for editing.

How To Format Headers & Footers

Although the method is little awkward, you can embed formatting commands and other instructions in the text of the header or footer of an *Excel* document. Insert the formatting commands in the header or footer boxes in the Page Setup dialog box. The following table shows what options are available:

COMMAND	EFFECT
&L	Align the characters that follow at the left margin.
&C	Center the characters that follow.
&R	Align the characters that follow at the right margin.
&P	Print the page number.
&D	Print the current date.
&T	Print the current time.
&F	Print the name of the document.
&B	Print the left, center, or right part of the header or footer in bold.
&I	Print the left, center, or right part of the header or footer in italic.
&&	Print a single ampersand (&).

MACROS

Only Use Macros From Open Macro Sheets

In *Excel*, you can use macros only from open macro sheets when building your spreadsheet. If you Close a macro sheet that contains a macro referred to by a cell of your open spreadsheet, the value of that cell will change to "#REF!" To recompute the functions, you must reOpen the macro sheet.

Order of Functions In A User-Defined Function

In a user-defined function macro, you must place the functions in a specific order. The macro must begin with one or more ARGUMENT functions and end with the RETURN function. The formulas that do the actual work must be between the ARGUMENT functions and the RETURN function. If your formulas are after the RETURN function, your user-defined function will not calculate properly.

MEMORY SIZE

Load *Excel* In the First Megabyte

Excel will not access any memory over the first megabyte. If you have more than a megabyte of RAM installed in your Mac, and are using the program in a *Switcher* configuration, be sure to install it in the first slot so it gets the lowest possible memory allocation.

Running *Excel* On A Single 400K Drive Macintosh 512

Need to use *Excel* on a single 400K drive 512K Mac? *Excel* doesn't require the full 512K of RAM. If you have a RAM disk, just create a 215K RAM disk that contains the *System*, *Finder*, and *ImageWriter* files. *Excel* works fine with the remaining memory. Some disk shuffling will arise when you save work files to a data disk.

NAMING

Automatic Naming for Cells To the Right of Their Labels

If you often find yourself entering a column of labels and then manually naming each of the cells in the column just to the right of your labels for use in formulas, try this trick. Select the first cell you want to have the same name as the contents of the label cell to its left. Now, use COMMAND-L (or choose Define Name in the Formula menu) and immediately hit RETURN, without waiting for the dialog box to appear. *Excel* automatically assigns the contents of the label cell to the left as the selected cell's name.

PASSWORDS

How To Remove Password Protection

If you have a legitimate reason to see a password protected spreadsheet, but don't have the password, try this. Use a disk editor (such as MacTools) to examine the file and find block 1, part B, position `0175`. If the flag is set (the spreadsheet is password protected) the indicator will be `01`. Change it to `00`, write the edited block to the disk, and you'll remove the password protection from the spreadsheet.

PASTE SPECIAL

Use Paste Special When You Only Want To Paste Values

If you want to Copy a section of your spreadsheet and Paste only its values (no formulas) somewhere else, use the Paste Special function when you Paste it in place. The resulting Paste will contain only the values that were shown in the original section when you Copied it and will not contain any formulas.

WINDOWS

Too Large A Document Window From A Mac/XL

On a regular Mac, when you display an *Excel* document created on a Mac XL, the document spills off the screen. To shrink it to fit the smaller screen, just double-click on the window title bar until you can control it with the grow box.

Filevision

BUTTONS

Create "HELP" Buttons For Others

For the convenience of other people using your *Filevision* database, you can establish HELP files in addition to the drawings. In the Types menu, add a type called HELP. Create one field in your data form and call it INSTRUCTIONS, and in the NAME field, type in a message such as, "For HELP, Double Click the Mouse." Take the rounded rectangle tool and place a small one in a convenient, but inobtrusive place on the screen. Now click on the rectangle to select it, and with the SHIFT key down, also select the text tool, and type HELP inside the rectangle. Finally, go back to the data form and type in your HELP text in the INSTRUCTIONS field.

DRAWING

Draw Oversized Objects and Shrink Them

To minimize the appearance of inaccuracies in your objects, draw them much larger than the finished size, reshape them until they're almost right, then grab them by a corner handle and shrink them to the appropriate size. This will reduce the imperfections by a corresponding amount.

Higher Quality Reshaping

Whenever possible, use the straight line tools to create your drawings in *Filevision.* Drawings created with the straight line tools use fewer points, giving you more latitude in reshaping.

Recycle Other People's Drawings

If you have a hard time creating the original drawings you'd like for *Filevision*, try looking through some of the examples on the *Filevision Ideas Disk* or the public domain files on *CompuServe*. You may find that you were trying to reinvent the wheel and that someone else has already created the graphic base you need for your files—or at least gotten you started so you can just modify existing work.

Use Symbol Editor To Create Graphic Elements

If you're not an artist and have a hard time creating æsthetically pleasing objects, use the symbol editor to create their graphic components and keep your main drawing simple. You'll have much finer control within the symbol editor and your mistakes will be less evident when the symbol is displayed in miniaturized form on the screen.

Use the Grid To Transfer Graphics

You can use an old-fashioned technique to transfer pictures from other media into *Filevision*. If you find a diagram in a magazine or newspaper that you'd like to copy into *Filevision*, draw a 1" grid on the artwork or place an acetate sheet with the grid on top of the drawing. Then, turn on the grid on the *Filevision* drawing screen and reproduce the original graphic, square by square.

FILES

Minimize Creating Objects or Drawing Files Used Often

If you are creating a drawing file that contains objects which you want to use in other files, you can Cut and Paste objects between files. For large groups of objects, a more convenient way is to duplicate the total drawing file. Then delete any information or objects you don't want in the new file. If you have custom designed symbols or data forms, and will use them repeatedly, use the same approach: Duplicate the drawing file containing the symbols and Clear all unwanted objects and data (leaving one object of each type to provide blank forms), then copy and rename this "template" file at the creation of each new file.

IGNORE

Clearer Pictures

When working with the "Highlight Some" selection, experiment with putting the background on "Ignore." The highlighted objects will come out with the background very visible, not grayed out like the other objects that are not selected. The IGNORE function also will prevent you from inadvertently clicking on the background when selecting an object.

MEMORY SPACE

Getting the Most Objects Possible

Two factors determine the total number of objects you can have in your drawing file: the complexity of the drawing itself and the length of its name. Symbols use up less memory than freehand drawings and the longer the name (i.e., the more characters you have in the name field), the more memory you need. *Filevision* will let you use up to 999 objects, but you're likely to run out of memory before you get there.

To get the most objects possible, try to use symbols rather than drawings, and then give them short, meaningful names. If you need mailing labels or full names in your reports, just make another space in your data form called "mailing name" and enter the full name there. That won't cut down the number of possible objects at all.

OBJECTS

Multi-element Objects and Bind

If you want to create multi-element objects which allow you to select a single element or the total object, use the SHIFT key when you select your drawing tool. Then, using the element or object selector tool, you can move the elements or the whole object around to place it anywhere in the drawing. The Bind selection from the Edit menu lets you bind all the elements in your object together and move it anywhere on the screen. You can Cut and Paste elements from an object into another object in the same file or into another drawing file, thus cutting down on your drawing time.

SCROLLING

Scroll By Number

To control the sequence of objects when using the NEXT or PREVIOUS buttons, number your objects in the NAME field. Numbers precede letters in the process *Filevision* uses to alphabetize things. Thus, to move items up to the top of the list, just give them names that are numbers. Another way to control their order is to use the same name (such as "Teleporter" but put numbers in front ("1Teleporter," "2Teleporter," "3Teleporter," etc.). This works very well when you need to show a series of steps or phases in your drawing file.

1st Base

FIELD LENGTHS

Create Merge Fields Longer Than 50 Characters

You can chain several 50-character fields together to form mergable paragraphs for form letters using *1st Base* and *1st Merge*. Simply put the number of 50-character fields you think you'll need in sequence in your form design. Then, fill in the fields, tabbing to the next field when the one you're typing in is full. Be sure to use hard spaces (OPTION-SPACE) at the ends of the fields to keep them from being stripped off when *1st Base* merges the abutting fields. When you design your *1st Merge* document in *MacWrite*, use the standard practice of enclosing the field names in brackets. Put the field names of the fields you want chained directly next to one another (no spaces between the brackets). This method works best when you put the chained fields in their own paragraph in the *1st Merge MacWrite* document.

HFS

Early Versions of *1st Base* Products Are Not Compatible with HFS

Early versions of *1st Base*, *1st Merge*, and *1st Port* are not compatible with HFS. The publisher suggests that you can try to run them under the old *System* on a Mac Plus, but does not guarantee that you won't still have problems. As of this writing (6/28/86), updates have just been issued for all three products that are compatible with HFS and add a few other improvements. We've not had a chance to review the updates, but they sound promising. The *1st Base* products are no longer published by DeskTop Software. The line of products has been purchased by Template Systems in Massachusetts. They plan to update the products to make them compatible with the Mac Plus. For more information, call them at (800) 522-2286.

INCOMPATIBILITIES

Incompatible with *BatteryPak Phone Pad*

1st Base and Batteries Included's *Phone Pad* are incompatible for Cut and Paste operations. If you try to Cut or Copy data from one of *1st Base's* fields and Paste it into the *Phone Pad*, not only does the data not appear on the *Phone Pad* as you requested, but it also disappears from the field in *1st Base* (regardless of whether you Cut or Copied it). The data can't be retrieved, so be careful!

Font/DA Mover

APPLICATIONS

DRVR Resource Conflicts In Installing DAs In Applications

If you choose to install desk accessories in applications instead of your *System* file, be aware of conflicts between the DAs DRVR resources. Later versions of the *Font/DA Mover* should adjust for this automatically, but it can be especially deadly to hard disk drivers if you're using an older version of the utility.

Use *Font/DA Mover* To Attach Fonts & DAs To Applications

You don't have to use the *Resource Editor* to attach fonts or desk accessories directly to resources or applications. You can use the Apple's *Font/DA Mover*. First, launch the *Font/DA Mover* (holding down the OPTION key if you want to go directly into desk accessory mode). You should see the fonts or desk accessories from the *System* file in the left-hand window and a blank window with an Open button in the right-hand window. Hold down the OPTION key while clicking on the Open button and the disk window that comes up will allow you to Open any file on the disk and install fonts or desk accessories in it.

BUGS

Version 3.1 Doesn't Copy DAs with DRVR ID=0

The *Font/DA Mover*, version 3.1 does not copy DAs with a DRVR ID=0.

Version 3.1 May Lock Up Mouse On Launch

Sometimes the mouse will lock when starting *Font/DA Mover* version 3.1. The solution is to reset and try again.

Won't Transfer Large Fonts In 128K Mac

Most or all versions of Apple's *Font/DA Mover* contain a known bug. On 128K machines, it won't transfer 18-point or larger fonts. To move these fonts, you'll have to use the old Font Mover that came with your machine.

DEMOS & INSTRUCTION

Install Fonts or DAs In Their Instructions

If you have a style sheet for a font or documentation on disk for a desk accessory, use Apple's *Font/DA Mover* to install the particular font or desk accessory that the document refers to. (See "Use *Font/DA Mover* To Attach Fonts & DAs To Applications.") By storing the font with its style sheet, you won't have to be sure that the fonts it uses are installed on the startup disk you're using. By storing a desk accessory with its documentation, you give the user a chance to try out the accessory while reading the documentation without having to make sure it's installed in the *System* file first.

EJECTING DISKS

OPTION-Close Ejects File's Disk

If you hold down the OPTION key when you click the Close button for a file, the disk containing the file will eject.

OPTION-Quit Ejects Both Disks

If you are running the *Font/DA Mover* on a two disk-drive system, you can eject the disks from both drives when you quit by holding down the OPTION key when you click on the Quit button.

FILES

Automatically Opens *System* File of Inserted Disk

You don't have to click the Open button in the *Font/DA Mover* display if you want to Open the *System* file on a new disk and one of the two "slots" isn't displaying a file. Simply insert the disk whose *System* you want to Open. The *System* file will Open and the fonts or desk accessories it contains will appear in the previously unused "slot."

New *Font/DA Mover* Doesn't Recognize "Old" DAs

The *Font/DA Mover* that was shipped with *Finder 4.1* doesn't recognize "old style" desk accessories. To make it do so, you have to change the creator and file types of the old desk accessories with a disk utility like *MacZap* or *ResEdit*. The old type probably is DESK —change it to DFIL. The old creator probably is DAMV—change it to DMOV.

LAUNCH

Launch Into Desk Accessory Mode

The *Font/DA Mover* defaults to font mode when launched. To Open directly into the desk accessory mode, press OPTION anytime after issuing the Open command or click on the Desk Accessory button as soon as it appears.

SIZES

Use OPTION Key To Find Out DA Size

If you hold down the OPTION key when you click on a desk accessory in Apple's *Font/DA Mover*, the display will show how many bytes are occupied by its code, pictures and "other."

FONTastic

SPECIAL CHARACTERS

Make a Font of Frequently Used Small Graphics

If you publish a newsletter or have another application that requires you to repeat a number of small custom graphics, you can save a lot of trips to graphics editors and the Scrapbook by creating your own font that contains all of your repeating graphics. You can make special characters to end articles, a graphic to lead-in every column, etc.

Fonts

BOSTON II

Hard Space Is Different In Boston II

Boston II is a shareware ImageWriter font distributed through many user groups. The hard space (unbreakable space available through OPTION-SPACE) is a different size in Boston II than in most fonts. In most fonts, this space is a little wider than a normal space. However, Boston II's designer intends that you use this space for fine adjustment (like extra room after italics). So it's a "micro-space"—only one pixel wide. Like its larger counterpart in other fonts, it's treated as a part of the previous word and won't be split by a word processor's line wrap function. This can be a very handy feature if you work exclusively in Boston II. However, be very careful when converting sections of Boston II to another font. Those five micro-spaces you put after an italic word could suddenly turn into an inch of space!

Boston II 14-Pt. Is Really 1-Pt. Line

The 14-pt. size of Boston II isn't made up of text characters like the other sizes. Instead, it is a 1-pt. underline character designed for constructing equations and other cases where a 1-pt. line might be required. Because *MacWrite* won't recognize a 1-pt. font, it's called 14-pt. to get it to appear on the menu.

Use *Key Caps* To Look For All the Special Characters

The designer of the Boston II font has gone to great lengths to include a large number of special characters, fractions, diacritical marks, etc. in the font. Use the new *Key Caps* (the one that lets you select the font it displays) to look at all of the OPTION and SHIFT-OPTION characters to make your writing more attractive.

CHARACTERS

Diacritical Marks

To use a diacritical mark (accent, umlaut, cedilla, etc.) with a letter of the alphabet, you must type the diacritical mark first. It won't appear on screen until you enter the character that goes with it. First, hold down the OPTION key and press the key that has the desired mark. Release both keys, then type in the letter that requires the diacritical mark. The character and the mark now will appear on the screen simultaneously. Use the *Key Caps* DA if you can't remember which key accesses the special mark you need.

Ellipsis

You can get a true ellipsis on the Mac. An ellipsis is a series of three periods used in text to indicate the omission of a word or words and it looks like… Use OPTION–SEMICOLON to get the character. This is a real advantage in justified text because the ellipsis remains attached to the word in front of it as a single character and the spacing between the periods isn't altered by text justification.

Em Dashes

You can make a true em dash—like the ones surrounding these words—on the Mac. It is equal in width to the letter "m" in the font you are using. Type SHIFT, OPTION and a hyphen, all at the same time.

En Dashes

You can make a true en dash–like the ones surrounding these words–on the Mac. It is equal in width to a letter "n." Type OPTION and a hyphen at the same time. To help you remember how to get an en dash or an em dash, notice that the hyphen key has a short line and a long line (normally for a hyphen and an underscore character). With the OPTION key down, the shift key selects the longer one, representing the longer em dash.

Hearts

Two fonts will provide a heart character. In New York, it's in the 18 point size, and you type OPTION-SHIFT-Tilde (~ is the top left character on your keyboard). In the LaserWriter Symbol font, the heart symbol is available in any size by typing OPTION-G.

Quick Row of Periods

Make a quick horizontal line of periods in any font with OPTION–SEMICOLON. The Mac treats each set of three dots as a character, so be careful with this feature if you fully justify your text—you'll get some strange spacing…

Tilde Characters

There's a "secret" key combination that's not shown in the old *Key Caps* desk accessory. Press OPTION-SHIFT-TILDE (~ is the key just to the left of 1). Depending on the point size and font selected, you can access the "secret" or special characters in most fonts. The shapes vary in usefulness. In 12-point Geneva, the combination results in a rabbit silhouette. In Microsoft's Seattle font, you get a Mac icon.

Use BASIC To Get Apple, Cloverleaf and Checkmark

The Chicago font has the Apple, Checkmark and Cloverleaf (COMMAND) characters hidden in the invisible portion of the ASCII character set. If you want to use them in a document, you can store them on the Clipboard from BASIC and then move them into the Scrapbook for later use. First, use the following BASIC program to get them to the Clipboard:

```
OPEN "O",1,"CLIP:"
PRINT #1,CHR$(17);CHR$(18);CHR$(20)
CLOSE
```

Then, move them to the Scrapbook. Because the Scrapbook displays its information in Geneva 12-pt., they'll appear as squares. Don't worry, they're still there, you just won't see them until you get them into a document where they can be displayed in Chicago. You can Paste them into your document from the Scrapbook and remove the characters you don't want. Be sure to keep them in Chicago font, or they'll go back to the squares you saw in the Scrapbook.

You Don't Have to Omit Ligatures

The age of the typewriter and its limited character set has led us to omit ligatures (æ, Æ, œ, Œ, etc.) from our written language. With the Mac OPTION key capabilities and most fonts, there's no reason to do so any more. Aesthetic's pronunciation is much more obvious when it's written as æsthetic. In most fonts, you can get æ and Æ with OPTION-Single-quote and SHIFT-OPTION-Double-quote, and œ and Œ with OPTION-q and SHIFT-OPTION-Q.

DESIGNING

Don't Alter Proportions When Designing Double-Sized Fonts

When you are designing the double-size of a font (making the 24 point version after the 12 point version, for example), make sure you keep the same proportions as you have in the smaller version. If you use the font in *MacWrite* and select the high quality option when you print, the ImageWriter will use the double-size version and reduce it to get better formed characters. If the proportions or the baseline of the double-size font are not the same as in the one you're using, you'll get garbage on the printout.

Use Type Catalogs As Font Sources

If you want to design your own fonts, don't feel you have to start by reinventing the wheel. Browse through presstype and other type catalogs (available at most art stores) until you find a font that's close to what you want. Use a digitizer or, if you have the patience, trace the characters of the font with the mouse. Now, you can Cut and Paste copies of the commercial font's characters into a font editor (like *FONTastic*) and modify them until you have the characters you want.

GENEVA

Geneva 12-pt. "Y" Is Different In High & Standard Qualities

As you probably know, when the ImageWriter prints a font in High Quality (Best) from many programs (like *MacWrite*), it looks for the double-size of the font on the disk and reduces it by 50% to produce the higher quality printout. A difference between the 12- and 24-point Geneva fonts causes an odd difference in Geneva 12-pt. printout between high and standard qualities. The lower-case "y" in Geneva 24-pt. is actually a subscripted upper-case "Y." The lower-case "y" in Geneva 12-pt. is a real lower-case y. If you print out the same Geneva 12-pt. document in high and standard qualities, you'll see the difference in the lower-case y's in your printouts.

ICON

Change Icon Font's Resource To Print On LaserWriter

The resource for the Icon font thinks it's a 12-pt. font, even though it's really 36. This won't make any difference for printing on the ImageWriter, but the LaserWriter will print it as a 12-pt. font. Use *FONTastic* to correct the resource for this font.

ID NUMBERS

Assigning Font ID Numbers

Theoretically, the Mac has a total of 511 font ID numbers. Apple has devised a numbering system for assigning these numbers. Fonts 0-127 are reserved for Apple. Fonts 128-383 are designated for outside developers but must be approved by Apple to avoid confusion. Fonts 384-511 are for "the rest of us." However, when assigning a font ID number, be careful, since resource tools don't always work with fonts numbered above 255.

LASERWRITER

Don't Try To Edit LaserWriter Fonts without Proper Software

Don't try to use a font editor designed for ImageWriter fonts to edit LaserWriter fonts. If you don't have the right software for editing LaserWriter fonts, you can make them unprintable with no trouble at all.

Updated Times, Helvetica and Courier Change Spacing

With the release of the LaserWriter Plus, Apple altered the Times, Helvetica and Courier fonts slightly to improve spacing when used on the LaserWriter from a Mac Plus. This may affect text spacing in existing documents. Check the formatting of your older documents before printing them out on the new equipment, and make adjustments, if necessary.

MAC ATTACK

Mac Attack's Fonts Can Be Used In Other Applications

Mac Attack uses four special fonts to create parts of its display—Tank, Missile, MaTitle and Landscape. These fonts are installed in the *System* file of the distribution disk for *Mac Attack*. You can use the *Font/DA Mover* to copy and manipulate them just like any other font. Who knows, they might come in handy for a letter to your grandmother about nuclear disarmament!

MANAGEMENT

Create Font Management Disk with No *System* or *Finder*

If you have two disk drives, you can create a font management disk that will simplify the process of altering the fonts on any current startup disk. On your font management disk, put a copy of the *Font/DA Mover* and files containing logical groupings of fonts (display fonts, picture fonts, text fonts, etc.).

When you want to modify the *System* on your current startup disk, put your font management disk in the other drive and double-click on the *Font/DA Mover*. The *System* file on your startup disk will Open automatically with the *Font/DA Mover* and you can then Open the other font files as you need. When you quit the *Font/DA Mover*, you'll be right back at the desktop of your newly modified startup disk.

MEMORY SIZES

Memory Sizes of Apple Fonts

The following table shows the memory sizes (disk space required) and font numbers for all of the standard issue Apple fonts:

FONT	FONT #	SIZE	FONT	FONT #	SIZE	FONT	FONT #	SIZE
Athens 18	7	4468	Helvetica 14	21	3350	Symbol 9	23	2380
Cairo 18	11	5840	Helvetica 18	21	5086	Symbol 12	23	3366
Chicago 12	0	2940	Helvetica 24	21	8154	Symbol 18	23	5902
Courier 9	22	2074	London 18	6	3268	Symbol 24	23	9238
Courier 10	22	2462	Los Angeles 12	12	2440	Taliesin 18	129	8074
Courier 12	22	2782	Los Angeles 24	12	6444	Terminal 12	241	1024
Courier 14	22	3322	Monaco 9	4	2026	Terminal 14	241	1846
Courier 18	22	4556	Monaco 12	4	2464	Times 9	20	2154
Courier 24	22	6906	New York 9	2	2032	Times 10	20	2396
Geneva 9	3	2152	New York 10	2	2200	Times 12	20	2806
Geneva 10	3	2200	New York 12	2	2734	Times 14	20	3574
Geneva 12	3	2734	New York 14	2	3352	Times 18	20	4978
Geneva 14	3	3568	New York 18	2	4516	Times 24	20	7966
Geneva 18	3	4864	New York 20	2	5260	Toronto 9	9	2200
Geneva 20	3	5848	New York 24	2	6832	Toronto 12	9	3034
Geneva 24	3	7568	New York 36	2	13780	Toronto 14	9	3658
Helvetica 9	21	2174	San Francisco 18	8	2984	Toronto 18	9	5688
Helvetica 10	21	2396	Seattle 10	?	2410	Toronto 24	9	8854
Helvetica 12	21	2978	Seattle 20	?	6302	Venice 14	5	3604

NEW YORK

Inconsistencies Between Screen & Printout

Apple's New York family contains a couple of strange mismatches between the diacritical marks you see on the screen and what you get on the printout. If you type an upper-case E with an acute accent in New York 9- or 18-pt., you get what you asked for on the screen (É). However, in the printout you get an umlaut (¨) instead of the acute accent. In New York 12- and 24-pt., a lower case i typed with an umlaut (ï) will appear on the printout with an accute accent instead (í).

PUBLICATIONS

U&lc Typography Magazine Subscription Information

If you truly want to produce superior textual output on the Mac, especially with the LaserWriter, you'll have to keep in touch with the traditional typography market and its applications. International Typeface Corporation offers a FREE publication called *U&lc*. To get your free subscription, write: *U&lc* Subscription Dept., International Typeface Corporation, 2 Dag Hammarskjold Plaza, New York, N.Y. 10017.

QUALITY

Double-Size Fonts For High Quality On the ImageWriter

If you are going to do high-quality printing on the ImageWriter, you should keep in your *System* file a font twice the size of the one you want to print. For some applications, the ImageWriter "shrinks" the double-size font by 50% to create higher quality characters on the page. New York 12, for instance, wants to use New York 24 as a "map" when it prints in high-quality. This is not necessary for printing on the LaserWriter.

RESOURCE NUMBERS

Calculating A Font's Resource Number

To determine the resource number of a font, multiply its font ID number by 128 and add the point size. For example, to determine the resource number of New York (font ID number 2), take 2 X 128 = 256 and add the point size. New York 12 point would have a resource number of 268 (256 + 12).

SIZE

Mac Point Sizes Aren't the Same As Standard Type

The point sizes the Mac uses are not the same as the standard point sizes used in typography. For example, 10-point Seattle single-spaced in *MacWrite* is about the same as a standard 12-point typeface with 2 points of leading. The LaserWriter fonts (Times, Helvetica, etc.) are standard type sizes. Try looking at a line of Times 9 point text next to a line of New York 9 point text, and you'll see the difference immediately.

Not All Fonts of the Same Point Size Are the Same Actual Size

The height and width of a font does not necessarily correspond to its assigned point size. The point size label is really at the discretion of the font designer. For example, 9-pt. Geneva and 9-pt. Boston II differ from each other a great deal in height and width.

Use *ResEdit* To Get Around Font Size Limitations

MacWrite, *MacPaint* and every other program that uses fonts accepts them as whatever size they really are, no matter what a font's resource ID says. If you want to install a 6-point font for use in *MacWrite*, you'll have to change its resource ID (using *ResEdit*) to something larger because 6-point isn't available on *MacWrite's* Style menu. Mini- and Micro-Boston II make effective use of this trick, for example.

SOURCES

Getting A Few Letters of A Non-Mac Font

If you are designing a logo or some other graphic image that needs just a letter or two of a font you can't get on the Mac, use a digitizer to transfer the letters you need from presstype catalogs or from any source that shows the letters of the font you need. If you don't have a digitizer, try using the mouse to trace the characters. Even if it's not perfect, you'll have a much better starting point than if you tried to draw the characters on the screen.

SPACING

Apple 9-pt. ImageWriter Fonts Print Six Single-Spaced Lines Per Inch

In *MacWrite*, *MacDraw* and many other applications, the 9-pt. Apple ImageWriter fonts (as opposed to third-party or LaserWriter fonts) print six single-spaced lines to the inch on the ImageWriter.

Nonproportional Fonts

The Mac provides several nonproportional (mono-spaced) fonts. A nonproportional font uses the same spacing for every character (like most typewriters). For example, a thin character (like an "i") takes the same amount of space as a wide character (like a "w"). These fonts are especially helpful if you are using columns of text or numbers and you need the character positions to line up with one another. The Apple nonproportional fonts are `Monaco` for the ImageWriter and `Courier` for the LaserWriter. Microsoft's Seattle font has proportional letters and nonproportional numbers to make columns of figures line up on a spreadsheet while allowing more attractive and legible text labels.

One or Two Spaces After Punctuation

In most touch-typing training, you are taught to use two spaces after the final punctuation in a sentence. This will not always produce the most pleasing spacing when working on a word processor or page layout program on the Mac. As a general rule of thumb, use two spaces after final punctuation if your copy is going to be printed out with either a ragged right or left margin (unjustified). If you are going to use fully justified text on your printout (both margins even, as in most magazines) use only one space after the final punctuation. The justification routines in most word processors and page layout programs align the text with both margins by expanding the spaces between words and letters. If they encounter two spaces in a row (such as after final punctuation), the routines may add too much space.

SPECIAL

Invisible Fonts

To incorporate into your documents a section of text which will appear and print with one version of your application, but disappear with another version, do the following: Create two versions of a font called "Invisible" with a font editor. One can be a copy of the font you want your "invisible" text to use (just change the copy's resource ID to the one you're going to use for "Invisible"), or you can create your own original font. For the invisible version of the font, create a font in which all of the characters are of zero width with one exception, the hard space (OPTION-SPACE). Make that character one black pixel. Be sure to give this font the same resource ID as the visible version. Now, create two startup disks with a copy of the application with which you want to use "Invisible" on each. On one disk, install the visible version of "Invisible." You will use this version to create and edit the document in which the "Invisible" information is located. On the other startup disk, install the invisible (zero character width) version of "Invisible." Be sure to use one hard space in every section of invisible text created on the first version so you'll have a reminder that it's there in the second version. Now, when you Open a document you've created with "Invisible" with the first disk, you'll see the text. When you Open it with the second disk, the "Invisible" text will disappear.

Make ENTER Characters Visible for Programming

When you are programming on the Mac, the invisible ASCII character generated by the Mac's ENTER key (03) can sneak into your files, especially in *Edit*. This will cause havoc with some languages. You can be sure you know about these spurious "ENTER" characters by using a resource editor to change them from invisible to a unique character in the font you're using for listings (for example, a sad face). Now, you'll be able to delete them like any other displayed character.

Modify Similar Characters To Make Them More Legible

For some applications (like programming), it's more important that you be able to distinguish among similar characters on the Mac's screen than for them to be pretty when you print them. For example 1 (one), l (lower-case L), and I (upper-case I), all look very similar, but mean very different things to a programming language. For applications such as these, use a resource editor to modify the similar characters to be more legible on screen. For example, you might add wide cross-bars on the top and bottom of the I so you can tell it from an l (or is that 1?).

Use Geneva 12-point for Microfilm Documents

If you are creating documents on the ImageWriter that are later going to be microfilmed, use the Geneva 12-pt. typeface in high (best) resolution for the most legible results. Of course, the LaserWriter, printing with Courier, will give you even clearer results.

SYSTEM FONT

Changing the System Font

If you're tired of seeing the system messages on your Mac in 12-point Chicago, you can change the system font. Use a resource utility (such as *ResEdit*) to change the Font ID and Resource numbers. First, check your *System* file with the *Font/DA Mover* to make sure that the font you want to replace Chicago is also in your *System* file. Then, start your resource utility. Before you can "install" your new system font, you'll have to reassign Chicago's Font ID and Resource numbers. Chicago's Font ID is 0 and its Resource number is 12. Change the Font ID to a currently unused number in your *System* file. Then, multiply the new Font ID by 128 and add 12 (the point size) to determine Chicago's new Resource number and reassign it. Now, change the Font ID of the font you want to become the system font to 0 and its Resource number to 12. The next time you boot this disk, your system messages should appear in your new system font. WARNING! FOR YOUR OWN PEACE OF MIND, ALWAYS TRY THIS OPERATION ON A BACKUP FIRST!

Resolving a Messed Up System Font

Does the typeface on your desktop look "wrong?" One of several possibilities may explain what has happened (especially if you're not the only person using your Mac). Someone may have changed the default system font, or the application's designers may have changed it for reasons of their own. Several public domain utilities are available for this purpose, such as the *Change Application Font* Desk Accessory and the *Change Application Font* utility (two different programs), or *PRAM2*.

If the Mac's battery is dead, it might be the cause of the problem. Check the date and time. If they are incorrect, the battery is weak, dead, or has a bad connection. In these cases, the best solution is to remove the Mac's battery for at least 30 seconds. If the battery is dead, it may be the cause of the problem. (Remember to reset the date and time when you start up again.) If that doesn't work, probably the *System* file on the disk you were using has been altered and one or more of the "unremovable" fonts has been altered or removed. Try starting up with another disk containing a *System* file you know has not been altered. If everything is back to normal, you may need to rebuild the *System* file on the disk that caused the problem.

Graphics Tablets

DRAWING SURFACE

Custom Fitting Acetate Sheets On Your Tablet

You can use acetate sheets on your graphics tablet for a number of special purposes. (See "Templates" hints.) If your graphics tablet isn't already equipped with alignment pins for attaching acetate sheets, you can modify it. First, buy three ProPins, a set of drafter's pegs, or animator's pegs. Also, buy a supply of the sheets you are going to use. If you buy pre-punched sheets and your pins or pegs are already fastened in a strip, make sure that their holes are properly aligned for the pins or pegs you'll be using. If you don't buy pre-punched sheets, also buy a precision punch (can be expensive) that will punch holes to fit your pins or pegs. If your pins or pegs are not already in a strip, use a punched sheet with the pins stuck through its holes to determine the alignment on the tablet and then securely tape the pins in place. Now you will have a smoother surface for drawing with the stylus and you'll be able to place materials under the acetate for tracing without fear of the original shifting or being damaged.

PLACEMENT

Disks, Disk Drives, and Graphics Tablets Don't Mix

A graphics tablet works on electromagnetic principles. Magnetic fields wreak havoc on all magnetic media. Unless you want to erase your disk, keep it away from the graphics tablet. Place your external disk drive away from the tablet and never put disks on the surface—even when the tablet isn't in use.

STYLUS

Keeping Stylus Under Control

If you keep a graphics tablet as a part of your Mac workstation, you've probably noticed that the stylus is always sliding off the tablet and getting in the way when you're working with other devices. One easy way to solve this problem is with peel'n'stick velcro fasteners available in any hardware or fabric store. Just put one side of the fastener on the stylus and stick the other side to the side of your keyboard or another handy, but out of the way, place. Now your stylus will always be where you expect it to be, but won't get in your way constantly.

TEMPLATES

Create Grids On Screen and Print On Acetate

If you frequently use two or three dimensional grids in your graphics software in conjunction with your graphics tablet, you can print them out on acetate as a handy tool. If your graphics software generates its own printable grids, just print them out on pre-punched acetate sheets. (See "Custom Fitting Acetate Sheets On Your Tablet" for instructions on how to modify your tablet.) Or, you can generate your own grids with the tablet and then print them. These tools should make drawing graphics aligned to your grid much easier.

Print Out Animation Cels on Acetate for Modification

If you do a lot of animation with your graphics tablet, you may want to print out progressive versions of your cels on acetate. This makes additional modification easier. (See "Custom Fitting Acetate Sheets On Your Tablet" for instructions on how to modify your tablet for use with acetate sheets.)

Print Out Frequently Updated Images On Acetate

If you frequently update graphics (maps, charts, etc.) with your graphics tablet, you can make the task much easier. Print out the images on acetate sheets and then use them as templates on your tablet. First, equip your tablet with pins to hold the acetate sheets. (See "Custom Fitting Acetate Sheets On Your Tablet.") Create your original AFTER you've equipped your tablet so that your printed sheet will align correctly with the screen display. Now, print the original on a prepunched acetate sheet. When you want to modify the graphic, you can place the printed sheet on the pins on your tablet and change portions of it very easily.

Use Acetate Sheets To Show Active Drawing Area

Not all graphics software supports the full drawing area on all tablets. You can print out acetate overlays to show the active drawing area for different applications and make your life much easier. (See "Custom Fitting Acetate Sheets On Your Tablet" for instructions on how to modify your tablet.)

Hard Disk 20

STARTUP

Hold Down Mouse Button To Make Floppy the Startup Disk

If you're running a system on Apple's Hard Disk 20 and want to make a floppy the startup disk, simply hold down the mouse button when you start up. The system will default to the floppy as the startup disk.

Hayden Speller

FILE SIZE

Don't Try to Check Files with More than 1,500 Different Words

Hayden Speller cannot check a file containing more than 1,500 different words (total word count can be more than 1,500). If you try, the file will not be checked and you'll get an error message telling you to split up the document into smaller files.

MAC PLUS

Speller Won't Work with *MacWrite 4.5* and HD 20

Hayden Speller (version 1.2C) appears to work fine on a floppy Mac Plus system. It will not work with *MacWrite 4.5* and a Hard Disk 20. However, it will work with *MacWrite 2.2* and text only files on an HD 20.

Hayes Modems

SPEAKER

Speaker Software Switch

If you don't want to hear all theose beeps, buzzes and clicks when your modem is dialing, you can turn the speaker off with the `ATM0` (last character is a zero) command. To listen in again, use `ATM1` (last character is a one).

WAIT TIME

Changing Carrier Signal Wait Time

If you're having trouble reaching an on-line service, you can adjust the length of time the modem waits for a carrier signal before it hangs up and redials. The command `ATS7 = x` sets the number of seconds it waits for the carrier. The default value for x is 20 seconds, but you can substitute a different length of time using this command.

Helix

ABACUS

Break Up Complex Calculations Into Modules

If you want to use one of *Helix*" abacus icons to perform a complicated calculation, take the time to plan it before you try to build it on the Mac. If possible, try to break up the calculation into modules and then combine them in your final calculation. This will not only make your final calculation less complicated, but will provide you the opportunity to use the modules in other calculations without having to start over from scratch.

Duplicate and Modify Abacus Icons for Similar Calculations

If you want to create a calculation with an abacus icon that differs only a little from another you've already created, duplicate the icon of the original calculation and modify the duplicate to create your new calculation. This can save you a lot of time if you need to create a series of similar calculations.

Moving Tiles and Arrow Segments

How to move tiles and arrow segments in a calculation window is not immediately obvious on the *Helix* screen. To move the tile only, click and drag anywhere on the tile, except in an arrow or blank space. To move an individual arrow segment, click on it and drag. To move a group of arrow segments and/or tiles, use the standard Mac SHIFT-Click procedure to select the individual elements you want to move, or surround the group of elements you want to move with a selection rectangle.

Plan Complex Calculations On Paper

If you can't break up the complex calculation you want to perform into modules, take the time to plan it out on paper before trying to construct it on the Mac. You don't have to get very elaborate in your paper plan, but a quick flowchart sketched out before you begin can save you from reorganizing a mess later.

Print Out Large Calculations To Review Them

Getting the "whole picture" of a complex calculation can be difficult because you have to view portions of it by scrolling the window around. To view the whole calculation at once, print it out on the ImageWriter by choosing Print Scaled Page from the File menu. Regrettably, the current versions of *Helix* do not support this feature on the LaserWriter.

DESKTOP NEATNESS

Take the Time To Keep Your *Helix* Desktop Organized

If you're constructing a complicated relation in *Helix*, before long, your desktop will be cluttered with lots of icons. Newer versions of *Helix* provide a Clean Up option to arrange the icons on a grid, but you really need to do more to keep from getting confused. First, name your most important and frequently used icons with all uppercase letters to make them stand out in the crowd. Then, move your less frequently used icons off to the side of the window and arrange your icons in logical groups so you can keep track of where you are. The time you spend on this task will pay for itself when you are manipulating your relation.

FIELDS

Format One Field and Duplicate It To Save Time

When you're setting up a Relation for the first time, several of your fields probably will have formats other than the default settings. For example, you might want many fields with the same dollar format. If you create the fields first, you'll have to Open each icon to format the field. To save time, create one field with each of the formats you plan to use (such as dollar format in the above example), replicate as many as you need for each format, and give the icons appropriate names.

INCOMPATIBILITIES

Be Careful with *System 3.1.1* and *Helix*

Helix seems to have some problems when used with *System 3.1.1* software. Some users have reported that entire collections have been trashed when they were stored. Keep backups and be careful!

LISTS

Show Selection Menu Option Prevents Immediate Listing

If you want to Open a List Selection (with a repeating rectangle), but don't want the list to execute immediately, select the Selection icon and then Show Selection from the Search menu. Using this option always Opens the Selection window (rather than the form) and keeps the listing from launching right away. You can make the form, query and index choices you want in the Selection window and then choose Show Form to launch the list.

RELATIONS

Duplicating a Relation Icon Doesn't Duplicate Data

When you duplicate a relation icon in the collection window, only the relation's structure is duplicated, not any data you've entered into the relation. This can be a handy option if you want to get rid of all the old data in a relation, but use its structure to enter new data. Simply duplicate the relation's icon, rename it, and throw the old relation in the wastebasket.

Keeping Relations Efficient

Remember that *Helix* allocates disk space in a record for every field that's defined in your relation, regardless of whether you've entered data into the field or not. For instance, if you have two forms in your relation that share no common fields, when you enter data in one of the forms, *Helix* is allocating blank space for the fields in the other form. If you find that you have two exclusively different forms, you should make the information from each of them a separate relation. You can then use the Lookup function between the relations when you want to use information from one in the other.

SPEED

Keep Your Filenames Short

For some reason, long file names slow down *Helix*' operation. For best results, keep your file and icon names short.

Many Icons In A Relation Can Slow Down *Helix*

The more icons you have in a *Helix* window (especially the Relation window), the slower the program will operate. Be careful to discard unused icons and make those you keep as efficient as possible. (See "Keeping Relations Efficient.")

HFS

CLIPBOARD

Use A Disk Utility To Make System Folder/Drive The Default

If you're working under HFS and the new ROMs, you know that *MacPaint* and many of the other graphics programs can get very confused as to what's on the Clipboard. Actually, they're getting confused and looking in the wrong place for the Clipboard file. The easiest way to solve this problem is to use a disk utility/desk accessory (such as *DiskInfo* or *DiskTools*) to make the System Folder/Drive the default. Then, the *System* always looks in the same place for the Clipboard file.

CONFIGURATION

Don't Use HFS On 128K Machines

Apple's Hierarchical File System (HFS) will work fine on a Macintosh Plus, Mac 512, and Mac/XL. However, it will run into problems on a 128K Mac. If you own one, continue to use *System 2.0*, *ImageWriter 1.0*, *Finder 4.1* and the older Macintosh File System (MFS).

DISK MENU

Single Sided Disks Don't Show Folders

When you are viewing the disk directory that applications use to Close and Open files, HFS will allow you to access folders on double-sided disks. However, if the disk has been initialized as single-sided, only documents will show in the directory. You can still Open any document on the disk, but you can't save new files directly to folders. You'll have to move them into folders on the desktop after you've quit the application.

FILES

Keep Track of Applications' Support Files

When you're running under HFS, be sure to keep the files an application uses in the same folder. For example, when a program looks for its help file, it will look in the folder the application's in first and then look in the folder where the *System* and *Finder* reside. If the help file is in another folder, it may have difficulty finding it.

HARD DISKS

Don't Keep Multiple Copies of Applications In Different Folders

The Hierarchical File System (HFS) has the ability to find the application for a document, as long as it's in an open volume on your hard disk. No longer do you have to keep multiple copies of an application (one in each volume) if you are using HFS on ALL of your hard disk and the application is in one of the volumes you have open. The only exceptions are certain applications that haven't been updated to use HFS. Some applications require that an application for the document you want to Open must be in the same folder as the document. Check with the publisher of your software to make sure you have the latest version and that it works properly with HFS.

Resource ID#s Are Very Important

If you are developing Mac software, be sure to use ICN numbers greater than 120. According to Apple's guidelines in *Inside Macintosh*, your application could destroy all of the user's files on an HFS hard disk if you don't follow this rule.

INCOMPATIBILITIES

Microsoft (Absoft) Fortran

Microsoft (Absoft) Fortran is incompatible with HFS and won't run at all.

Neon 1.5 Not Compatible with Mac Plus ROMs

Version 1.5 of *Neon* is incompatible with the Mac Plus ROMs. It may work with disk based HFS (*Finder 5.0*), but be very careful. The problems should be corrected in version 2.0.

Q&D Filer Runs Very Strangely with HFS

Don't run *Q&D Filer* under HFS. It exhibits some strange behavior and has been known to cause hard disk crashes.

SkipFinder 5.3's Open Button Performs Strangely

SkipFinder 5.3 won't do you much good when you're running under HFS (Hierarchical File System). When you click on the Open button to Open a document, you'll go to the *Finder* instead.

INITIALIZING

How To Make A 400K HFS Disk

Normally, when you initialize a disk as single-sided under HFS, the Mac treats it as an MFS volume and the folders won't show in the disk menu within applications. However, if you hold down the OPTION key when you click "OK" after naming the new disk, it will become an HFS volume and you'll be able to use folders in the disk menu within applications.

PERFORMANCE

Optimize Performance with Lots of Small Folders

The most efficient way to use the Hierarchical Filing System (HFS) is to use a lot of folders and keep just a few files in each one.

STARTUP DISK

Hold OPTION Key While Launching An Application To Switch Startup Disks

Under the old Macintosh File System (MFS), if you launched an application from a startup disk other than the current startup disk, the Mac would make the necessary transfer of Clipboard and Desktop information and make the new application's startup disk the current startup disk. Under HFS, this doesn't happen. The current startup disk remains the current startup disk until you change it. If you want to change startup disks under HFS with the procedure described above, hold down the OPTION key when you double-click on the new application and the Mac will switch to its *System* files as the startup disk.

SYSTEM FILES

All *System* Files Must Be In the Same Folder

With the Hierarchical File System, you must keep all of your *System* files in the same folder. This includes the *System*, *Finder*, *MiniFinder* (if you are using one), any printer driver and prep files, and any desk accessory files you are using.

WINDOWS

Distinguishing Between HFS Windows and MFS Windows

Apple chose a VERY subtle way to indicate whether a window relates to the Hierarchical File System (HFS) or to the Macintosh File System (MFS). Look at the double lines under the second line of text in the window, where it says how many items are in the disk or folder. At the extreme left end of the lines, HFS windows have an extra pixel before the vertical border-line. If the pixel is missing, the disk or folder is from the MFS.

ZOOM BOX

Use the Zoom Box To Expand Window to Screen Size

HFS windows have another box on the right side of the grab bar that looks similar to the Close box on the left side. If you click on this Zoom Box, the window will expand to the size of the screen. Click on it again and the window will return to its previous size. Some new applications also support this feature and updates to most software probably will incorporate it.

HFS Backup

ARCHIVES

Freeze Your Backup At A Particular Time By Backing Up Your Backup

If you want to freeze the state of your files (for archive purposes) at the time of a particular backup, just make a backup of your backup disk. That way, even after you've used your first backup in conjunction with subsequent incremental backups, you can still use your "frozen" copy to go back to the versions of your files from the time of the first backup. Be sure to mark it clearly and put the date on the label so you don't confuse it with a regular backup disk.

DISK CACHE

Don't Use Disk Caching with *HFS Backup*

HFS Backup operates more efficiently if you turn off the disk cache on the *Control Panel*. The program doesn't use the cache option, and the cache will keep the program from running at all on a 512K Mac.

DISKS

HFS Backup May Reject Disks Accepted By the *Finder*

The *Finder* is less choosy about slightly flawed diskettes than *HFS Backup*. If *HFS Backup* rejects a disk, you'll have to use another one. However, you may be able to use the same disk with the *Finder* and other applicatons with no problem.

Hold Down OPTION Key To Use Single-Sided Disks

If you are using *HFS Backup* on a Mac system with double-sided drives, the program assumes that you are using double-sided diskettes. To tell it you are using single-sided disks, hold down the OPTION key when you insert a diskette.

HyperDrive

BAD BLOCKS

Click On Drawer Icon In *Manager* Dialog for Bad Block Count

To find out how many bad blocks are on your HyperDrive, click on the drawer icon in the About the HyperDrive Manager… dialog box.

DESKTOP

Close Drawer By Dragging To the Trash To Update Desktop File

When you Close a drawer on the HyperDrive with the *Drawers* desk accessory, the drawer's desktop file isn't updated and the positions of your icons on the desktop may be lost. However, if you drag the drawer's icon to the trashcan to Close it, the drawer's desktop file will be updated and your icons will be where you left them the next time you Open the drawer.

DRAWER NAMES

Adding Type Styles To Drawer Names In the Menu

You can make the names of drawers appear in different type styles on Hyperdrive's *Drawers* desk accessory menu. Following their names, type the character "<" and the first letter of the style you want (<B is Bold, <I is Italic, <U is Underline, <O is Outline, and <S is Shadow).

Never Use Parentheses In A Drawer Name

Never use parentheses in the name of a drawer for General Computer's Hyperdrive. An open parenthesis will disable the drawer's name in the Drawers menu and it will be impossible to access.

FORMATTING

Trick for Formatting HyperDrive with Hardware Timeout Problem

If your HyperDrive refuses to format and continually gives you a hardware timeout error, try booting from the HyperDrive floppy. Hold down the COMMAND and Period keys and Open the *Manager*. This should solve your problem.

INCOMPATIBILITIES

Be Careful When Installing *Camera* DA On HyperDrive

The *Camera* desk accessory (available on *CompuServe*, or from many user groups) can cause serious problems with your HyperDrive if you don't install it properly. Make sure you make a backup of your HyperDrive before you install the DA in case something goes wrong, and be sure to run the *HyperInstall* utility after installing *Camera*.

Be Careful When Using *MacTracks* on HyperDrive

Be very careful if you try to use *MacTracks* on a HyperDrive. It's been known to wreak havoc with the HyperDrive system software and cause problems with other hard disks.

Don't Run *Billiards* On the HyperDrive

The Rascal demo *Billiards* program reportedly can eat HyperDrive directories. Don't run the program from the HyperDrive or you may be sorry.

Don't Run *NiftyBase* with Cache Turned On

Don't run *NiftyBase* on a HyperDrive-equipped Mac with any RAM cache turned on. *NiftyBase* will crash.

Don't Use *ClickArt Effects Installer* with HyperDrive

Don't try to use the *ClickArt Effects Installer* on a HyperDrive equipped Mac. It will destroy the *System* file on your HyperDrive.

Total Music Has Problems With Some Versions of HyperDrive Software

Some versions of the HyperDrive software have problems when you run *Total Music*. To get around the problems, start the system up from the HyperDrive floppy. Then, mount the Startup drawer and pass control to it.

OTHER HARDWARE

Change Dasch RAM Disk's Resource ID To Use with HyperDrive

The Dasch External RAM Disk and HyperDrive drawers have conflicting Resource IDs. To use the two together, use *ResEdit* to change the resource ID of the Dasch to an unused number to avoid conflicts. Then, be sure that you start the HyperDrive before the Dasch.

PROBLEMS

Balky Startup from Floppy Disk

When you can't get your HyperDrive to startup and try to boot it with the HyperDrive floppy disk, you may still get an error message such as, "The only function you may execute at this point is 'Format.'" Ignore the message and try to restart it again. If that doesn't work, replace the *System* file.

Problems with HyperDrive 20

Some applications don't work well with the HyperDrive 20. A good way to bypass a balky startup is to boot from the HyperDrive floppy disk.

SYSTEM DRAWER

Reconstruct *System* Drawer If You Modify It Often

If you frequently modify the *System* file on your HyperDrive, your *System* file gets spread all over the disk, linked by many pointers, so the Mac can retrieve all the pieces. When this situation gets out of hand, you're tempting fate for a crash. If you think this might be the case, back up your *System* drawer and delete it. (Remember to do this from the HyperDrive floppy and to reset the Preferences options.) Now, recreate the *System* Drawer, restore your *System* files, and all should be OK.

ImageWriter

ABORT

Emergency Stop For Printing

A few programs don't stop printing when you press COMMAND-Period. If the program also doesn't respond to clicking on the Cancel button, or if you need to stop immediately (for example, when the print-out starts winding around the roller), just turn off the ImageWriter's power switch. The Mac will still think it's printing and will continue until it's finished, although the print time will be shorter than usual.

DRIVERS

ImageWriter 2.0 Causes Occasional "Drunken Letters"

Version 2.0 of the *ImageWriter* printer driver will cause an occasional "drunken letter" when you print out in standard resolution. Get the 2.2 upgrade.

LABELS

Don't Roll Labels Backwards In the ImageWriter

Rolling sheets or strips of labels backwards in the ImageWriter is not a good idea. Although you may save a few pennies on the the labels you might rescue, it may cost you a lot in time and inconvenience to take your ImageWriter to your dealer and have them remove the labels that stuck to the bottom of your platen when you rolled them backwards.

MAINTENANCE

Lubricating the Carriage-Bar

The ImageWriter manual recommends that you lubricate the carriage-bar on the ImageWriter once a year. However, it says "Do not use electric motor oil or any lubrication that contains rust inhibitors." That advice no longer applies, and you can use sewing machine oil, even though it contains rust inhibitors. According to Apple, the metal that the carriage-bar is made from is not the same one that was specified when the manual was written. The new metal is not subject to problems with oils containing rust inhibitors.

PLACEMENT

Magnet On Cover—Disks Beware

The cover of the ImageWriter I has a permanent magnet on the left side. Don't put a floppy disk on top of it or you could lose all of your data. On the ImageWriter II, the magnet is hidden away on a little tab on the bottom right corner of the cover, just above the power switch. You won't damage a disk if you put it on top of this new placement, but don't inadvertently remove this part of the cover and put it on top of a floppy disk. The purpose of this magnet is to trip a switch to let the printer know the cover is in place, so it can go ahead and print.

PRINTING

Extra Sheet When Printing

If your ImageWriter scrolls an extra sheet through when printing, fill in the From and To boxes in the Print… dialog box. If your document is six pages long, type in From 1 to 6. If it's a single page, type in From 1 to 1. Also check the end of your document to make sure it doesn't have an accumulation of blank spaces after the final period.

Faster Quality Produces Darker Pictures Than Best Quality

When using the new *ImageWriter* driver (version 2.2 or later), picture quality is darker for Faster quality than for Best quality. This is a feature, not a bug.

Prompting the Last Line

To cut down on the time the ImageWriter pauses before it prints the last line in a document, press the

SELECT button once. The printer immediately prints the line. Hit SELECT again to advance the paper forward enough to tear off or remove the page.

Squished First Line of Print

The ImageWriter often squishes or distorts the first line of a page, especially when printing in high resolution. The line is not actually distorted; the paper was slightly wrinkled.

In standard printing, the ImageWriter's print head makes two passes to create a line of text, and in high resolution, it makes four. In both cases, it prints the top portion of the first line of text first, and the other parts on successive passes. Now, if the paper in the printer is not fixed firmly in position between these passes, it prints the next portion partly over the top part—giving the effect of squishing the line.

Obviously this is not supposed to happen, but sometimes it does when the ImageWriter is sorting out where to start printing on a page, and where the paper itself is stiff and the perforated fold lifts the paper slightly away from the platen when printing starts.

The only solutions are to leave one extra blank line at the top of documents—putting a Return at the beginning of a header in *MacWrite* for instance—and to buy cheap thin paper that fits flush to the platen at all times. These aren't real answers, but they're the only ones available until Apple finds a way to solve it.

RIBBONS

Alternative Ribbons

If you can't find ImageWriter ribbons in your local store, buy NEC 8023, C.Itoh 8510, or DEC LA50 ribbons. They'll work just as well.

VERSATERM

Change DIP Switch To Print Graphics with *VersaTerm*

VersaTerm won't print graphics correctly with the ImageWriter's normal DIP switch settings. Turn the power off and set Switch 2-3 to its closed position. When finished printing graphics, return the switch to its normal open position.

ImageWriter I

CABLES

Longer ImageWriter Cable

Is your ImageWriter I cable too short? A handy replacement from Radio Shack is ten feet long and costs only $3.99. It's actually a joystick cord (part #276-1978). However, any non-standard cable has the potential for causing serious problems with either the Mac or the ImageWriter I, so don't blame us if your system blows up. Try this at your own risk.

MACCHARLIE

Reset ImageWriter I DIP Switches To Print

To print directly to the ImageWriter I with MacCharlie, you need to reset the DIP switches inside the printer. On SW1, switches 1, 2, 3, 4 and 8 should be closed, with 5, 6 and 7 open. On SW2, switches 3 and 4 should be closed, with 1 and 2 open. If printing is still a problem, check the number on your ImageWriter cable. The first 6,000 printers had cable #5900121. MacCharlie is designed to work with the later cable #5900169, although updated software may correct this problem.

PRINTHEAD

ImageWriter I's Printhead May Overheat

If you are doing printouts of many pages with a high concentration of black space, the printhead on the ImageWriter I may overheat and need to be replaced. Graphic images with dark backgrounds are more likely than normal text to cause problems. For long printouts, avoid using more than 25-30% solid black on a page. Or, you can print out your document a page or two at a time, allowing the printhead to cool for a few minutes between each printing. The ImageWriter II has built-in protection to guard against this problem.

PRINTING

Use Masking Tape To Cover Single-Sheet Slot

The ImageWriter I suffers from a design fault you may notice if you use tractor feed paper. Quite often, the very top sheet of paper, especially if left overnight to take the shape of the platen, curls back into the sheet feed slot, causing the printer to get thoroughly fouled up. Place a piece of masking tape over the slot to solve this problem. Be careful, though, only to fix the tape at the front, so you can still remove the back cover over the tractor feed.

ImageWriter II

BUGS

ImageWriter 2.2 Can Get Confused with ImageWriter II

The 2.2 version of the *ImageWriter* driver sometimes forgets how to recognize an ImageWriter II, and assumes it has different paper handling routines than it actually does and no color. This will be fixed in the next driver version.

INCOMPATIBILITIES

No Print Spoolers With ImageWriter II

The ImageWriter II confuses most print spoolers because it sends a message back to the Mac indicating that it is an ImageWriter II. The LaserWriter also sends its own message back. You see the results on the *Chooser's* printer menu. Many spoolers don't know what to do with that signal. Those spoolers that work usually pretend to print to a hard disk, which in turn sends the data stream to the printer.

MICROSOFT PRODUCTS

Use Old *ImageWriter* Driver with Microsoft Products

Microsoft products will print slower in medium mode on the ImageWriter II than on the ImageWriter I. You can speed things up by using an old version of the *ImageWriter* driver, but you'll have to give up some of the ImageWriter II's features.

PAPER THICKNESS

Adjust the Paper Thickness Guide To Fit Two Sheets of Paper

You'll get the best results on your ImageWriter II printouts if you adjust the clear plastic paper thickness guide so it will allow two sheets of the paper you're using to pass through. The paper thickness lever is (inconveniently) located under the cover of the ImageWriter II, to the right of the platen.

RESOLUTION

Draft Mode Defaults To ImageWriter's Print Quality Setting

If you print on an ImageWriter II in draft mode, the output defaults to the setting of the print quality switch on the printer's front panel. This is how you get access to the ImageWriter II's three built-in fonts. The NLQ (Near Letter Quality) printout looks almost like it was done on a regular typewriter. It may sound a little silly, but some uninformed members of the business world aren't ready for all of the Mac's font and formatting capabilities. On the LaserWriter, the Courier font serves a similar purpose.

SELF-TEST

How To Run the Self-Test

The ImageWriter II is capable of running self-test samples in all three printing modes—draft, standard and high.

1. To do this, turn the printer off, hold down the Form Feed button, and turn the printer back on. This will start the "draft mode" test.
2. While the printer's printing, deselect the printer by pushing the Line Feed button. Then, push the Print Quality button to select a new mode and reselect the printer by pushing the Line Feed button again. When the printhead reaches the left margin and begins a new line, you'll see "standard" quality print.
3. To preview "high" quality, repeat step two.

TROUBLESHOOTING

Printhead Foil Can Be Removed If It Gets Torn

If you're getting smeared printouts, check the little piece of foil on the printhead of the ImageWriter II. You may have inadvertently torn it in the process of loading paper. If you have, it may smear your printouts. The foil appears to serve no particular purpose and you can remove it if you're having this problem.

Installer

BUGS

Version 2.1 May Lock Up Mouse On Launch

Sometimes the mouse will lock when starting *Installer* version 2.1. The solution is to reset and try again.

FONT/DA MOVER

Make Sure *Font/DA Mover* Is In System Folder

When using Apple's *Installer* program to upgrade any disk, make sure that the *Font/DA Mover* is in the System folder of the disk with the *Installer*. The *Installer* looks for it in its own System folder if it needs to make any modifications to the Fonts or Desk Accessories on the other disk in the process of updating it.

UPDATES

System Update 3.1.1b Doesn't Work with *Installer*

If you upgrade to *System* software 3.1.1b (on the Mac Plus), don't think that anything's wrong when the Apple's *Installer* application doesn't work—they're incompatible. The easiest way to update your disks in this case is to copy all the fonts and DAs from the *System* file you want to update into a copy of the new *System 3.1.1b* file. Then, when you copy the new *System* back to your old disk, you'll still be working with the same fonts and DAs as before.

Jazz

BUGS

This File Can't Be Printed

Jazz sometimes tells you that "This File Can't Be Printed." And when it does, you're not going to print THAT file, no way, no how. This bug appears for no apparent rhyme or reason—some files just seem to fall victim. It occurs more often if your Mac is attached to an AppleTalk network.

The real cause is that sometimes *Jazz* gets confused and scrambles its port configuration memory. Restarting the Mac does not reset *Jazz's* brain, since the port configuration is stored in that tiny bit of RAM powered by the battery. That's the RAM that remembers the day and time while the Mac is shut off. To reset the Parameter RAM, you must disconnect the battery for at least 30 seconds. (Remember to reset the date and time after you perform this surgery.)

The most convenient solution is to make sure *Jazz* knows what printer it should use, and where that printer is connected. Apple's *Choose Printer* desk accessory is the perfect cure. Simply install it in *Jazz's System* file and use it at the start of each *Jazz* session.

COMMUNICATIONS

Use Cut and Paste To Send Pre-Written Messages

When using *Jazz's* communications facility, you can use Cut and Paste to send text. With all the messages you wish to send stored in a word processing file displayed on one side of the screen, you can Cut each one at the time you want to send it and Paste it into the communications window at the appropriate point.

GRAPHICS

Copying Graphs Doesn't Change the Worksheet Link

If you make a copy of a worksheet and its accompanying graph, the new graph remains linked to the old spreadsheet. In other words, just making a copy of the graph does nothing. To link it to another worksheet, use a resource editor to edit the graph's "LFRF" and change the old worksheet's name to the name of the new one.

MEMORY SIZE

Memory Allocation for Applications

Here is a list of the memory sizes that *Jazz* allocates to each of its applications. Remember that if you Close an application that you're not using, *Jazz* will allow another application to use the extra memory to create and Open larger documents.

APPLICATION	MEMORY
Operating Program	237K
Spreadsheet	70K*
Database	97K**
Graphics	45K
Word Processor	70K
Communications	26K

*Spreadsheet requires only 3K if the database is already open.
**Database requires only 30K if spreadsheet is already open.

QUITTING

Always Shut Down

Before and after using *Jazz*, be sure to turn the Mac's power switch off rather than Shutting Down or hitting the reset button. *Jazz* puts a few things into memory that don't get erased by the reset button, and you may find "ghosts" haunting the next application you use.

SYLK FILES

Make Sure SYLK File Has No Formatted Cells

If you are converting a SYLK file from another spreadsheet (such as *Multiplan* or *Excel*) to *Jazz*, make sure that none of the cells in the SYLK file are formatted. The Mac will grind away for days trying to convert a file with formats, but will accomplish nothing. Converting an unformatted file takes only a few minutes.

Just Text

COMMANDS

Undocumented Commands {sb} and {eb}

Two *Just Text* commands, {sb} and {eb} are not documented. A careful reading of the example documents in the manual indicates that these codes mean "start a box" and "end a box." Thus, placing {sb} at the beginning of a text block and {eb} at the end creates a ruled box around the text block.

LaserWriter

BUGS

LaserWriter 3.0 Can Release System Font and Crash

Version 3.0 of the *LaserWriter* driver can un-install the system font (Chicago 12) on a Mac Plus behind the back of the Font Manager. The next time your Mac Plus needs the system font, it crashes because it can't find it. This is rather rare.

CARTRIDGES

Refilled Cartridges May Produce Lower Quality Printing

Although you can get your LaserWriter cartridges refilled, they don't always provide good quality printouts. In addition to the toner, the cartridge contains parts that get quite a lot of wear in the operation of the LaserWriter. For instance, the coating on the drum will wear out after so many passes. The drum might work well with a second round of toner, but it's not designed for that kind of use. For best results in your printouts, always use new cartridges.

FONT SUBSTITUTION

Font Substitution Doesn't Change Spacing

For the highest quality results on your printouts, always manually change the fonts in your document to the LaserWriter's built-in fonts (Helvetica, Courier, Times and Symbol on the first model) rather than using Font Substitution. Also, remember to turn off Font Substitution and Smoothing on the Page Setup dialog box. Yes, the printer driver's font substitution option really does change the characters from ImageWriter fonts to LaserWriter fonts. However, the spacing between the characters remains the same as in the original ImageWriter fonts. The results can be quite disappointing, and don't take full advantage of the LaserWriter's capabilities.

LaserWriter Driver 3.0 and Later Do Better Job

The font substitution option (from Page Setup) in the *LaserWriter* Driver 3.0 and later do a better job than previous drivers. The spacing still is not the same as if you had converted your document to LaserWriter fonts yourself, but this driver does a better job of closing up some of the spaces between letters and words, so the output is much more acceptable.

FONTS

Change of Style and Back Will Confuse *LaserWriter 3.0*

When the *LaserWriter* driver (version 3.0) encounters a change in style, and then a change back, in a downloaded font (or in a Macintosh bit-mapped font), it re-downloads the original style. This fills up the LaserWriter's virtual memory very quickly, and the LaserWriter resets in the middle of the print job.

ImageWriter Fonts Must Be "Resourced" Properly

If you are using ImageWriter fonts on your LaserWriter, they must have been "resourced" properly in order for them to print in the right size as bit-mapped characters. In other words, if a font is 36 points, you must give it the proper resource number when you create it. An error in its resource number won't show up on the ImageWriter, but the LaserWriter will print it out in the point size the font's resource number specifies. (The Icon font is a good example. Although it's 36 points, its resource number says that it's 12 points, so the LaserWriter prints it that way.) Correct these resource number problems with *FONTastic*.

Keep Largest Versions of Non-Laser Fonts

When you're using ImageWriter fonts (such as Venice, London, Hollywood, etc.) in documents you want to print on the LaserWriter, always keep the largest version you can make room for in your *System* file. The LaserWriter uses the largest version and scales it down. The larger the font it scales from, the smoother the appearance of the printout.

FORMATTING

You Can Format for the LaserWriter If It's Not Hooked Up

If your LaserWriter isn't connected to your Mac, or if you don't own one, you can still format documents to be printed later on a LaserWriter. First, install the LaserWriter fonts you want to use and the *LaserWriter* drivers on your startup disk. Then, use the *Choose Printer* desk accessory and choose "no printer" by clicking in the white space below any printers listed. (With the new 128K ROMs, turn on AppleTalk on the *Control Panel* and click on the LaserWriter icon in the *Chooser*.) Now, you can format your documents for printing on a LaserWriter or Linotronic typesetter. You'll get better results if you change your fonts to LaserWriter fonts yourself rather than using the Font Substitution option (see "Font Substitution Doesn't Change Spacing").

GRAPHICS

Speed Correspondence By Preprinting Letterhead Containing Graphics

The LaserWriter takes a long time to print the first copy of a document containing complex graphics because of the tremendous amount of information it must generate and store in its memory. But it prints subsequent copies fairly rapidly after it has crunched all the numbers that define the page. If your letterhead has graphics in it, you can speed printing of your letters on the letterhead by preprinting a quantity of sheets with the letterhead only. Create the usual word processing template for your letters to position the text in the correct place on the page. Then, simply load the preprinted letterhead into the cassette. The LaserWriter will print your letters much faster than if it had to construct and print the graphics of your letterhead with each letter. Preprinting from *MacDraw* is usually the quickest method.

Use 96% Reduction for Bit-Mapped Graphics

When you use the LaserWriter to print a document containing bit-mapped graphics, set the Reduction to 96% in the Page Setup dialog box. This establishes an exact 4 to 1 relationship between dots on the Laser-Writer and dots on the screen. The Mac's screen has 72 dots per inch (dpi) resolution, and the LaserWriter has 300 dpi. But 96% of 300 is 288, and so is 4 X 72. When the relationship is an exact integral multiple, the LaserWriter doesn't have to interpolate extra dots to fill in the gaps, and the results look much sharper. For example, an 80% reduction doesn't work as well as a 72% reduction (3 X 72 = .72 X 300 = 216).

Use *MacDraw*, Not *MacPaint* For Original Art

Try to use *MacDraw* instead of *MacPaint* when creating original art for the LaserWriter. The printer can scale *MacDraw* objects more accurately than *MacPaint* images. Thus, it produces sharper printouts from *MacDraw* than from *MacPaint*. Even after you Paste them into a *MacWrite* document, the Mac can scale *MacDraw* objects without losing too much of their clarity. Also, the fill patterns you've used will maintain their original scale in *MacDraw* art when you rescale the object. *MacPaint* treats the patterns just like the rest of the image and rescales them by the same proportions when you stretch or compress the art. It can look as if you've put a magnifying glass over the image.

MANUAL PRINTING

How Much Time You Have to Insert Paper

When printing with the Manual Feed option on the LaserWriter, you have up to 90 seconds to insert the next sheet of paper after it finishes each page. If you fail to feed it the next sheet during this period of time, the LaserWriter will time out and cancel the print job.

MARGINS

There's a .45 Inch Border Around the Printable Area

The LaserWriter won't print within a 0.45 inch border on the two long edges of a standard or legal sheet of paper. If your margins are wider, it ignores them. This border is built into the standard Apple printer driver for the LaserWriter. That's simply a matter of making a choice, and some printer drivers (such as *Aldus Prep* for *PageMaker*) allow you to print closer to the edge. However, you should always allow a small margin to make sure all of your image gets printed.

Use A Wider Right Margin On LaserWriter Documents

When you are composing text for printing on the LaserWriter, always allow a wider right margin than you normally do for the ImageWriter. The LaserWriter prints out text in longer lines, so you need to make them proportionally shorter on the screen with the wider right margin.

PAPER

Paper Thickness

Although the LaserWriter manual says you can use paper as thin as 8-pound stock, the printer tends to feed double sheets or curl the paper excessively when printing on anything lighter than paper of 20- to 24-pound weight. The curling is especially frustrating if you're trying to print on both sides of the sheet. The curl produced on the first pass can jam the machine on the second pass. Try to use paper with a high rag content. High rag content paper has a surface that's easy for the LaserWriter's feed mechanism to grab.

POSTSCRIPT

Creating A *PostScript* File

You can make the Mac create a *PostScript* file on your disk instead of sending the print file to the Laser-Writer. Simply hold down the COMMAND and F keys right after clicking on the OK button in the print dialog box. You'll see a different set of messages than you're used to seeing, and the Mac will write the *PostScript* file to your disk. You can examine this file with *MacWrite* or *Microsoft Word*. This technique can be especially useful if you plan to transmit a file to a remote *PostScript* driven typesetter. By having your Mac do the processing to create the *PostScript* file, you'll save expensive time on the typesetter.

PRINT DENSITY

Try Turning the Print Density Dial Down

Many users report that they get clearer output on the LaserWriter when they turn the Print Density Dial down almost to the lightest setting. Experiment with different settings until you get the output you want.

PRINTING

Making Two-Sided Copies

To print your work on both sides of the paper with the LaserWriter is a bit tricky, but if you follow these instructions you'll save yourself a great deal of time:

1. Make sure your document file includes everything. All spreadsheet data, graphics or other information should be included in the document and the disk should have plenty of room for the Print File.
2. Print one copy of the document from the paper cassette.
3. Take the finished pile from the output tray and place it FACE DOWN in front of you. Restack the printout, removing two sheets from the first pile and putting them on the other pile — the top two sheets of the first pile become the bottom two sheets of the new pile. (A 10-page document would be reordered to 9,10,7,8,5,6,3,4,1,2 with page 9 on top.)
4. Place the stack back in the paper cassette, FACE UP, TOP TOWARD THE PRINTER. The next to last page of your document should be on top. Be sure to remove any excess curl from the paper.
5. Choose Print again. If the printer jams during the second printing, use better paper next time. When you unjam the printer, look at the top two pages in the cassette to determine where to stop the printing and restart the print from page 1 to the page where it jammed (if your application prints out your document from back to front).

Printing Envelopes

Printing envelopes on the LaserWriter rarely works well because they jam frequently. But if you need to print an envelope with the LaserWriter, this will make things easier: 1) For a regular business envelope, set the left margin at 5 inches; 2) On the Page Setup dialog box, select Landscape mode; 3) Select manual feed; 4) After the yellow "ready" light on the LaserWriter comes on, insert the left end of the envelope, face up.

SMOOTHING

Use Smoothing for Most Applications

In most applications, the smoothing function in the LaserWriter printer driver will give you more attractive printouts. Except in special applications, you won't want bit-mapped graphics or text to remain jaggy.

TROUBLE SHOOTING

Getting Rid of Micro Jaggies

If you suddenly start getting little jagged edges on some of your fonts (making them look as if they had been printed on the ImageWriter), you can try several possible cures. First, reinstall all your fonts—but use the latest version of the *Font/DA Mover* (3.1 or later). If you still have the problem, make sure that you're using the latest versions of all the system software (*System*, *Finder*, *LaserWriter*, *Laser Prep*, etc.) and that all of the Macs connected to your network are using the same versions of the software. As a last resort, reconstruct your work disk with "clean" system software from a disk that doesn't have the problem when you print from it.

Light Printing With A New Toner Cartridge

If you've just set up or moved your LaserWriter, the print quality may be too light. This is a fairly common situation that's easily corrected. First, make sure that the toner material is loose and evenly distributed throughout the cartridge. If you gently rock the cartridge back and forth on its long axis several times, the toner will disperse properly. After you've distributed the toner in the cartridge and reinstalled it, run off 20 or 30 black pages from *MacPaint* or *MacDraw*. This will "break in" the drum on a new machine. When you move or ship the LaserWriter, remove the cartridge from the machine and keep it horizontal until you reinstall it.

LaserWriter Plus

APPLICATIONS

Applications Must Support New Fonts, Too

You may be disappointed to find out that the new fonts on the LaserWriter Plus must be supported by your application program as well as by the printer and your system software. *PageMaker 1.1*, for example, prints out bit-mapped versions of the new fonts instead of fetching them from the LaserWriter Plus ROM. *PageMaker 1.2* will support the LaserWriter Plus fonts and upgrades to other software should be out shortly.

BUGS

LaserWriter Plus Can Lose Track of Apple To Adobe Character Mapping

The LaserWriter Plus can lose track of the Apple to Adobe character mapping on the new fonts. Some optional characters won't print and others will print incorrectly. This doesn't always happen. The solution is to power the LaserWriter Plus off and then on again.

NAMES

Most Applications Require LaserWriter Plus be Named "LaserWriter"

When you first install your LaserWriter Plus on your AppleTalk network, it will appear as LaserWriter Plus on the *Chooser* desk accessory menu. Many applications on the Mac (including version 1.1 of *PageMaker*) require that the LaserWriter – plussed or not – be named "LaserWriter." Use the *Namer* utility that came with your LaserWriter to change your LaserWriter Plus' name back to "LaserWriter."

POSTSCRIPT FONTS

Fonts for Downloading Must Be On Same Disk As *System*

If you're working with documents containing *PostScript* fonts which must be downloaded to the LaserWriter Plus, make sure that the fonts are stored on the same disk as the *System* and *LaserWriter* driver. If you're working under HFS, they must be in the same folder as the *System* and driver.

Localizer

IDIOSYNCRASIES

Localizer Changes *System*, But Not Applications

Using the *Localizer* program from Apple to customize your Mac for the country you're in does not have any effect on application programs. For instance, changing the *System* file and its associated *Finder* date routines has no effect whatsoever on the date functions of *Microsoft File*. How a program handles time, date and even keyboard characters is up to the programmer, who, according to whim or his or her superiors, can be flexible or not, internationally-minded or American parochial. The *Localizer* can only help with things within its domain—the Macintosh's Desktop.

Mac/XL

BOOTING

Express Reboot on Lisa or Mac/XL

To avoid the long wait (while the Lisa or Mac/XL checks its memory) every time you turn the power off, hold down the COMMAND (or Apple) key when you push the power button to reboot from the hard disk. Alternatively, hold down the OPTION key when you press the power button. The machine will reboot and ask for a floppy.

EXPERLISP

Don't Try To Run *ExperLisp* On A Mac/XL

ExperLisp and *ExperOPS5* have real problems running on a Mac/XL under *MacWorks*. They are full of bugs and can cause system crashes and power shutdowns.

STARTUP

Hold Down OPTION Key To Boot From A Floppy

You can boot your Mac/XL from a floppy disk by holding down the OPTION key after the memory test.

Mac240

DIALING

Hayes Compatible Modems Must Have Carriage Return After Dial String

For a Hayes compatible modem, always end a dial string with a carriage return character. You can get this in the *Mac240* terminal software by typing ^M.

MODES

Use VT125 Mode to Ignore Eighth Bit

Some DEC VAX software (such as the *ReGIS Graphics Editor*) always sends the eighth bit of every character "on." *Mac240* considers the eighth bit a control character and will misinterpret seven-bit characters with the eighth bit set. Use *Mac240's* VT125 mode to ignore the eighth bit of incoming characters.

VMS

Use NOLINE Editing With *ReGIS Graphics Editor*

When you're working with the *ReGIS Graphics Editor* under *VMS*, set *Mac240* to NOLINE editing to make it work properly.

MacAdvantage UCSD Pascal

MACINTOSH PASCAL

Compile *Mac Pascal* Programs with *MacAdvantage Compiler*

You can directly compile programs written in *Macintosh Pascal* with the *MacAdvantage UCSD Pascal Compiler*. After a successful run of your program, save it under a name containing only lowercase letters. That way, you can use the *MacAdvantage* editor and compiler to access your program directly.

SPEED

Use RAM Disk To Speed Program Development

A RAM disk can make the Mac hum when you're developing programs with the *MacAdvantage UCSD Pascal* development system. Use a *MiniFinder* and *System* installed in a RAM disk along with the *MacAdvantage Pascal* editor, compiler, *Pascal* runtime, p-machine, and empty file.

MACBACK

BACKUP

***Backup V. 3* Will Hang System If No Tape In Drive**

The *Backup* utility for the MACBACK streaming tape drive will not work properly if you have no tape in the drive. The initial screen will come up, but the system will hang until you put a tape in the drive. If you insert a tape at the point of the hang, the prompt line will appear and everything will continue as usual.

TAPES

Always Retension A New Tape

Always run the Retension Tape menu option in the MACBACK *Backup* utility when you're going to use a brand new tape. Doing so will insure that you get an accurate backup of the data on your hard disk. Also, always retension a tape if it's been in storage for an extended period of time.

MacDraft

PROBLEMS

***MacDraft* Is Buggy with New ROMs**

MacDraft appears to be nearly unusable with the new ROMs. It has extreme problems with text and users have reported many other problems. Get in contact with the publisher about an update for the new ROMs.

RAM DISKS

MacDraft Has Problems with Some RAM Disks

MacDraft can behave rather strangely with some RAM disks. In some cases, if you double-click on a document to start *MacDraft*, the *MacDraft* blank drawing will come up without the document you specified. However, if you then Open your document from within *MacDraft*, it will appear on your screen with no problem. It's a little quirky, but shouldn't prevent you from using *MacDraft* with RAM disks.

MacDraw

ARCS

Make A Pattern To Draw Arcs of Ovals

The Arc shape on *MacDraw's* Tool Palette is very useful, but it's difficult to use when you want to create the arc portion of an oval. The easiest method is to use the oval tool first to create a full oval the size of the one from which you want to create an arc. Then, use the arc tool to "trace" the arc you want and delete the full oval. This is a little tricky and will take a little practice. However, it's a lot easier than trying to create arcs of ovals with no help.

BUGS

Click Only On Buttons In Version 1.7 Dialog Boxes

Don't experiment with clicking anywhere but on the buttons in *MacDraw 1.7's* dialog boxes. The system may crash or you may cause permanent damage to your drawing.

Filetype Isn't Changed When Your Convert Old *MacDraw* Files To PICT

Versions 1.7 and 1.9 of *MacDraw* have a confusing bug. It appears when you convert a *MacDraw*ing (previously saved in *MacDraw* format) to PICT format by loading it and using Save As... without changing the file's name. The file's filetype remains DRWG, rather than PICT. When you try to load it into *MacDraw*, you'll get a blank document. To fix the problem, use a disk editor (like *MacTools*) to change your file's filetype to PICT.

Text and Non-Text Items Don't Always Drag Together

MacDraw versions 1.7 and 1.9 both have a bug that sometimes shows up when you drag several items. When you drag text and nontext items together (either because you've grouped them, or selected them with SHIFT-Click), sometimes they move different distances, losing their relative alignment. This happens only if the grid is on, and you've made certain custom ruler settings. Specifically, to keep the bug from showing up, the denominator of the major division sizes must be a divisor of 24. For 1 inch, for example, the bug appears when you specify 32, 16, 10 or 5 divisions, but not when you use 24, 12 or 8 divisions.

DUPLICATING

Intelligent Duplication Anticipates Your Spacing

You can duplicate any object, or group of objects, by selecting them (press the SHIFT key to select more than one object), and choosing the Duplicate option from the Edit menu. This is a much more powerful system than *MacPaint* has, and is "intelligent." If you move the first copy (in relation to the original), and then duplicate the copy, the new copy will be placed in exact relation to the first copy as the first copy was in relation the original. A simple application would be making a row of objects. Put the first copy next to the original, and then simply duplicate successive copies to fill out the row. Try it—it's easier to demonstrate than to describe.

ERASERS

Create Borderless Objects In Background Pattern As "Erasers"

You can't erase areas of a *MacDraw*ing the way you can a *MacPaint*ing. However, you can use borderless objects (either white or whatever background texture you're using) to obscure areas you would otherwise "erase." It's the electronic equivalent of typewriter "whiteout" correction fluid, except you can have it in patterns, too. Simply create an object the exact size and shape of the area you want to erase, fill it with the background texture, and select None from the pen menu to make the borders disappear. You can then move the "eraser" into place and manipulate it with Smooth and Reshape Polygon to make any fine adjustments. If your "eraser" gets obscured when you select the object you placed it in front of, just select the eraser again and Move To Front.

FONTS

Customizing Fonts To Appear In First Eleven Slots of Font Menu

MacDraw's Font menu has only eleven places before the area where the font sizes appear. As a result, if you have installed more than eleven fonts in your *System* file, some of them won't be accessible from *MacDraw*. See below for how to fix this problem on a Macintosh Plus. If you're working with a machine with the old 64K ROMs, do the following: Install the fonts you want to use in *MacDraw* directly into the application with the *Font/DA Mover*. (To install fonts and DAs in applications, hold down the OPTION key when you click on the Open button in the *Font/DA Mover*.) When you launch *MacDraw*, those fonts installed in the application will be the first to appear on the menu, followed by those installed in your *System* file.

Customizing Fonts To Appear In First Eleven Slots On A Mac Plus

On the Mac Plus, the fonts in the font menu of any application are arranged in alphabetical order. As a result, in *MacDraw*, only the first eleven fonts, alphabetically, appear in the available slots in the Font menu. (The others appear after the font size portion of the menu, but you can't select them.) To get around this problem, use a resource editor to put a space in front of the first letter of the name of the eleven fonts you want in *MacDraw*. The alphabetic sort considers the space character as a "pre-A" character and puts those fonts first on the menu. If you want those fonts to be the first eleven fonts in all of your applications, make the name changes to the fonts installed in the *System* file you'll be working with. If you want to change the order only in *MacDraw*, use the *Font/DA Mover* to install the fonts you want directly into *MacDraw*. (Hold down the OPTION key when you click on the Open button in the *Font/DA Mover* to select *MacDraw* to install the fonts.) Then, use the resource editor to change their names after you've distinguished them from those in the *System* file. This is all a little complicated, but worth the effort if you do a lot of work with *MacDraw*. Write to Apple and urge them to fix these font problems.

PATCH TO SOLVE FONT SLOT LIMITATIONS

If you have the guts to use *Fedit* and go at a copy of *MacDraw 1.7*, here's a patch that should allow you to use all of the fonts in your *System*. Remember, work ONLY on a copy of the program and test it thoroughly before entrusting the modified version with any valuable data. Within *Fedit*, find the hex string in the first column of the table below and replace it with the one in the second column. You will have to replace the string the number of times shown in the third column.

FIND HEX STRING:	CHANGE TO:	OCCURRENCES
41ED FAD6	41ED F360	9
0000 0C60	0000 0CA0	1
0014 6F02 7C14	001F 6F02 7C1F	1
000B FACE	0016 FACE	2
70E1	709D	3
0001 00E1	0001 009D	3
10E1	109D	1
0C47 0015	0C47 0020	1
4E56 FFBE	4E56 FF9E	1

Default Font Is Most Recently Installed If Geneva Not Present

If the Geneva font is installed in your *MacDraw* startup disk's *System* file, but is not displayed in *MacDraw's* font menu, the topmost font (most recently installed with the old ROMs or first, alphabetically, with the new ROMs) will become the default font.

Text In Fonts Not In Menu Will Be Displayed In Top Font

If a *MacDraw* document contains a text item that was created with a font that's not displayed in the eleven available slots in the menu, the Mac will display the item in the default (topmost) font.

FORMS

Use Custom Rulers for Forms To Be Typed

When you are using *MacDraw* to create printed forms that other people will fill out using a typewriter, you can use custom rulers to make the job much easier. Set the number of divisions in an inch to six in the Custom Ruler dialog box and vertically align your blanks with the division markers. Six vertical spaces on a typewriter are equal to one inch.

FREEHAND DRAWING

Approximate Your Drawing with Shapes

If you have a hard time using the Freehand tool in *MacDraw* to create the objects you want, try approximating them first with the shape tools. Create a group of shapes that together are the general shape and size of the finished freehand drawing you want to create. Select all of the objects that are a part of your pattern and group them before you start your freehand version. That way, when you have finshed your drawing, you can select the first pattern with one mouse click and delete it by hitting BACKSPACE.

Smooth A Freehand Drawing To Allow You To Reshape Polygon

If you pull down the Edit menu after you've created a freehand object that's still selected, the Reshape Polygon option is dimmed, indicating that you can't use it at this point. However, that doesn't mean you can't use it at all on a freehand object. First, with the freehand object selected, choose Smooth from the Edit menu. Then, when you pull down the Edit menu again, Reshape Polygon won't be dimmed any more and selecting it will place handles on your freehand drawing so you can reshape it.

GRID

Hold Down SHIFT To Turn On Grid Temporarily

When you have turned the grid off in *MacDraw*, you can turn it back on temporarily by holding down the SHIFT key as you move an object. Be sure to press the SHIFT key after you've depressed the mouse button to pick up the object you want to move. If you depress SHIFT before clicking, you'll be making a selection "on top of" the object you intended to select (see "SHIFT-Click To Select On Top of Another Object").

LINES

How To Get Dotted Lines In *MacDraw*

Dotted lines are very easy to get in *MacDraw*. Choose the appropriate pattern from the Pen menu before you select a drawing tool, and the tool will draw lines or objects in the pattern you selected. Experiment with different pen patterns to get the dotted pattern you want. You may have to use different patterns for horizontal and vertical lines to get approximately the same pattern of dots in each. You can also change lines to a different pen pattern by selecting the line you want to change and then selecting the appropriate pen pattern.

MAC PLUS

Run *Chooser* From *MacDraw* Even If You Did From the *Finder*

MacDraw doesn't seem to recognize changes made with the *Chooser* in the *Finder*. To make sure that you're set up for the right printer options, run it after you've started *MacDraw*, too.

MEMORY SIZE

Watch Out On 128K Macs

Users of the 512K or larger Mac can ignore the space used and remaining information that appears when they select About MacDraw… on the Apple menu, but

128K users must pay careful attention to this information, since it's extremely easy to run out of memory. Few things can be more frustrating than nearly completing a drawing, only to find out that you don't have enough memory available to finish it.

MOVING IMAGES

Precise Positioning

When moving images around on the page, press the OPTION key while moving the object to see the graphic image instead of a rectangle. This is especially useful when you are doing fine positioning of objects.

OTHER PROGRAMS

Create Unusual Sizes of Fonts In *Microsoft Word*

Do you need a font in an unusual size? Create your text in *MacDraw*, then Copy it into *Microsoft Word*, where you can stretch it to any size you want. The best news of all is that it prints out perfectly on the LaserWriter. (Printing doesn't work as well on the ImageWriter.)

*MacDraw*ings Resize Better In *MacWrite* Than *MacPaint*

Images from *MacDraw* maintain their quality better when resized in *MacWrite* than in *MacPaint*. Resizing the images in *MacWrite* doesn't cause any loss of quality, because the files are still stored as attributes. This is not true when passing *MacDraw*ings into *MacPaint*, however, because *MacPaint* instantly converts pictures into bit maps.

MacPaint Graphics Are Transparent In *MacDraw*

Most *MacPaint* patterns appear transparent when Pasted into *MacDraw*. This means that lines can show through the white spaces in the patterns. Experiment with this "feature" and you may be able to use it to your advantage.

Pasting Charts from *Jazz* or *Microsoft Chart*

Both *Jazz* and *Microsoft Chart* store their images in the same form as *MacDraw* (as QuickDraw "descriptions"). This is an advantage when you Paste a chart from *Jazz* or *Chart* into *MacDraw*. You can select and manipulate all the individual elements of the chart just as if you had originally created it in *MacDraw*. For most applications, you'll find this is an easier way to enhance a chart than by Pasting it into *MacPaint*.

Use *MacDraw* Instead of *MacPaint* To Trace Digitized Images

If you want to use a digitized image as the basis for your graphic, but don't want to include the original image in the final product, *MacDraw* is a better tool for the job than *MacPaint*. Digitizing it and Pasting it into *MacDraw* means that you can work on top of it, tracing the outlines. When you're finished, just delete the digitized image, leaving the outline intact. In *MacPaint*, removing the original digitized image would involve a great deal of work in FatBits.

PAGE SETUP

Wide Layouts

Get a feel for the way horizontal layouts will look by selecting Wide from the Page Setup... dialog box. The screen will display the pages horizontally. Be sure to do this before switching between a LaserWriter and ImageWriter. The margins will change!

PATTERNS

Create Custom *MacDraw* Patterns with *ResEdit*

If you are frustrated by the limited choice of patterns in *MacDraw*, you can use *ResEdit* to create your own custom replacements. Open the PAT# resource with *ResEdit* on your copy of *MacDraw* by double-clicking. Then, double-click on the pattern you want to replace and you'll be able to edit it in a manner similar to FatBits in *MacPaint*. When you have the pattern you want, Close the window and save the changes when *ResEdit* prompts you. When you Open that copy of *MacDraw*, your new pattern should be available on the Patterns menu. However, if you Open a document created with the new pattern in a different copy of *MacDraw* that hasn't been customized, *MacDraw* uses the old pattern in place of your custom pattern. No damage will occur—just make sure to use your customized *MacDraw* with the documents you created with it.

PRINTING

Create White Type Double Size and Reduce 50% for Clearer Printing

If you're having trouble LaserPrinting small white type in a *MacDraw* document, create it double the finished size and reduce it with the LaserWriter. First, type the text in Outline style and fill in the background. Specify 50% reduction in the Page Setup dialog. That should solve the problem.

Don't Rotate Images from *MacPaint* for the LaserWriter

The LaserWriter will print a bit-mapped image (such as a *MacPaint* document) with white "seam" lines if you Copy the image to *MacDraw* and then rotate or flip it. This is probably a *MacDraw* bug. One workaround is to rotate the *MacPaint* image to the desired orientation using T/Maker's *Click-Art Effects* in *MacPaint*, before you Copy the image to *MacDraw*.

Error in *PostScript* Message

The LaserWriter won't print *MacDraw* objects that it cannot convert to its *PostScript* language. The message "Error in *PostScript*" usually means that the document contains such an object, even though it is not visible. The typical cause is charts Pasted in from other applications, such as *Jazz*, *Chart*, or *Excel*. The cure is to standardize all the objects in your document. Select All objects, then choose the appropriate font and point size. Select the line weight you want, and erase all objects you don't want.

Patterns Don't Change Orientation with Page Setup

If you change the orientation of a drawing from tall or tall adjusted to wide in the Page Setup dialog box, the patterns will fill their objects in their new positions on the page, but the patterns themselves will maintain the same orientation to the page as they do in tall or tall adjusted. To illustrate this problem, create a simple drawing of a house in the tall orientation and fill its walls with the staggered brick pattern. Then, change the orientation to wide with the Page Setup dialog box and print out your graphic. The house will shift its orientation on the page and will be filled with the brick pattern. However, the bricks will look like they're stacked on their ends instead of their sides. If you need the patterns in your art to change orientation along with the rest of the art, you'll have to stick to *MacPaint*.

Reduction Or Enlargement May Cause Text Clipping On LaserWriter

If you use more than 150% enlargement or 75% reduction in the Page Setup dialog box, the Mac may clip off some of the text in your drawing when printing it.

RESCALING

Click-SHIFT To Maintain Proportions As You Rescale

You can use the SHIFT key to constrain rescaling of your drawing in *MacDraw*, similar to the way you do in *MacPaint*. The difference is that you have to depress the SHIFT key after you have clicked on the handle you want to drag. If you hold down the SHIFT key before you click, you'll get a whole different effect (see "SHIFT-Click To Select On Top of Another Object").

Create Complex Drawings Oversized and Then Shrink

If you want to create a highly detailed drawing, and have difficulty manipulating *MacDraw* in small scales, create the whole drawing in a larger size. Then, when you've completely finished the drawing, use Select All from the Edit menu and shrink the whole drawing at once. Hold down the SHIFT key after you've selected a handle to make sure the drawing stays in proportion to your original as you shrink it. Always save a copy of the oversized drawing under another name before shrinking it so you have a way to recover and try again in case you save the reduced drawing and later discover you don't like the results.

Surround Large Areas with A Rectangle To Rescale

If you have very large areas you want to rescale, go into the Reduce or Reduce to Fit mode and surround the whole area you want to rescale with a large rectangle. Then, select Move To Back to put the rectangle in the background, Select All from the Edit menu, and rescale your drawing with the lower right handle on the large rectangle. You can then delete the rectangle, if you want.

Use *MacWrite* or LaserWriter Reduction To Scale Text with Art

When you rescale an object, or group of objects, containing text in *MacDraw*, the program will try to reposition the text in its appropriate position in the rescaled image. However, it will leave the characters the same size. You can force the text to rescale its size as well as its position in one of two ways: Produce your art and text oversized and use the reduction mode of the LaserWriter (in the Page Setup dialog box) to reduce the whole image to the size you want; or Paste the art and text as a single object into *MacWrite* and rescale it there. In both cases, the text will rescale in the same proportion as the art.

RESHAPE POLYGON

Think of A Rubber Band Stretched Around Nails

To get a better idea of how Reshape Polygon works, think of your polygon's perimeter as a rubber band that's stretched around nails on a board. Every handle that appears when you select the polygon is the equivalent of a nail. Simply move the nails around to reshape the polygon.

ROTATE

How To Remember the Rotation Direction

The Rotate command in *MacDraw* rotates the selected object 90° to the left (or counterclockwise if you prefer)—the same direction you twist a jar lid to remove it. To remember it, just pretend you're unscrewing the screen of the Macintosh—Rotate will go the same direction.

SAVING

An Explanation of PICT Format

When using the Save As... option in *MacDraw*, you always see a radio button labelled "PICT Format." The *MacDraw* manual is rather vague about its use, and therefore the default format of "*MacDraw* Format" seems the obvious route to choose.

Saving *MacDraw* documents stores them on the disk in the same format as they existed in the Mac's memory. However, if another program wants to read a *MacDraw* file, it cannot do so unless you have chosen the "PICT Format"—a sort of universal means of storing pictures, in much the same way as the "Text Only" option offered when saving in *MacWrite*. Under normal conditions, always choose the "*MacDraw* Format" option. But, if you want other programs (like *PageMaker*) to access the files, save a second copy in the "PICT" format under another name.

MacDraw 1.7 Can Forget Fonts In "*MacDraw* Format"

MacDraw 1.7 can forget which fonts it used for text if you load the file into a different *System* that does not have those particular fonts. Saving diagrams in the "PICT Format" ensures that it remembers, although the cost is that the saved file will be slightly larger.

SELECTING

Hold Down COMMAND Key to Select Object As You Draw It

You can select an object while you are creating it. Hold down the COMMAND key as you draw the object. This can be handy if you want to draw an object and immediately move it to another position.

SHIFT-Click To Select On Top of Another Object

If you want to select a portion of your *MacDraw*ing without selecting the objects behind your selection rectangle, hold down the SHIFT key as you click to start the selection rectangle. This is especially handy if you want to select several small objects overlapping a larger object, but without selecting the larger object itself. Be careful to depress the SHIFT key before you click or you'll get a whole different effect (see "Click-SHIFT To Maintain Proportions As You Rescale").

SMOOTHING

Adjust Effects of Smoothing with Reshape Polygon

After you have chosen Smoothing to change the shape of your object, you can use Reshape Polygon to make fine adjustments in your finished drawing. If you have smoothed the object, the handles will "resmooth" as you manipulate them with the pointer.

Experiment To Understand How It Works

The Smoothing option in *MacDraw* has varying effects on different shapes and angles. In rounding some angles, *MacDraw* may cut them almost in half. The best way to learn how to predict smoothing is to create a document of many different shapes and angles and experiment with Smooth and Unsmooth until you get a better feel for how the function works.

TEXT

Cut Text to *Note Pad* and Re-Paste To Get It Under Control

You can control your text in *MacDraw* with this trick. First, type in a sample of your text in any font or style until it's as wide as you want the finished product and hit ENTER. Now, Cut the text, Open the *Note Pad*, and Paste. Nothing will appear on the *Note Pad* because the *Note Pad* "thinks" the text is a picture, but a subtle change will be made to the text on the Clipboard. Now, go back to your *MacDraw*ing and Paste the text there. Now, the right and left edges of the text are set. Make the font, size and style choices you want, put the insertion point at the end of your text and enter the rest of it. The text will wrap to fit between your margins. You can also manipulate the text with the black handles when it's selected as an object.

Forcing Word-Wrap In Original Text

Here's a way to make *MacDraw* word-wrap text for you. Make a box and type in your text, but DO NOT SELECT THE TEXT TOOL. Your text will appear in the box, and *MacDraw* will wrap the lines within the limits of the box. To change the width of the text, select it and drag the lower right handle to lengthen or shorten the lines. This method permits you to reshape a text block even if you delete the rectangle.

Formatting Existing Text

Reformatting text once you've entered it into a *MacDraw*ing is difficult. However, the way to do it is to put it inside a rectangle. First, select the block of text you want to format by triple-clicking on it. Then Copy or Cut it. Draw a rectangle the size and shape you want for your block of text. While the rectangle is selected (mouse button still down), type any two letters (as "dummy text"), and release the mouse button. Immediately select Paste from the Edit menu, and your text will appear in the rectangle, following the two dummy letters you typed. Delete the dummy letters. You can now resize and reshape the rectangle and the text will reformat accordingly. After you have the format you want, you can remove the rectangle by selecting it and hitting BACKSPACE.

How To Get Inverted Text In *MacDraw*

Although it's not obvious, it's possible to get inverted text (known in the graphics arts trade as "reverse") in *MacDraw*. First, create a rectangle the size of the background you want and fill it with black. Then, create the text you want, using the Outline style option. You can either select the rectangle and begin typing inside it after choosing the Outline option, or create your text separately and move it into the rectangle. The first method will allow you to reshape and resize the rectangle and the text will adjust accordingly.

Select Whole Block of Text with Triple-Click

MacDraw has one of the few triple-click options on the Mac. With the text icon selected, if you click once, it places an insertion point. If you click twice, it selects the whole word. If you triple-click, the whole block of text you clicked is selected.

Title Option Capitalizes the First Letter of Every Word

When you choose the Title option from the *MacDraw* Style menu, the program capitalizes the first letter of every word of the text that was selected when you invoked the option. This can be especially handy for modifying text you bring in from another program so you don't have to retype it.

TOOLS

COMMAND-Click will Reselect the Last Tool You Used

Are you tired of having the cursor revert to the pointer every time you complete a drawing operation? Hold down the COMMAND key while clicking the mouse button to select the last tool you used.

MacNifty Switch

INCOMPATIBILITIES

BERNOULLI WARNING!

If you're using the Bernoulli Box, avoid the temptation to use the MacNifty accessory switch box. This combination can cause damage to both the Bernoulli Box and to your Mac. For advice on how to solve the problem, call Iomega at (801) 778-3000.

MacPaint

BRUSH SHAPES

Create Custom Brush Shapes with A Font Editor

You can edit the brush shapes in *MacPaint*. Just use a font editor that can access fonts stored as resources with applications. When you Open *MacPaint* with the font editor, you'll see that it has only one font stored with it: "12." Open this font, and you'll recognize the characters with ASCII values 120-151 as *MacPaint's* brush shapes. Simply use the font editor's edit mode to alter these characters to the new brush shapes you want and save your changes. The next time you run that version of *MacPaint*, your custom brush shapes will be displayed in the Brush Shape dialog box.

Double-Click On Paint Brush For Quick Brush Shapes Window

To see the Brush Shapes window quickly, double-click on the Paint Brush in the tool palette.

Drag Borderless Objects with OPTION-COMMAND for Custom Brushes

You can create your own custom brush shapes in *MacPaint* by using the OPTION-COMMAND-Drag technique that usually creates multiple copies (see "Multiple Copies While Dragging"). First, create an object the shape of the brush you want to use. Then, with the object selected, choose the dotted line option (no border) for its border. Now, while holding down the OPTION and COMMAND keys, click on the object and drag it as you would a brush.

Largest Brush Shape Is Also Eraser Tool Shape

If you alter font "12" (in *MacPaint*) to change the brush shapes available in the brush shape menu, be forewarned that the Eraser tool also uses the largest rectangular brush shape. If you alter that brush shape, you'll also alter the eraser shape.

COMMAND KEYS

You Don't Need To Hold Down Key Combinations for Complete Drag

When using one of *MacPaint's* special key combinations in combination with the mouse to stretch, drag, etc., you don't have to keep holding down the keys once you've started the mouse movement. Just hold down the keys when you start dragging the mouse and then release the keys. The keys' effect on the mouse motion will stay active until you release the mouse button.

CONSTRAINING

Constraining Movement and Painting

Hold down the SHIFT key while dragging a selected *MacPaint* image, or scrolling the screen, to constrain the movement to horizontal or vertical. When held while using the spray can, paint brush, pencil, eraser or line tool, it will constrain the effect of the tool to horizontal or vertical.

SHIFT Works In Show Page, Too

The SHIFT key works the same way in Show Page as it does in the regular or FatBits modes. When held down while dragging the image in Show Page, it will constrain the movement to horizontal or vertical.

Squares, Circles & Polygons

Hold down the SHIFT key when using the rectangle and oval tools (filled or outline) to create squares or circles. Holding down SHIFT while using the polygon tool constrains all sides (except the last side, which the Mac automatically completes when you double-click) to horizontal, vertical, or diagonal lines.

COPIES

Controlling Space Between Copies

The distance between multiple copies made while dragging is directly proportional to the line width currently selected. Choose a wide line width for a lot of space between each copy. Thin line widths result in copies spaced closely together.

Multiple Copies In A Straight Line

Keep multiple copies of an image in a straight line by pressing SHIFT, COMMAND and OPTION while dragging.

Multiple Copies While Dragging
Make multiple copies of a *MacPaint* picture by typing COMMAND and OPTION while clicking and dragging the image.

Picking Up A Copy
You can use the OPTION key to peel off a copy of a selected image. After using the lasso or rectangular selection tool to select the area you want to copy, hold down the OPTION key, push down the mouse button while the arrow is in the selected area, and drag the copy to its new position.

Preserving Patterns
To keep multiple copies' patterns intact, choose Grid to turn the grid on before making the copies. Grid lines are eight pixels apart.

DISK SPACE

Leave Some Room For *MacPaint* To Work
MacPaint requires some room on the disk it occupies so it can save its various temporary files as it operates. Be sure you leave about 100K on your work disk.

Multiple Illustrations In One Document
To save disk space, store several small *MacPaint* illustrations in a single file. The empty screen space around a document in *MacPaint* requires more than 2K of disk space. The extra 2Ks can add up quickly if you store a lot of images on a disk.

Throw Away ImageWriter Driver
Free up disk space on your *MacPaint* startup disk by deleting the *ImageWriter* driver file if you're not going to be using the disk with any other applications. *MacPaint* doesn't require the driver to print.

Trimming Short Cuts & Intro Screens
MacPaint has two resources that you don't need, and you can save about 13K of disk space by deleting them. Use the *Resource Editor* to remove the Short Cuts and Introduction screens, which are stored as PICT resources 2401 and 2400.

DRAWING SIZE

Use *MacWrite* To Expand Drawing To Full Page
Drawing a full-page sized drawing in *MacPaint* can be a tedious experience, requiring a lot of scrolling and toggling between Show Page and Regular Size. However, you can create a smaller drawing in *MacPaint* and then expand it to full page size in *MacWrite*. First, create the small version of your drawing in *MacPaint*. Be careful not to make it bigger than the screen window, so you can select the whole thing with the selection rectangle. When finished, select the whole drawing with the rectangle, Copy it, and quit *MacPaint*. Then, start up *MacWrite* without switching startup disks, and Paste your graphic in the upper left corner of a new document. Select the graphic by clicking on it, and use the handles on the lower edge of the frame surrounding the graphic to stretch it to the full size of the page.

ERASER

Custom Size Erasers
Customize the size and shape of the eraser from the 16 X 16 pixel square by selecting the paintbrush and choosing white as the paint color.

Double-Click On Eraser To Erase the Whole Screen
To erase the whole drawing area shown on the screen, double-click on the Eraser icon in the tool palette.

Use Lasso Or Selection Marquee To Erase Large Areas
Erase large or oddly-shaped areas in *MacPaint* with the lasso or the selection marquee. Select the area by either outlining it with the marquee, or for unusual shapes, draw around the object with the lasso. Then, hit BACKSPACE.

FATBITS

All the Tools Work
Don't forget that all of the tools on the menu work when you're in the FatBits mode, as do all of the modifier keys (SHIFT to constrain, etc.). Too often, users get into the habit of using only the pencil, eraser and grabber when working in FatBits. Some of the tools are more practical than others, but don't draw a line pixel by pixel—the line tool works much better.

Express FatBits
Take the express route into FatBits by selecting the pencil tool, then hold down the COMMAND key and

point to the place you want to work on. Click the mouse and presto! Instant FatBits. (You must release the COMMAND key to draw in FatBits, otherwise, you'll go right back to the full-size drawing.)

Print Out FatBits Images In *MacDraw*

Occasionally, you need a *MacPaint* document printed out in FatBits mode. Normally, the only way to accomplish this is with lots of SHIFT-COMMAND-4 snapshots and a lot of Cut and Paste. *MacDraw* provides a much easier way. First, Copy the *MacPaint* document onto the Clipboard and quit *MacPaint*. Without resetting the Mac, boot up *MacDraw* and choose Paste from the Edit menu. Next, press COMMAND-G to group the pixels together, and you have the normal-sized *MacPaint* image.

Choose the Wide option from the Page Setup dialog box (or you can use the Drawing Size option to make your document a couple of pages bigger and choose Reduce To Fit to give you a reduced version on the screen). Click once on the collection of pixels to give it some handles. Then, depress the button on the mouse while the arrow is on one of the corner handles, depress the SHIFT key, and drag the corner diagonally to stretch the whole image. You can stretch it as much as you like, using the Normal Size option to see its real size. When you're satisfied with the results, print it out and you'll find it will be much higher quality than *MacPaint* normally would allow.

FREEHAND DRAWING

Create a Pen for Smoother Drawings

For freehand drawing in *MacPaint*, you can create a pen that behaves a little differently than the pencil. The pen will give you smoother movement and better freehand curves. First, use the Pencil to create a single dot on the screen. Then, lasso the dot, hold down the COMMAND and OPTION keys, place the pointer on the dot and depress the mouse button. You can now release the COMMAND and OPTION keys and drag the repeating dot to draw with your new pen.

Use Clear Transparency On Screen As A Guide

If you need to transfer a design into *MacPaint* or *MacDraw* and don't have either the artistic skill to draw it on the screen or a digitizer to enter it electronically, try this trick. The object is to put the image on a transparency, so you can place that over your screen and trace it with the mouse and drawing tool. First, use a photocopier to reduce or enlarge your design to make it fit the Mac's screen. If possible, make the copy of your design in green on the transparency. If not, place a piece of transparency film over your black and white design and trace it with a light green marker. Then, tape the film over the screen of your Mac and use the green design as your guide for freehand drawing. Be sure to use a light green marker so the black line of the freehand tool shows through your tracing lines.

GRABBER

Quick Grabber

When the pencil is selected, hold down the OPTION key to turn the pencil into a Grabber hand. When you release the key, you're back at the pencil.

GRAPHIC SOURCES

Take Snapshots of Program Graphics for Your Personal Use

A good trick for non-artists who want to build up a disk of useful graphics is to borrow pre-defined images here and there from other programs using the snapshot facility of the Mac (SHIFT-COMMAND-3). For example, you can use the keyboard image from *Key Caps* on the Apple menu or *MacPaint*, rulers from *MacWrite*, and the disk and Wastebasket icons from the *Finder*. Just look around and you'll see lots of images that could be useful — especially if you modify them for your own needs. Remember, however, that graphics are covered by copyright laws so be sure to use these images only for your own personal applications and not for anything you're going to sell.

GRID

Grid Measurements

The lines of the invisible grid in *MacPaint* are eight dots apart. When you have the Grid option turned on, it causes operations affected by the grid to jump to these invisible 8-dot increments.

Operations Affected By the Grid

MacPaint has five operations in *MacPaint* that are affected by the grid when it's turned on. They are: 1) Dragging and duplicating objects selected with the lasso; 2) Selecting, dragging and duplicating objects with the selection rectangle; 3) Drawing straight lines; 4) Drawing filled or open rectangles, ovals or polygons; and 5) Placing the text insertion point. See hints under "Patterns" for examples of how the grid affects patterns used in these operations.

INVERTING

Three Kinds of Pixels

If you use the lasso to invert a section of a drawing, you'll soon discover that *MacPaint* has three kinds of pixels, two of them identical in appearance. *MacPaint* has black, white and transparent (appearing white) pixels. See the hints on transparent paint and transparent objects to understand how to create transparent pixels. When you use the Invert command on a lassoed area, black pixels turn white, white pixels turn black, and transparent pixels remain transparent (still appearing white).

LASSO

No Need To Complete the Loop

When using the lasso, you don't need to complete the loop to lasso an object. *MacPaint* automatically completes the lasso in a straight line back to the point where it started when you release the mouse button.

LINES

How To Get Dotted Lines

Many people misunderstand the line thickness (border) menu in *MacPaint*. The dotted line option does not create dotted lines. Instead, it chooses an invisible border (for objects filled with a pattern other than white), and a one-pixel border for white objects.

However, *MacPaint* provides a way to get dotted lines. Select Brush Shapes… from the Goodies menu, and pick the single-pixel brush. Then, select any of the patterns from the bottom palette, hold down the SHIFT key, and draw. This will give you nice horizontal or vertical dotted lines with various patterns of dots. You can also get dotted outlines of objects and dotted lines drawn with the line tool by holding down the OPTION key while you draw with the tool. The tool will draw in the currently selected pattern. Experiment with different patterns until you achieve the dot pattern you want.

Making A Curved Dotted Line

To create a curved or irregular dotted line in *MacPaint*, lasso a single dot. Then, select a line width to control the spacing between the dots (see "Controlling Space Between Copies"). Hold down the OPTION and COMMAND keys, select the lassoed dot, and drag the multiple copies in the pattern you want for your dotted line. You may have to experiment a bit to get this technique under control, but it works quite well once you get the feel for it.

MARQUEE

Double-Click On Marquee To Select the Whole Screen

To select the whole drawing area shown on the screen, double-click on the Marquee icon in the tool palette.

MEASUREMENTS

Converting Dots to Inches

In *MacPaint*, nine dots (pixels) are equivalent to 1/8 inch on your ImageWriter printout. That means one inch contains 72 dots. If you really need to count exact dots, use FatBits to avoid eyestrain.

OUTLINES

Use OPTION Key for Gray Outlined Filled Objects

If you hold down the OPTION key while you draw a filled shape, its outline will be gray instead of the usual black.

PAINT BUCKET

Avoiding "Spilled Paint"

When you use the Paint Bucket to fill objects in *MacPaint*, the objects you fill MUST BE CLOSED. If even one pixel is open in the line bordering the object, the paint will spill through that hole into the rest of your drawing. If you want to fill an object that isn't completely enclosed, select it with the lasso and choose Fill from the Edit menu. Another method is to close the border of the object temporarily with lines or pixels, fill the object with the Paint Bucket, and use FatBits to remove the temporary border.

Fill Tiny Areas with the Paint Bucket in FatBits

When you're trying to fill areas with the Paint Bucket, you can miss the tiny areas. However, don't forget that all of the tools, including the Paint Bucket, work in FatBits mode. Simply scroll to the portion of the drawing you want to work with in FatBits and choose the Paint Bucket and the pattern you want to use. Don't forget that the pattern you see in the spaces you fill is also being displayed in FatBits mode, and it may not resemble the pattern sample in the palette. It will look fine when you return to the regular size of the drawing.

PASTING

Pasting A Graphic To A Particular Size and Position

If you want to Paste a picture into a specific area and have it appear a specific size, use the selection marquee to create a "marching ant" box in the size and position you want, then Paste the graphic into the box. Your image will be resized to fit into your box and will appear within it.

Presize QuickDraw Images Before Pasting

A convenient *MacPaint* function is its ability to presize and place an image you want to Paste into a *MacPaint* document (see "Pasting A Graphic To A Particular Size and Position"). This is even more advantageous when Pasting an image that you're importing from an application that stores its graphics as QuickDraw "descriptions" (like *MacDraw*). If you want to resize a QuickDraw image, make sure you select a rectangle the exact size you want it to be in *MacPaint* before Pasting. Then, the Mac's QuickDraw routines will resize the image before it appears on the screen, and will maintain the fill patterns in their original proportions—but in the new size. If you try to resize the image after Pasting it, *MacPaint* treats the patterns and the rest of the object as bit-mapped (as opposed to QuickDraw) graphics, and will distort the image when you reshape it.

PATTERNS

Copying A Pattern from A Drawing

If you have a pattern on-screen that you'd like to add to your permanent collection, select a pattern you can live without and choose Edit Pattern from the Goodies menu. Instead of copying the pattern pixel by pixel on the grid, just click the mouse on the part of the screen showing the pattern you want. The new pattern replaces the old one and becomes a permanent part of your Patterns menu for that document.

Creating A Custom Pattern Template

When you save a *MacPaint* document, any custom patterns you've created in its palette are stored with it. This leads to a useful trick. Create and save a document with a library of custom patterns in its palette, but with no drawing in the window. The next time you Open the document, you'll have a blank template pre-equipped with your custom patterns. When you're done creating a document with your new patterns, be sure to use Save As... from the File menu and save it under another name. Then your template will remain a blank page for your next work session with the custom patterns. Make sure you save your template with a meaningful name so you know how to find it again and lock it from the Get Info dialogue box in the *Finder* to prevent anyone else from throwing it away or renaming it.

Drawing In Patterns

You can make any of the drawing tools create lines and borders in the currently selected pattern by holding down the OPTION key while drawing with the tool. The line tool will draw in the currently selected pattern and the shape tools will create shapes with borders of the currently selected pattern.

Drawing In Transparent Paint

Hold down the OPTION and COMMAND keys simultaneously while using the drawing tools to draw in transparent paint. The line tool will create transparent lines in the currently selected pattern. The hollow shape tools will create shapes with borders of the transparent pattern and the filled shape tools will create shapes with borders and "filling" of the transparent pattern.

Express Pattern Edit Window

To bring a pattern's edit window onto the screen quickly, double-click on it in the patterns palette. The double-click also makes the pattern the current active pattern.

Screening Images for Litho or Offset Printing

If you intend to use a printout from your ImageWriter or LaserWriter as a master for litho or offset printing methods, you'll get much better results on your graphics if you screen them with a gray pattern of dots before printing them out. To screen an image, first enclose it with the selection marquee. Then, choose Invert from the Edit menu. Select the shade of gray you want from the pattern palette and, while holding down the COMMAND key, draw a filled rectangle over the top of your graphic image. Now, select your image again with the selection marquee and Invert again from the Edit menu. You may have to experiment with various shades of gray to get the effect you want.

Transparent Patterns & Paint

Place one patterned shape over another without blotting out the original shape by pressing the COMMAND key while selecting the paintbrush, spray can, paint bucket, or shape tools. At the point of overlap, both shapes' patterns change to reflect the blend.

Use *MacPaint* Document To Store Large Library of Patterns

You can use *MacPaint's* ability to pick up a pattern design from anywhere in a document to allow you to store large libraries of custom patterns in a single document. First, create your library of custom patterns in one document and fill a small rectangle (only slightly larger than the pointer) with each one until the document contains all the patterns you want. To use one of your custom patterns in another *MacPaint* document, Copy the rectangle of the pattern you want to the Clipboard (using *MacPaint* or a desk accessory that allows you to Copy information from a *MacPaint* document like *Paint Cutter*). Then, Paste the pattern in an unused section of your new document. Choose Edit Pattern and a pattern you want to replace. Click the pointer in your imported pattern (making sure that all of the pointer is inside the pattern). Your custom pattern will now be installed in your document's palette.

Use the Fill Command To Replace the Pattern In An Object

If you've filled an object with a pattern using the paint bucket, using the paint bucket to replace that pattern with another one is difficult. An easy way to do it is to use the Lasso to select the object. Now, select the new pattern you want from the palette, and choose Fill from the Edit menu. The new pattern will replace the old pattern. Experiment with this one. You'll get interesting effects with overlapping objects. Also, try using the selection rectangle instead of the Lasso.

Use Transparent Paint To Create New Patterns

You can use the transparent pattern feature of *MacPaint* to create new custom patterns. Simply overlap sections of various objects drawn with transparent paint (while holding down the COMMAND key) until you have a combined pattern that you like. Then, see "Copying A Pattern From A Drawing" for a method to transfer your new pattern into your pattern palette.

POSITIONING

Create A Visible Grid

You can create a visible grid in *MacPaint* by turning on the invisible grid from the Goodies menu and then filling the blank page with one of the wide-spaced, even-dot patterns. Then, you can use the dots as a visual cue for drawing objects or lines of a specific size. If you want your drawing to have specific measurements, print out the page filled with the dotted pattern before you start your drawing and, measuring on the printout, calculate how many dots make up an inch, centimeter or whatever unit of measurement you want to use.

Finding The Screen's Center

If you need to find the absolute center of a *MacPaint* screen, type a period, lasso it, Cut it, then Paste it. It will reappear at the very center of the screen. Actually, the lower right corner of the dot is the exact center of the screen, because the screen has an even number of dots both horizontally and vertically.

Remote Control Movement for Lassoed Images

If you try to manipulate very small images after selecting them with the Lasso, the pointer can get in the way and keep you from seeing the exact position of the image. To get around this problem, *MacPaint* provides a "remote control" method for moving objects selected with the Lasso. First, select the image you want to move with the Lasso. Then, move the pointer into the thin gray area between the left and bottom edges of the drawing area and the tool and pattern palettes. When the pointer changes from the Lasso into an arrow, you can move it within the gray area and the lassoed object will respond accordingly.

POWER FAILURES

MacPaint Attempts To Save Your Work

If the power fails or your system crashes while you're working on a *MacPaint* document, the program makes a last ditch effort to save your work (and usually succeeds). When the power returns, start *MacPaint* again by double-clicking on its icon (not on the icon of any file). When it starts up, the document will be titled "Rescue" and your document will be stored in the files called "Paint1" and "Paint2" on your disk. Simply save the document under the name you want to use and you should be right back where you were when the lights went out.

PRINT CATALOG

Get a Catalog of Miniatures with Print Catalog

The Print Catalog menu option in *MacPaint* does not operate in the same way as the same command at the desktop level. If you choose the menu option, it will print out miniature images of the currently active disk (approximately nine miniatures to a page). Although you won't be able to discern much detail in the miniatures, this option can help you keep track of the major characteristics of the images on a disk.

Changing Active Disks To Print Other Catalogs

The Print Catalog menu option in *MacPaint* prints miniatures of the files on the active disk. To change active disks, simply Open one of the files on the disk you want to catalog and it will become active.

PRINTING

How To Print Multiple Copies

MacPaint uses its own printer driver and doesn't offer you an option to designate multiple copies when you're printing a document. However, you can print multiple copies of a document at the *Finder* level. If your document is on a crowded disk, move a copy of it to a disk with lots of free space. Then, use the Duplicate command from the File menu to duplicate as many copies of your file as you want to print or can fit on the disk. Now, select all of the copies with a selection rectangle or by SHIFT-Clicking and choose Print from the File menu. *MacPaint* will print all of your copies.

Paste Images Into Program That Allows Smoothing for LaserWriter

MacPaint cannot smooth an image as it sends it to the LaserWriter. However, you can Paste the image into another program that allows smoothing (like *MacWrite* or *Microsoft Word*) before you print it. This may improve the appearance of your image substantially when the LaserWriter prints it.

PROTECTION

Open and Hide A Desk Accessory To Protect Drawing

If you want to take a break from your session with *MacPaint*, but want to leave the drawing on the screen until you get back to it, Open a desk accessory and drag it nearly off the screen so that it's hard to notice. No one will be able to make any changes to the *MacPaint* drawing until you return and put away the "hidden" desk accessory.

QUITTING

Use COMMAND Quit To Reset System

When you're finished with *MacPaint*, use this easy method to reboot the Mac. Hold down the COMMAND key while choosing Quit from the File menu. The Mac ejects the disk and resets. This is particularly useful if *MacPaint* is the startup application and you have deleted the *Finder* to save space. This high-speed system reset will eject only the *MacPaint* disk, and will ignore any disk in the other drive.

RULERS

"Stealing" a Ruler from *MacWrite*

You can use the Mac's built-in capability to make a *MacPaint* document out of any screen to transfer a ruler into *MacPaint*. First, Open *MacWrite* and make sure one of its rulers is showing on the screen. Then, use the grabber bar and size box to make the maximum measurement of the ruler show on the screen. Press COMMAND-SHIFT-3 to "take a picture" of the screen for *MacPaint*. Quit *MacWrite* and startup *MacPaint* with the new Screen 0 document that's on your desktop. You can now edit the picture until just the ruler is left. Use the selection rectangle to duplicate the first inch of the ruler and shift it over to the left end of the ruler to create the first inch. You can now Copy the ruler into the Scrapbook for use with any other *MacPaint* document.

Make A Pixel Ruler In FatBits

You can make a pixel ruler of any length you want in FatBits. This kind of ruler can be handy when you need an accurate measurement device for constructing graphics that will be used only on the Mac's screen (as opposed to being printed out). First, go into FatBits and make a line 10 pixels long (or whatever pixel increment you want to use). Then, put one black pixel beside the last pixel in the line. Now, you can duplicate and join this section several times to create a ruler of the length you need.

SCREEN

Number of Pixels On a Screen

The *MacPaint* screen contains 99,840 pixels. That's a lot of FatBits!

SELECTING

Number of Positions You Can Select

MacPaint's grid has 52 horizontal positions and 30 vertical positions where you can click and place the cursor. With the grid off, the screen has 416 horizontal positions and 240 vertical positions.

SHAPES

Making a Circle or Ellipse Template

When using the ellipse tool, remember that it actually defines a rectangle that the ellipse fits into, not the edge of the ellipse itself. That makes controlling the size of the ellipse difficult. But, you can use the rectangle tool to create a template to help you draw an ellipse to exact size. First, draw a rectangle exactly the size of the outermost edge of the ellipse you want to draw. Then, erase all of the rectangle except the upper left and lower right corners. Now, choose the ellipse tool (hollow or filled). Place the crosshairs exactly on the corner pixel of the upper left rectangle corner and drag to the opposite corner. You can now erase the corner guides and have a finished ellipse exactly the size you wanted.

Making an Object "Transparent"

If you want to move one object or drawing in front of another and still be able to see the back object through the gaps in the front object, you need to understand how *MacPaint* deals with those gaps or voids. If a white area is completely surrounded with black pixels, *MacPaint* assumes that space is closed and opaque. If there is any break in the bordering black (even one pixel), *MacPaint* assumes that space is open and transparent. Before you move an object in front of another, you have to make sure that any spaces you want to be transparent are not completely bordered in black. Make one-pixel breaks in your border with the pencil or line tool, move the object where you want it with the back object showing through, and then use FatBits to repair the "holes."

Transparent Filled Shapes

If you hold down the COMMAND key while using the filled shape tools, the shapes' fill patterns will be transparent (see "Transparent Patterns & Paint").

SHORTCUTS

Shortcuts Menu Option Will Help You Remember Key Combos

The Goodies menu has an option called Shortcuts. If you select it, you'll see a screen of cues on using various key combinations for special effects. Who knows, it could save you a few trips back to this book!

SHOW PAGE

Double-Click On Grabber For Quick Show Page

To go to Show Page quickly, double-click on the Grabber in the tool palette.

STRETCHING

Stretching Or Compressing A Rectangular Selection

Hold down the COMMAND key when dragging the edges of an image that's been selected with the rectangular selection tool to stretch the image. If you drag from one of the edges, one dimension of the image will be modified. If you drag from one of the corners, both of the dimensions will be altered.

Preserving Patterns

To keep the pattern of an image intact while stretching it, hold down the SHIFT (Constrain) key.

Proportional Stretching and Compressing

You can control the proportions of a rectangular image by holding down SHIFT-COMMAND while stretching or compressing it from the edges. If you drag from the corner while holding down the keys, the Mac maintains the proportions of the image in both directions. If you drag from one of the sides, the horizontal stretch or compress will be limited in magnitude in proportion to the vertical position of the cursor.

TEXT

Change Font and Size from the Keyboard

You can change the font and its size from the keyboard without having to pull down the menus with the mouse. COMMAND-SHIFT-< and COMMAND-SHIFT-> will change the font. The font you change to is determined by the order of the fonts in your Font menu. COMMAND-SHIFT-< will take you to the next lower font and COMMAND-SHIFT-> will take you to the next higher font. Use COMMAND-< and COMMAND-> to change the size of your font. COMMAND-< takes you to the next smaller point size and COMMAND-> takes you to the next larger point size.

Changing Font Size of Pasted Text

When you Paste text from a word processor into *MacPaint*, it always appears in 12-point Geneva. If you choose a font size larger than 12-point before deselecting the text, the selection rectangle stays the same size and only part of the text is left showing. If you deselect the text at this point, the Mac will Paste only the text showing in the rectangle into your document. However, if you select Undo after enlarging the font size and then Paste again, the text will appear in the larger font size you selected in a selection rectangle large enough to show all of the text you Pasted.

Changing Fonts and Styles without Changing Position

If you want to change fonts or styles in the middle of adding a text line, without selecting a new insertion point, press the ENTER key and select the new font or style. The only drawback to this method is that you can't backspace past the point where the cursor was when you pressed ENTER.

Enter Text with Grid On To Make Alignment Easier

When you enter text in *MacPaint*, turn the Grid on. If you enter more text later, alignment will be easier.

Formatting Pasted Text

When you Paste text into *MacPaint*, it appears in a selection rectangle. Don't click the mouse button! You can change the format of the text in several ways before you deselect it—but not after. First, if you hold down the COMMAND key, you can change the size and shape of the rectangle with the mouse and the text will shift to fit the new space. Second, you can choose any of the text formatting options and they will apply to the text in the rectangle. Add or change as many options you want as long as the text is still "active" (not Pasted down).

How To Get Inverse Text

MacPaint provides a method for getting inverse (white on black) text. First, create the black background on which you want to place your text with any of the drawing tools. Then, in a blank white area of your document, create your text in regular black on white. Use the lasso to select the text and move it into place on the background. With the text still selected, choose Invert from the Edit menu and deselect the text. Voilá, white text on a black background.

Pasted Text Appears Only In 12-point Geneva

MacPaint can't interpret the invisible codes that word processors use to indicate the font, size and style of text. So, if you put some fancy text on the Clipboard from another application and then Paste it into *MacPaint*, it will appear as plain 12-point Geneva. This happens whether the text has come directly from a word processor or from the Scrapbook.

Psychedelic Text
Give lettering a psychedelic feel by selecting it with the marquee and pressing SHIFT, COMMAND and E simultaneously several times. With each successive press, the letters become more strangely outlined.

Repairing Typos
When you've made a typo in a piece of text and have gone on to other things, erase only the letters of text that are in the wrong location. In a blank area of your document, type the replacement text in the identical font, size and style, including one or two characters from one side of the space in which you intend to place the repair. Lasso the new text and move it into the correct position, using the duplicated letters to align the repair. Note: You may have to make some fine adjustment to the letters around the repair to correct the spacing between the letters. However, this fix is a life saver in situations where you can't simply replace a block of text containing a typo.

Tightly Spaced Shadowed Text with Shifted Tracings
You can get shadowed text that's more tightly spaced than the shadowed style option will allow. First, enter your text as plain or bold text. Then, select the text with the selection rectangle and press COMMAND-SHIFT-E to trace the lower right edges. Your text will be shadowed, but with its original and spacing.

Ultrabold Characters
Get ultrabold characters by entering text using OUTLINE from the Style menu, then fill in the white space with the paint bucket.

Use Screen Snapshot To Import Formatted Text
If you have a section of text that's formatted exactly as you'd like in *MacWrite* or any other Mac program, you can import it into *MacPaint* easily. Use the SHIFT-COMMAND-3 combination to take a *MacPaint* "snapshot" of the screen. If your section of text is large, you may have to take several snapshots and use the Scrapbook to store sections from several *MacPaint* documents and then incorporate them into one. It's a little awkward, but if your text has a lot of complex formatting, this may be the simplest way to get it to *MacPaint*.

Use the *Note Pad* As *MacPaint's* Word Processor
Pasted text offers much more leeway in its format and placement than does text created originally in *MacPaint*. (See "Formatting Pasted Text.") Because of this, you may want to put yourself in a "Paste-only" mode whenever you enter text in *MacPaint*. Type whatever you want in the *Note Pad* first, Copy it to the Clipboard, and then Paste it into the *MacPaint* document for reformatting.

You Don't Need Double-Sized Fonts for Printing
MacPaint doesn't handle text the same way as *MacWrite* and other applications do. When you print in High or Best resolution on the ImageWriter with *MacWrite*, the Mac takes the double-size of the fonts you're using (if they're installed in the *System*) and scales them down to give you better looking text. *MacPaint* doesn't do this, even if you have the double-sized fonts installed. If you create a lot of *MacPaint* documents using only smaller fonts, you can save some disk space by removing the larger sizes of your fonts from the *System* file.

TOOLS

Combining Key/Mouse Effects
You can use more than one COMMAND, SHIFT or OPTION key combination to combine their effects. For example, if you hold down the SHIFT and OPTION keys while drawing with the line tool, the direction of the drawing will be constrained to horizontal, vertical or diagonal (the effect of the SHIFT key) and the lines drawn will be in the currently selected pattern (the effect of the OPTION key). Adding the COMMAND key to the combination will make the pattern of the lines transparent.

TRACE EDGES

Shifted Tracings
COMMAND-SHIFT-E will give the same effect as the Shadow style in *MacWrite*. Notice that you can get some amazing graphic effects by issuing this command and its non-SHIFTed variation on the same selected area of the screen—or by giving one or both commands several times over. The result will vary, depending on the order in which you give the commands.

UNDO

Tilde Key Is Same As Undo or COMMAND-Z

The tilde key (the top left key with the shift key down) does the same as choosing Undo from the Edit menu or pressing COMMAND-Z. By holding the key down, you can get an interesting animation effect. This is true only in *MacPaint*.

MacPascal

BUGS

Version 2.0 May Be Dangerous To Your System's Health

Be very careful if you're working with version 2.0 of *MacPascal*. Some dealers have pulled it off their shelves as of this writing because of some fatal bugs. For instance, if you try to run it on a Mac with the old 64K ROMs but with the new (3.1.1) *System* and (5.2) *Finder*, you'll get quite a showy system crash.

DEBUGGING

Quick and Dirty Debugging

For quick debugging, select a program on the desktop and then choose OPEN from the File menu. Be sure your ImageWriter is on. If you make any errors, both the *MacPascal* error messages and the statement where the error occurred will be printed out.

RUNNING PROGRAMS

Run Two or More Programs from the Desktop

Run two or more programs in a row by selecting them on the desktop and then choosing OPEN from the File menu. If an ImageWriter is attached and running, you will also get a log of the activities performed.

WINDOWS

Open Windows Only As Necessary To Conserve Memory

If your *Macintosh Pascal* program is very large, or it's just a memory hog, avoid "out of memory" problems by using the "hideall" command to hide all the windows. Then, show them only as called for and necessary during execution of your program. An open program window can consume over 20 percent of the available memory in a 512K Mac!

WRITING PROGRAMS

Write Programs In *MacWrite*

MacPascal can read text-only files saved from *MacWrite*. This provides an easy way to write and edit programs. Write your program in *MacWrite* and save it as text-only. Choose the option that places returns after paragraphs, not lines.

MacProject

MAC PLUS

Guided Tour Is Not Compatible

The guided tour disk that comes with the *MacProject* package is not compatible with the Mac Plus. Although the demos will run, they cannot find the files they're supposed to work with. All you get is the cursor running around on an "Untitled" document. We've tried updating the *System* file on a backup, but can only create a disk that hangs the system.

MacServe

ARCHIVER

***Archiver* Is Not Compatible with HFS**

The *Archiver* provided with version 2.0 of *MacServe* is not compatible with HFS. You'll have to use a backup utility provided by the manufacturer of your hard disk drive, back your hard disk up with a tape drive, or back up your files individually to diskettes. If your files are too large to back up on a single diskette, copy them to MFS volumes and use the *Archiver*.

CHOOSER

Remove *Chooser* Or *Choose Printer* After Installing *MacServe*

MacServe does an excellent job of managing AppleTalk on your network. Its desk accessory takes over all the functions of the *Chooser* or *Choose Printer* desk accessory. First, install *MacServe* with its Installer utility. Then, to make sure there's no confusion, turn off AppleTalk with *Choose Printer* or the *Control Panel* on newer *Systems*, and use the *Font/DA Mover* to remove *Chooser* or *Choose Printer* from your *System*. *MacServe* will take over management of AppleTalk from then on.

Sometimes *MacServe* DA Can't Find AppleTalk ImageWriter

When you're first installing *MacServe* on your system, its desk accessory may not be able to find AppleTalk ImageWriters connected to your network. If this happens to you, reinstall the *Chooser* and use it to choose the AppleTalk ImageWriter. You can now remove the *Chooser* and the *MacServe* DA will be able to find the ImageWriter from then on.

CRASHES

Crashed User System Can Hang *MacServe* DA At Server System

Sometimes, if one of the Users on a *MacServe* network experiences a system crash, the Server's system will hang if you select the *MacServe* DA from the Apple menu. We experienced this once, called InfoSphere, and have not been able to duplicate the problem. Our only way out was to restart the Server Mac with the power switch.

Don't Try To Initialize Floppies At Active Server

The one operation on your Mac that cannot, under any circumstances, be interrupted by *MacServe* is initializing a floppy. As a result, if your system is functioning as the Server on a *MacServe* network, you'll not be able to initialize a floppy or you'll crash your system and freeze the network. Either use another system to initialize your diskette, or wait until you can shut down the network and initialize the disk on your system running on a local basis. If you run into this problem frequently, you may find it useful to keep a supply of pre-initialized disks at your work station so you can avoid it.

MacServe Performs Magic and Reconnects Users

MacServe can perform what seems like magic if the Server on your network experiences a system crash. Somehow, if you restart your Server immediately, and if no Users have requested extensive disk operations, it will re-establish the links to your Users' application and document files. To make sure this works, let your Users know immediately if your Server crashes and ask them to stop working until you're restarted. In most cases, *MacServe* will restore your network with no problems for your Users.

ERASE DISK

Hidden Files May Disable Erase Disk Button

If you try to erase a disk containing open files, *MacServe* will not allow it. If all files are apparently Closed, check the disk for a discarded Clipboard file, or for other hidden files that might be open.

Hold Down COMMAND-OPTION When You Start the *Manager*

The *MacServe Manager* will not allow you to erase the disk on which it resides. If you want to erase your hard disk, be sure to hold down the COMMAND and OPTION keys when starting up the *Manager* from the floppy so that the Mac switches to the *System* on the floppy and makes it the current Startup disk.

HFS

You Must "Erase" A New Volume To Make It HFS

Volumes created with the *MacServe Manager* utility are always in MFS (Macintosh File System) format. To format a new volume with HFS, you must "erase" it after choosing the HFS format in the dialog box available from Erase Disk on the File menu.

INCOMPATIBILITIES

Check Applications' Port Configuration

Some applications for the Mac access the printer port directly. (Terminal emulators are common examples.)

To be sure that you can use such programs with *MacServe*, especially its print spooler, make sure that you can configure the applications to use the modem port instead.

Don't Use *Font/DA Mover* Version 3.0

Version 3.0 of the *Font/DA Mover* has serious problems with *MacServe*. For example, sometimes it will boot the Mac when you double click on its icon. Don't use it; get a later version.

NAMES

Limit Name Length If You Have Any *XL/Serve* Nodes

If your network has any *XL/Serve* nodes on it, be sure to keep the length of the names for your disk and print servers under 14 characters.

PRINTING

Enter A Dummy Printer Name If You Disable Print Spooler

If you want to disable *MacServe's* print spooler, make sure you enter a dummy printer name that's definitely NOT a variation on ImageWriter in the appropriate dialog box in the *MacServe Manager*.

Rename *ImageWriter* Driver If *AppleTalk ImageWriter* On System

MacServe's print spooling utility may get a little confused if you have both an *ImageWriter* and *AppleTalk ImageWriter* driver in your *System* file. To prevent this problem, rename the *ImageWriter* driver to some other distinctive name so you can identify and select it from the *Manager* and *MacServe* desk accessory for print spooling. If you're not using print spooling, remove the *ImageWriter* driver and leave the *AppleTalk ImageWriter*.

RAM-BASED HFS

MacServe Has Problems with RAM-Based HFS

MacServe version 2.0 has problems dealing with the RAM-based HFS released with Apple's Hard Disk 20 prior to the introduction of the new 128K ROMs. Infosphere recommends that you not even attempt to run *MacServe* with RAM-based HFS.

SCSI DRIVES

Early SCSI Software May Cause Problems

Some of the support software provided with early SCSI hard disk drives has a bug which causes problems in reading and writing to the disk. This bug won't show up in *MacServe* until you erase the disk and its name doesn't reappear in the Erase Disk dialog box. If this happens to you, don't try to use *MacServe* until the drive's manufacturer has provided you with corrected software.

SYSTEM

Don't Make Modifications To *System* File with Users On Network

In general, don't make modifications to your Server *System* files while other Users are logged on to the network. Operations with your *System* files are more likely to crash your Mac than other kinds of operations—and crashes at your Server can cause problems for other Users on your network. You should be able to make most of the standard modifications, like adding or removing fonts, without causing any problems.

UPDATES

Update *MacServe* After Updating *System* Software

When you update the version of the *System* file on your hard disk, you may damage the *MacServe* files on your disk. For best results, always immediately update *MacServe* with its *Installer* utility (click the Update button) after you've made any serious changes to your *System* software.

VOLUMES

HFS Volumes Must Be Contiguous

HFS requires that each volume on your hard disk must be internally contiguous. In other words, a volume cannot be fragmented into several different sections of the disk. To use *MacServe* with HFS, give careful thought to the volume number and sizes you need before you allocate any volumes on the disk. Don't plan to make any changes or additions until the next time you want to restore your disk completely. (See "Use Dummy Volume Next To *System* Files.")

Superimpose *MacServe's* Volumes Over Drive's Organization

Most hard drive manufacturers provide software to subdivide the disk. When using *MacServe*, you'll find it's usually most efficient to use the manufacturer's software to make the drive one large subdivision and then superimpose *MacServe's* volumes on top of that.

Use Dummy Volume Next To *System* Files

When you create volumes with *MacServe's Manager*, it starts at the outside of the hard disk and works in toward the center. Your *System* files are on the outermost rim followed by your first volume, second volume, etc. If you modify your *System* files later, and happen to make them larger, they won't have room in their volume to expand. The hard disk will spread them all over the disk, using any available space, with pointers leading from one fragment to another. This will slow down the performance of the hard disk and the network. To leave some room for the *System* to expand and prevent this problem, create an empty dummy volume with an appropriate amount of room for expansion, and designate that as your first *MacServe* volume. Then make your real first volume the second, and so on. When you've created all of your volumes, go back and delete the dummy volume you created at the beginning. Now, when you expand your *System* files, they'll have room to grow.

MacSpell+

BOSTON II

MacSpell+ Incompatible with 14-Pt. Boston II Text

Don't try to use *MacSpell+* on text containing lines of Boston II 14-pt. text. (Actually, the 14-pt. size of Boston II is a special one-pixel underline font that fools *MacWrite* or *Word* into thinking it's text.) MacSpell+ won't be fooled by 14-pt. Boston II. Even worse, it will get confused and crash or lock up the system. To prevent this problem, make sure that if your document contains Boston II 14-pt. linest, they are not in the section being checked by *MacSpell+*. Or, you can add them after checking the document.

MacTablet

CURSOR

Lift Puck One Inch Off Tablet After Menu Selection

When you slide *MacTablet's* puck off the drawing screen area (for instance, to make a menu selection), the cursor probably won't be aligned properly when you slide the puck back into the drawing area. To solve this problem, lift the puck approximately one inch off the surface of the tablet after making a selection and place it back in the drawing area. Everything should realign properly.

MacTerminal

BACKSPACE

Use COMMAND-BACKSPACE For Destructive Backspace

When you are communicating with mainframe computers, hitting BACKSPACE in *MacTerminal* may correct your screen display, but it will not correct the data as it is stored in the mainframe. To make your backspace destructive (so it removes the character you backspace over), use COMMAND-BACKSPACE.

BUGS

Bundle Bit Problem Patch for Version 2.0

Version 2.0 of *MacTerminal* will prevent the Mac from setting the Bundle bit when you're transferring files via the MacBinary protocol. Among other things, this will keep you from getting the icons for the files you're transferring. To fix the problem, you'll have to CODE resource 15. Change `2F3C 0000 00E8` to `2F3C 0000 E800`. Find and make the change twice to fix the problem.

MACTERMINAL COMMAND KEYS

Hidden COMMAND Key Combinations

Several undocumented COMMAND key combinations are available to direct cursor movement and other actions in *MacTerminal*:

COMMAND	EFFECT
COMMAND-H	Moves the cursor back one space.
COMMAND-I	Moves the cursor to the right, stopping at the next tab marker.
COMMAND-J	Moves the cursor down one line.
COMMAND-K	Moves the cursor down two lines.
COMMAND-M	Moves the cursor to the start of the current line.
COMMAND-G	Sounds the Mac's tone (the bell character left over from teletype days)

These key combinations don't always work when you're on-line. However, they should always function when you're off-line.

CURSOR MOVEMENT

Simulated Cursor Keys

MacTerminal lets you simulate the cursor keys while you're connected to a remote computer. Hold down the OPTION key to transform the cursor into a four-way VT100 arrow cursor, move it where you want it, and click. *MacTerminal* transmits the appropriate cursor key sequences to the remote computer.

MAC PLUS

Use the OPTION Key To Make ENTER Key Work Properly

The ENTER key on the Mac Plus doesn't act the same way on the Mac 512. To make the Mac Plus' ENTER key behave the same way as on the Mac 512, hold down the OPTION key, too.

SETTINGS

Creating a Mac-to-Mac Document

MacTerminal supplies a Mac-to-Mac document with all the terminal settings preconfigured. However, should you accidentally trash that document, here's how to create a replacement: 1) First, pull down the Settings menu. Under this menu you will have to make changes in the three dialog boxes you get by choosing, in turn, Terminal, Compatibility and File Transfer. 2) In the Terminal Settings dialog box, click the mouse in the following boxes to "on" (if they don't already have an X in them): New Line, Local Echo, On Line, Auto Repeat, and Auto Wraparound. 3) In the Compatibility Settings dialog box, choose: 8 bits per character, No parity, No handshake, and the baud rate the host computer will be using. 4) In the File Transfer Settings, choose: XModem, Retain Line Breaks, Word Wrap Outgoing Text, and Remote System equals *MacTerminal*. 5) For all other choices, the program default values are fine. Once you have configured all the settings, use the Save As... option to save this document at "Mac-to-Mac."

If *MacTerminal* Hangs Up After Answer, Add Pauses To Phone Number

Sometimes, *MacTerminal* will hang up shortly after the host computer answers the number you're dialing. If you're using a Hayes compatible modem, you can solve this problem by placing a few commas after the phone number. Each comma will cause the modem to wait two seconds and will allow *MacTerminal* time to register the fact that the phone has been answered at the other end.

VERSION 1.1

Wait For Call Option Is Reversed

The Wait For Call option in *MacTerminal 1.1* is reversed. You don't have to tell it to wait for a call if you want it to answer and it won't answer if you tell it to. Don't try to understand it, just get the version 2.0 upgrade from your dealer.

MacType

BUGS

Certificates Won't Be Awarded for Exact Results

MacType has an obscure bug. The program requires that you achieve test results of 30 words per minute at 99% accuracy—or higher for it to award you a certificate. The problem is that if you get exactly 30 WPM at 99% accuracy, the program won't award the certificate. You'll have to do just a little bit better than the program asks to get its certificate.

MacUser

SUBSCRIPTIONS

Call 1-800-MAC-USER

If you'd like to subscribe to *MacUser*, call 1-800-MAC-USER. That's also the number to call if you'd like to renew your current subscription or if you're having any kind of problem with your subscription. Don't miss an issue. Every month, you'll find a tip sheet with some of the latest additions to this book.

MacWrite

APPLICATIONS

Poor Man's Database Manager

MacWrite can serve as a poor man's database manager. Arrange your data in a *MacWrite* document as if it were a record in a database, and use SEARCH, FIND and FIND NEXT to zip through the document for keywords. For example, if you use it as an address book, you can search for names, phone numbers, cities or addresses, ready to Cut and Paste elsewhere.

Using *MacWrite* As An Address Book of Envelopes

You can keep your address book as a continuous document in *MacWrite*. Put only one address on each page (insert a page break after each address). Position the addresses correctly to print on envelopes and make the font and style choices you want to use. You can look up an address via the Find window by searching for the name or other portion of the address. Once found, you can print the envelope immediately, Copy the address, Close the address book, and Paste the address into your letter template.

CHARACTERS

Use Outline & Underline To Give Visual Character Count

Need to count the number of characters in a line, series of lines, or an entire document in *MacWrite 4.5*? Select the line or lines and choose underline and outline from the Style menu. If you look closely at the on-screen underscoring, you'll notice a small dot inside the double underscore lines once every 15 characters (including spaces). Count the dots, multiply by 15, and add the characters to the right of the last dot. The dots don't appear in the lines when they're printed if you leave the styles the same.

CURSOR

Finding A Lost Cursor

Lost the cursor in a large document? Hit ENTER to scroll rapidly to the cursor's present location.

DELETING TEXT

Cut Removes One of the Spaces Around Double-Clicked Word

When you select a word to delete by double-clicking on it, pressing BACKSPACE removes only the text, but leaves both of the spaces on the ends of the word. However, if you choose Cut from the Edit menu (or use COMMAND-X), the Mac also removes one of the spaces, so that the remaining words close up, with only one space remaining between them.

Double Backspace After Double-Click

To delete a word and remove one space in one fast operation, double-click on the word, then double-press the Backspace key. After a few days, it will be a habit.

ENTER-Double-Click Deletes Single Word

Hold down the ENTER key when you double-click on a word to delete it automatically. Undo will put it back. Develop the habit of hitting the BACKSPACE key immediately after double-clicking, and you'll also remove the extra space between words.

Express Delete with the ENTER key

Use the ENTER key to delete areas of text quickly. Holding down ENTER while selecting text causes the selection to disappear as soon as you release the ENTER key.

Un-Backspace

If you inadvertently BACKSPACE over text and can't Undo, place the insertion point where you want to restore the text and press COMMAND-BACKSPACE. If you haven't used BACKSPACE since you deleted the text you want, it should reappear, one letter at a time, up to 50 characters. This works only if you back-spaced over text, one letter at a time, not if you selected a block of text and hit BACKSPACE.

DISK SPACE

ABOUT *MACWRITE*

Keep an eye on how much disk space is left by choosing ABOUT *MACWRITE* from the Apple menu.

DOCUMENT SIZE

Document Sizes for 128K and 512K Macs

The maximum size allowed for a *MacWrite* document on a 128K Mac is about 27,000 characters, or approximately 5,000 words on 20 double-spaced pages in 12-pt. type. On a 512K Mac, the limit is about 108,000 characters, or approximately 20,000 words on 80 double-spaced pages in 12-pt. type. The actual size of your document will be limited by the number of fonts and graphics you use. The more fonts and graphics, the smaller the document. In any case, we don't recommend a *MacWrite* document of more than 45 pages. The program will bog down and editing and saving operations will be tediously slow.

DOCUMENT WIDTH

Wider-Than-Screen Documents

Although the procedure is somewhat obvious, the *MacWrite* manual fails to document how to get documents wider than the screen. To move the right margin beyond the edge of the window, pick up the window with the grabber bar across the top and move it as far left as you want to expand the right margin. Open the window to the right with the sizing box in the lower right-hand corner of the window. You'll now be able to move the right margin marker to where you want it. Reverse the procedure to bring the left-hand margin back into view. Be sure to resize the window before you move it or you won't be able to use the elevator.

ENVELOPES

Put Copies of Addresses At the End of Your File

You can combine your letters with envelope addressing documents in the same file. This is especially convenient if you type more than one letter in a file and want to print them on continuous form paper. First, write one or more letters in your file, putting a page break between each letter. Then, Copy and Paste the inside address from each letter onto the last page of the document and insert page breaks between each address. When you print, select continuous forms and print only the pages containing the letters. Then, select Print again, but use the Cut Sheet option and print out only the pages containing the addresses, feeding an envelope into the printer each time it requests the next sheet. If you write several letters at a time, this can save you a lot of time.

FIND & CHANGE

Search and Replace Tabs Using *Note Pad*

MacWrite doesn't provide a direct way to enter a Tab character in the "Find What" field in its Find and Change boxes. However, you can use the *Note Pad* to create Tab characters and then Cut and Paste them into the "Find What" field.

For example: Here's a handy way of making use of the Tab command to change the entire look of a document. If you have used a Tab to indent each paragraph in an eight-page document and you want to replace each Tab with a bullet (• = OPTION-8), you would have quite a time-consuming task on your hands. However, a simple method of carrying out this operation is to type in a Tab character on the *Note Pad*. Select the Tab character, Cut it and then Close the *Note Pad*. Using the Search menu, select the Change option and Paste the Tab character into the "Find What" box. Now type your bullet character into the Change To box, click in the Change All box (if the indents are the only Tabs you've used) and, voilà, the task is done.

FONTS

Create Tiny Text In *MacDraw* and Paste In *MacWrite*

For documents that require fonts smaller than 9 points (the smallest size *MacWrite* will support), create the original text in the smaller point size in *MacDraw*. Type it into a box the width of the space between your *MacWrite* margins. Then, Paste the text into your *MacWrite* document. This works especially well if you're printing on the LaserWriter and use LaserWriter fonts.

Fool *MacWrite's* Font Size Limitations with FNTLIB.UTL

A special *MacWrite* document (common in public domain and user group libraries) allows you to use fonts in any size from 3 to 48 points. The document is called FNTLIB.UTL on the *Club Mac Bulletin Board*, "MacWrite Fonts" on the Boston Computer Society's *Font Disk 1*, and WRTFNT.BIN in DL7 of *CompuServe's* Mac User group (PCS-23).

To use a particular font size, just Copy a section of the text of that size onto the Clipboard from the FNTLIB document. Close the document, Open your own, and Paste the text into the document in which you want to have the font size appear. The Pasted text will retain its size attributes from FNTLIB. Place your cursor in the middle of the Pasted section and type the text you want in that size. When you're finished, delete the superfluous Pasted text from the ends of your new work.

Small LaserWriter *System* Files with FNTLIB.UTL

Here's a way to save space on your *MacWrite* Startup Disk for the LaserWriter fonts. Use FNTLIB.UTL (see "Fool *MacWrite*'s Font Size Limitations with FNTLIB.UTL") as a substitute for storing a range of sizes for each font in your *System* file. With that document on the startup disk, you need to place only one small version and one large version of each font in the *System*, because the Mac will use the FNTLIB.UTL file as a repository of font sizes. The actual fonts used by the LaserWriter when it prints are built into it and only need to be in the *System* file to improve the screen appearance. The drawback of deleting fonts is that the scaled fonts do not look as crisp on the Mac screen. However, saving 80K or more on your Startup disk could be worth the sacrifice. By retaining only the two smallest and the largest font sizes of Courier, Helvetica, Times and Symbol, you can free up nearly 33K on the *System* disk. The screen images for the sizes above 9 point are quite readable.

FOOTNOTES

Use *Note Pad* To Store Footnotes, Then Paste Them In

MacWrite doesn't have a footnote option, but you can use the *Note Pad* to store the notes as you write. Later, you can Paste all the notes at the end of your paper, or put a single footnote at the bottom of the appropriate page of your document.

FORMATTING

You Don't Always Have To Use Rulers To Format

MacWrite 4.5 added several new formatting commands (viewable under the Format menu) that allow you to format paragraphs without using a Ruler. To use them, simply place the insertion point anywhere in the paragraph you wish to format and select the option from the Format menu or use the COMMAND key combination. The options are: Align Left (COMMAND-N); Align Center (COMMAND-M); Align Right (COMMAND-R); and Justify (COMMAND-J). If you change your mind and want to return to the ruler's formatting, type COMMAND-D (Use Ruler).

FORMS

Form Letters

Preconfigure the form letters you use often, then save the form with its own file name (such as "Invoices").

Whenever you need that form, simply Open it, and fill it in. To retain a copy for your records, use the Save As... option and give it a specific title ("Teleporter Invoice"). This keeps the generic form ready to use the next time.

GLOSSARY

Use Abbreviations and Change Option As A Glossary Function

One of *MacWrite's* shortcomings is its lack of a Glossary function so you can store long strings of text and then recall them with one or two keystrokes. However, the Change option, combined with abbreviations, provides a way to emulate this function. While typing in your document, create a distinct abbreviation for each word or phrase (/JCD for the *Journal of the CD-ROM Society*, or *MU for *Mac-User*, or ;FD for "For further details on this product, please call me." etc.). To avoid confusion with short words such as to, at, me, etc., start each abbreviation with a character that won't have a space character before it in normal text (such as a slash, an asterisk, or a semicolon). Then, when you use the Change option to flesh out the abbreviations, ask it to search for all occurrences in the document that have a space character followed by the abbreviation string. For convenience, enter all your abbreviations and their equivalent text on the *Note Pad* as you create them. Paste them from there into the Find What and Change To boxes.

GRAPHICS

Moving A Graphic From *MacPaint* To *MacWrite*

One of the greatest advantages of the Mac over other computers is its ability to transport graphic or text information from one program to another. However, the first time you try to move a graphic image from *MacPaint* to *MacWrite* may be a little confusing. First, select the graphic in *MacPaint* with the lasso so you leave as little white space around it as possible. Then, either Cut or Copy the selected graphic, quit *MacPaint*, and start *MacWrite*. Place the insertion point in the document where you want the graphic to appear and Paste. You'll be able to type above and below the graphic, but not beside it. Don't type anything while the graphic is selected (a black rectangle around it), or you'll replace it with what you type. You can move the graphic by grabbing anywhere on it besides the three "handle" boxes at the bottom. Drag on those handles to resize the graphic. Afterwards, in *MacWrite*, you can treat the graphic just like a section of text for Cutting, Copying, Pasting, etc.

Mixing Graphics and Text On the Same Line

MacWrite doesn't allow you to enter text on the same line as a graphic image in a document. However, the way to get around this problem is to create both the text and the graphics in *MacPaint* or *MacDraw*. Then, Paste the whole thing into *MacWrite* as a graphic. You should print documents created with this technique in Standard or Faster resolution to make all of your text appear the same. If you use High or Best resolution, the text next to your graphics will appear in much lower quality than the rest of your document.

Replacing A Graphic with One Already On the Clipboard

Replacing a graphic image in a *MacWrite* document can be confusing if you have the replacement already sitting on the Clipboard. If you Cut the old graphic, it will move to the Clipboard and destroy the graphic you wanted to put in its place. However, the Mac has two good ways to perform this operation without destroying the image on the Clipboard. You can select the old graphic, hit BACKSPACE, and then Paste in the new graphic. (Hitting BACKSPACE doesn't move the old graphic to the Clipboard.) Or, you can select the old graphic and Paste in its replacement. The new graphic will replace the old.

Resizing A *MacPaint* Picture

When Pasting a *MacPaint* picture into *MacWrite*, you can stretch or shrink the image by placing the cursor over one of the three squares ("handles") on the bottom border. Drag the mouse while still clicking. The drawing reshapes itself when the mouse button is released. Once changed this way, only immediately choosing Undo returns the picture to its original proportions.

Tall Adjusted Corrects Distorted Pictures

When Pasting *MacPaint* pictures into *MacWrite*, the image might look distorted. This is especially true with circles. To keep the image looking the way it should when you print it out, choose Page Setup from the File menu and click the Tall Adjusted box in the Orientation option. This stretches the picture horizontally, usually correcting distorted images.

Wide Page Setup Corrects Distorted Pictures

Choosing the Wide box under Page Setup will correct distortion in *MacPaint* pictures Pasted into *MacWrite*. The text, of course, remains in the same relationship to the image, but not to the page.

HEADERS & FOOTERS

Date & Time Icons Automatically Change

The date and time icons in headers and footers automatically enter the current date and time whenever you have the document on screen or are printing it. The ony way to prevent these from changing is to type the date and time you want to use instead of using the icons. If you choose to use the icons, always type the date in the body of your document if you want to know when you wrote it.

Maximum Lines In A Header or Footer

MacWrite's headers and footers can contain a maximum of seven lines each.

Overlap Text and Graphics with Header Icons

Although you can't actually place text on top of pictures in most of *MacWrite*, the text generated by the time, date and page number icons (in headers and footers) will print on top of either text or graphics. To take advantage of this, just Paste the graphic you want into the header or footer and position the appropriate icon on top of the space in the graphic where you want the text to appear. Try, for example, putting the page number inside a graphic image that looks like one of the Mac's document icons in the *Finder*—or put the time in a box that makes it look like a digital clock. You may need to do a little experimentation to get the text exactly where you want it, but the results can be quite pleasing.

Starting Page Numbers On the Second Page

If you are numbering the pages of your document with the page number icon in a header or footer, the number won't print on the first page if you've checked the Title Page menu option. The first page number printed will be "2" on the second page. If you want the second page to be numbered as "1," go to the first page, select Set Page #..., and make it page "0." The only disadvantage to this technique is that you won't be able to print the first page by itself. If you tell the Print dialog box to print pages 0 to 0, it will print the whole document. You can change the page number back to 1 temporarily if you need to print it by itself.

Time, Date & Page Number Icon Text Format

How do you control the font, size and style of the text generated by the time, date and page number icons in headers and footers? Selecting the entire header or footer has no effect on the icon-generated text. The icons derive their instructions from the choices you've made for the first character or space in the header or footer. (The default font is 12-point Geneva). If you want the first line of a header or footer to be in a different font, size and/or style than the icon-generated text, put one blank space at the beginning of the first line. Select that space only, and choose the format you want for the icon-generated text. Then, make your choices for the remainder of the line (and other lines).

Title Page Option Turns Off Header & Footer Text

When you select the Title Page menu option for a document, the headers and footer text won't be displayed or printed on the first page of your document. The Mac substitutes the proper number of blank lines to keep your top and bottom margins the same as the other pages.

Use Header or Footer As A Style Sheet

If you're willing to sacrifice the use of your header or footer, you can use one of them as a style sheet or "well" to store frequently used rulers and type styles. Just Paste the rulers and font samples (in the styles you want to use) into the header or footer. Choose the Remove option from the Format menu for the header or footer, depending on which you're using, but leave it on the screen. Now, move your document window slightly to one side or the other so you can click on the edge of the header or footer window to make it active. When you want to get a ruler from your style sheet, make the window active, Copy it, and Paste it into your document. If you want to get a font/style sample, Copy it from the header or footer, Paste it into your document, select the pasted text, and start typing. Your text will appear in the same font and style as the Pasted sample.

OTHER PROGRAMS

Create Tables in A Spreadsheet for Easy Editing

Editing tables in *MacWrite* is a little difficult. The easiest way to handle tables is to create them in a spreadsheet (such as *Multiplan*, *Click-On*, etc.) and then Paste them into your *MacWrite* document. This allows you to format or edit whole columns or rows at a time in the spreadsheet before moving them into *MacWrite*. Save a temporary copy of your file in the spreadsheet form. That way, if you discover you need to make large editing changes, you can make them in the spreadsheet version and "re-Paste" the table into your *MacWrite* document.

Paste Large *MacDraw* Graphics Into Blank *MacWrite* Document First

If you try to Paste a large *MacDraw* document into a *MacWrite* document that already contains some text, you usually get a message informing you that the Clipboard is too large to transfer. To make matters worse, the Paste command fails. To get around this, first Paste to a new, empty *MacWrite* document, then Cut and Paste into the desired target document.

Transferring Blocks of Cells from Spreadsheets

Transferring blocks of cells from a spreadsheet into *MacWrite* is easy. The data from each of the cells is separated by a Tab, with a Carriage Return at the end of each row. First, select the block of cells you want to transfer from your spreadsheet, and Copy them to the Clipboard. Quit your spreadsheet and, if it gives you the option, be sure that the Clipboard saves the format of the values. Now, Open the *MacWrite* document where you want to Paste the cells. Insert a ruler just before the place where you want to Paste the cells and position a Tab marker for each column in your block of cells. (Be sure to use Decimal Tabs if applicable.) Now, Paste. If the columns don't line up the way you want, adjust the Tab markers.

Transferring *Microsoft Word* Documents

Microsoft Word and *MacWrite* use different file formats for storing documents. Regrettably, this means that the only way to transfer files from *Word* to *MacWrite* is to save your file in the Text Only form. The Mac retains your Returns and Tabs, but none of the formatting—margins, fonts, styles or point sizes.

PRINTING

Click On Cancel Button To Eject Last Page Quickly

When printing *MacWrite 4.5* documents on an ImageWriter, the program often takes a long time to scroll the page out of the printer after it has finished the last page. The delay's length is in direct proportion to how much scrolling it has to do. Avoid this time-waster by choosing the on-screen Cancel box as soon as the ImageWriter finishes the last line of output. This causes the printer to take over and scroll the page out, while *MacWrite* regains immediate control.

Document Too Long

If *MacWrite* says it can't print a document, it may be too long. Try printing it a few pages at a time.

Extra Page When Printing

If your file produces a blank page from the printer when you print the file, you may have space characters at the end of your document that trail onto an extra page. Place the cursor directly after the last character of your file. If it's not already on the screen, use the elevator to bring the bottom of the last page onto the screen. Hold down the SHIFT key and click the mouse in the lower right hand corner of the document. Press BACKSPACE to delete the unwanted invisible spaces.

MacWrite Doesn't Accurately Show LaserWriter Format

The margins on a *MacWrite* document aren't accurate for what will print on the LaserWriter. You can experiment until you find margins that are acceptable for your purposes. As a general rule of thumb, you can format your document's margins as they are for the ImageWriter and then print at 90 or 95% reduction.

Not Enough Disk Space

MacWrite saves a bit map of each page to the disk before printing it out. If the startup disk doesn't have enough space left, it will give you a "disk full" message. Either delete some files from the disk, or print the document with *MacWrite* from another start-up disk that has more free space available.

Print Envelope Before Writing Letter

If you are only going to write a single letter in your document, you can save some time by printing the envelope first. First, Open a new document or your correspondence template. Type the inside address of the letter you're about to write and stop. Insert a temporary ruler above the address and alter the margins and line spacing so the address is in the center of the page (or wherever you want it to appear on your envelope) and the first line is at the top of the page. Insert your envelope into the printer with the printhead on the line where you want it to start printing the first line of the address. Print the envelope using the Cut Sheet option. Then, return to your file, remove the temporary ruler, restore the space at the top of the page, and type the rest of your letter, using the address you typed for the envelope as the inside address of the letter. This technique will also work with *Microsoft Word*, but you'll have to use a slightly different method for altering your margins temporarily.

Print File for Version 2.2 Is Twice the Size of Original Document

If you are using *MacWrite 2.2*, you'll have to leave enough space on your startup disk to accommodate a print file twice the size of the document being printed.

Printer Not Properly Connected

MacWrite won't print a file if the printer isn't hooked up properly (you know this is the case if the trouble occurs right after the Mac says "Looking for the ImageWriter or LaserWriter."). If the connections are all hooked up properly, go to the *Chooser* (*Choose Printer* with older *Systems*) under the Apple icon and select the appropriate hardware. If nothing shows up in the dialog box, you'll have to Quit the application and check to make sure the disk contains the correct printer driver files.

Use Footers and Avoid Headers for Draft Printing

When you are using draft quality on continuous form paper, place information you want to appear on every page in a footer and avoid using headers entirely. Otherwise, the printer will scroll backwards on each page after printing the body copy so it can print the header. Not only will this cost you time, but the ImageWriter is much more vulnerable to jamming when running paper backwards. If you want headers in your finished copy when you print it in Standard or High quality, keep the information you want in the footer while you're writing and printing draft copies and then Cut and Paste it into a header just before printing your final copy.

Use the LaserWriter To Produce Extra Large Fonts

MacWrite does not support font sizes greater than 24 points or less than 9 points. For very large fonts on the LaserWriter, you can often create the entire document with the right margin set at 4 1/4 inches and print at 200% enlargement of the original size. This works very well for single page posters.

QUITTING

Fast Quitting from the Disk Menu

MacWrite is not permanently damaged if the power goes off while it's running (although unsaved documents may be lost). If you plan to shut the computer off when you finish with a *MacWrite* session, you can quit quickly from the disk menu without having to go back to the desktop. First, Save the file and Close it. Then, choose Open from the File menu and make sure all of your diskettes are ejected. With the disks out of the drives, just turn off the power switch. *MacWrite* will be fine the next time you start it.

RULERS

Creating A Ruler "Well"

When setting up multiple columns (see "Multi-Column Text"), or repeating a number of different ruler settings, create a ruler "well." At a convenient place in your document, place one copy of each of the rulers you'll be using. By Copying rulers from this common source, you'll avoid repetitive resetting of ruler settings and will assure that the settings will all be the same for the sections you want to look the same. Also, Copying rulers assures that you won't be surprised by things you forgot to do when you re-created each new ruler. If you're not using headers or footers, you can keep your ruler well in one of them.

Faster Ruler Changes

When you want to make several changes to the settings on a ruler with a large amount of text follwing it, speed up the process by inserting a ruler immediately below the ruler you want to change. Make the changes on the upper ruler, then select the lower ruler and hit BACKSPACE. This will avoid waiting for the text to reformat after every ruler change—it will reformat only when you delete the temporary ruler.

Keep Complex Rulers In the Scrapbook

If you frequently need to use a complex ruler setting in a new document, you can keep a library of one or many rulers in the Scrapbook. This can be especially helpful if you use the same rulers for repeating sections of a document which are many pages apart.

Using *Localizer* To Get Metric Rulers

Here's a cheat method of displaying a metric ruler in *MacWrite* without resorting to the *Redit* utility. All you need is the *Localizer* program from Apple. When you boot up the *Localizer*, you are asked to specify in which country you are using your Macintosh. If you click on any of the buttons other than the United Kingdom and the USA—such as Germany or France —*MacWrite* will come up with a metric ruler. The only two countries that sport the Imperial ruler are the USA and the UK. However, be careful using this approach, because each of the country selections in the *Localizer* menu makes changes to keyboard layout and other features of *MacWrite*.

SCREEN

Number of Pixels On a Screen

The default *MacWrite* screen contains 175,104 pixels. Just thought you'd like to know.

SELECTING

Double-Clicking On A Word Doesn't Include Punctuation

The shortcut way to select an entire word is to double-click on it. But, that won't include commas or period characters after a word, nor quotation marks before and/or after the word. However, the double-click will grab the apostrophe and characters following it in contractions.

SPACING

Check for Extra Spaces After Cut & Paste Operations

When you make changes in a document (especially with Cut & Paste), the spacing between words is sometimes altered by spaces brought in by the change. Usually, you'll see the extra spaces, but if they occur at the end of a line, you won't see them. The word wrap routine will fill the line with as many extra spaces as necessary, but they may be preceded by extra spaces from your Cut & Paste operation. When you make other changes earlier in the document, those extra spaces may get pushed onto the next line, where they are visible. A document with columns controlled by Tabs can lose its neat appearance for no apparent reason because of this. If you suspect that this is the cause of a line formatting problem in your document, select the entire space between the last character of the suspect line and the first character of the next line. Delete it or replace it with the number of spaces you really wanted. Although it won't always be necessary, it's quick, sure—and avoids formatting problems and spoiled pages at printout time.

Correcting Forced Space After Decimal Tabs

If you try to move a decimal Tab up against the right margin, you'll notice that it forces you to leave at least one space between the Tab and the margin. If the material you're tabbing doesn't have any places after the decimal, this can throw off the appearance of the right margin of your document. To correct this problem, create a ruler for the tabbed material with a right margin 1/4 inch to the right of the right margin of the rest of your document. After your tabbed material, insert another ruler to move the right margin back to where it was before. If you need to use this setup often, you can keep a ruler adjusted for the tabs in a "Ruler Well." (See "Creating A 'Ruler Well.'")

Correcting Uneven Line Spacing

Don't forget that blank spaces have a point size, too. If you have uneven line spacing in a section of text and have used the same point size for all of the text, you may have stray space characters of a different point size. Select the section of text with all of its surrounding spaces, and select the point size you want from the Style menu. The spaces will change to the same point size as your text and the line spacing should even out.

Custom Line Spacing

Do you want different spacing between your lines than you can get with the three built-in space controls? Select any blank space on the lower of two lines and change its size to the font size just larger than the one you're working with. (For example, when using 12-point fonts, put a 14-point space in the second line).

Cut Off Italics

MacWrite sometimes cuts off part of the last letter of an italic word at the end of a line, especially when you justify the right margin. To avoid this, hold down OPTION when you space after the word. This creates what typesetters call a "hard space." *MacWrite* treats it like a character attached to the previous word when it adjusts the spacing for justification. Be sure to insert another regular space after the hard space if you want *MacWrite's* word wrap function to be able to break the line after the italic word. (See "Non-Breakable Spaces.")

How To Accomplish Vertical Centering

Here's a method for centering text vertically on a page. First, type in the text at the very top of a page. When finished, put the cursor after the last character of the text and insert carriage returns until you generate a page break. Now, select half of the space between the text and the page break by dragging over it with the cursor, and Cut it. Put the insertion point in front of the first character of the text and Paste. Remember that the human eye perceives the center of the page at a place slightly higher than the actual center, so you should leave a little less space above the text than below it.

Irregular Spaces After Italics

The last letter of an italic word usually runs into the first letter of the next (non-italic) word. To avoid this, always use a "hard space" (OPTION - SPACE) after an italics word. For better results, follow the hard space with a regular space. This will adjust the space between the words and still allow *MacWrite's* word wrap function to break a line after the Italics. (See "Cut Off Italics")

Look For Spaces If Text Doesn't Center Properly

If you center a piece of text and it still doesn't appear to be centered between the margins, check for extra spaces before or after the text. The centering routines in *MacWrite* consider the spaces as part of the text when formatting it. Simply select the space(s) and hit BACKSPACE to correct the spacing. Remember too, that the centering is in relation to the margins, not the full width of the paper.

Multi-Column Text

The ImageWriter can print two or more columns, but the method is awkward, and prone to jamming the printer. The concept is to print the first column, then re-insert the page, or roll the paper back to the beginning, and print the second column. Set your margins to half the page width, minus your left margin and half of the space you want between columns. For example, set your left margin to one inch, and your right margin at the 4-inch mark. On a regular 8 1/2 inch wide sheet, that will give you a half-inch space between columns. At the top of page 2, insert a new ruler and set the left margin to the 4 1/2-inch mark, with a right margin at 7 1/2 inches. When you choose Print, select the Cut Sheet option, whether or not you're using tractor-fed paper. After the printer finishes the first column, it will stop and ask for the next sheet. Instead, either re-insert the page or roll the paper back to the top of the page. Exact vertical alignment is, of course, crucial. Now click OK and the ImageWriter will print out the right column on the other half of the page.

Non-Breakable Spaces

If you need to have two words together on a line and want to be sure *MacWrite* doesn't insert a line break, press OPTION and the space bar when spacing between the words. This inserts a non-breaking space that tells the Mac to treat the words as one. Telephone numbers, model numbers, dates, and catalog numbers with spaces in them often benefit from using the "hard space" so that *MacWrite* doesn't break them apart.

Use Six Lines Per Inch To Fill Out Pre-Printed Forms

MacWrite has a special option to make filling out forms designed for typewriters quick and easy. Most typewriters always put six lines of type in a vertical inch of space. To make your Mac do the same thing, use the "six lines per inch" check box on the ruler. You'll find that 9-pt. type usually works best for this purpose to prevent any of the upper part of the letters from getting clipped. However, you may want to experiment with other sizes in various faces until you find what works well for you. Monospaced fonts, such as Monaco or Courier, are best because typewriters use monospaced fonts too (all the characters occupy the same space on the line).

STARTUP

You Don't Need To Wait Before You Start Typing

When you double-click on *MacWrite* to start it, you only need to wait about four seconds before you start typing. As soon as *MacWrite* gets its first screen up, the characters you typed will appear. It's great if you have a hot idea or are in a hurry and just can't wait to get those thoughts to a keyboard.

STYLE

Change Styles As You Type

Once you learn the keyboard equivalents for the options on the Style menu, you'll save time by entering them from the keyboard as you type rather than entering your text and then pulling down menus to enter the styles. The COMMAND Key combinations are mnemonic and easy to learn. Most of them are the first letter of the Style menu option with the exception of superscript and subscript. For the last two, just think of (H)igh for superscript and (L)ow for subscript.

For example, if you want to enter the title of a magazine in a letter in plain text, use COMMAND-I-U to turn on the Italic and Underline styles before you type the title and COMMAND-P afterwards to go back to Plain text. The commands also act as toggle switches to turn themselves off. If you type COMMAND-B after a word in bold, it will return to plain text just as if you had typed COMMAND-P. Here are the Style keyboard equivalents:

MACWRITE STYLE COMMAND KEYS

STYLE	KEY COMBINATION
Plain	COMMAND-P
Bold	COMMAND-B
Italic	COMMAND-I
Underline	COMMAND-U
Outline	COMMAND-O
Shadow	COMMAND-S
Superscript	COMMAND-H
Subscript	COMMAND-L

TEXT ONLY FILES

Creating and Re-Opening Text Only Files

Saving a document as Text Only stores the words of the document only, but without all the data for the fonts, styles, margins, and so on. This may not appear useful at first, but Text Only is the format that permits you to exchange *MacWrite* documents with other programs, such as spreadsheets and database managers. When you try to save a document as Text Only, a dialog box asks if you would like the document saved with Carriage Returns at the end of each line or only between paragraphs. For use with most applications, (such as a database manager), click on the Paragraphs radio button—but check the manual of the destination program to find out what it expects to see in the file.

When you Open a Text Only file, select the Paragraphs radio button and then format the text on-screen to your requirements. If you want to create or edit text created from another program usung *MacWrite*, try out the various options offered by the Text Only dialog box to determine what you should answer, before using the process on a larger document. Many, but not all, word processors use the Carriage Return character to mark the ends of paragraphs. Spreadsheets and database managers frequently use Tab characters to separate cells or fields, and Carriage Returns to separate rows or records. To preserve those relationships, click on the Paragraphs button.

Use Text Only Option for Space-Efficient Backups

If you are concerned only with the text contained in a document, and don't care if you save its formatting in your backup, use the Text Only option. The backed up file will take approximately 30% less disk space.

TRASHED FILES

Change File Type of Damaged Files To TEXT To Recover

Sometimes, you can rescue a damaged *MacWrite* document by changing its file type with a disk editor. Normally, when you save a *MacWrite* document, its file type is WORD and it includes all the formatting and font information you included. A Text Only file's file type is TEXT. *MacWrite* is a lot less picky about what it expects when it tries to open a TEXT file than it is when it tries to open a WORD file. If you can't get a document to open, change its file type from WORD to TEXT and try again. You may have some garbage in your rescued file and may have to do a little cleaning up. You'll lose all of your formatting information, but at least you'll have saved your text.

Recovering With *Microsoft Word*

Microsoft Word can recover trashed *MacWrite* files if you don't have a utility to help you recover them. When you start up *Word* and Open the *MacWrite* files, *Word* converts them to its own format, and in the process, recovers them.

UNDERLINING

Double Underlines

Headings really stand out with a double underline at each end. To accomplish this, first choose Underline from the style menu (COMMAND–U), then hit the SHIFT and the hyphen keys. Type a few double underlines, move the cursor back to the center of them and click the mouse while the cursor is positioned between double underline characters. Now, type in the heading.

MegaForm

CELLS

Getting Around Manually Completing One Cell In Each Form

MegaForm requires that each form has one cell that is filled out manually. However, you can circumvent this restriction by designing a form that uses its manually filled cell to force the completion of many more forms. For example, filling in a name on a master index card could force the creation of an index, a new record, and an updated customer record.

Microsoft BASIC

BUGS

Version 2.1

In *Microsoft BASIC 2.1*, don't use a Tab character before a label name. If you do, you'll get an error message.

DEBUGGING

Debugging Programs Typed In From Printed Listings

Typos can create considerable mischief when you try to run a program you've entered from a magazine or newsletter listing. If you need to stop the errant execution of the program, use the break command (COMMAND and the period key held simultaneously). Usually, you'll get a disabled menu bar after the break command. To reset the menu bar, ask for the Command window by typing any character, and type `MENU RESET` to return to the *BASIC* menu.

An especially troublesome typo revolves around *BASIC's* reserved word, `DATA`. Any mistakes in lines containing the word `DATA` can foul things up when your program tries to execute with bad data.

FILES

Some *BASIC* Filetypes

Files that are created by *BASIC* can have any one of a number of filetypes. Datafiles default to type TEXT, as do all *BASIC* programs saved in text format. The other types of files created from *BASIC* are:

TYPE	DESCRIPTION
MSBB	Decimal *BASIC* programs, compressed format
MSBP	Decimal *BASIC* programs, protected format
MSBC	Binary *BASIC* programs, compressed format
MSBD	Binary *BASIC* programs, protected format

Remove ON ERROR GOTO Routines

If your *M-BASIC* program doesn't seem to run correctly, temporarily remove all your `ON ERROR GOTO` statements. You'll now see error messages that would have been suppressed by `ON ERROR GOTO` routines.

Text Only Program Files Will Run In Binary Or Decimal Version

You can save a program as Text Only and it will run with either the binary or decimal version of *Microsoft BASIC*. However, remember that the two versions of *BASIC* store data to random access files in different manners. If you run a program in one version and create files, then run it in the other version, it may not be able to read the files it created. The single- and double-precision arithmetic used by the two versions causes this difference.

FONTS

Changing List & Command Window Fonts

Although *Microsoft BASIC* allows you to select font type and size for the output window using `Textfont`

GRAPHICS

A *MacPaint* To *BASIC* Utility

The following listing is for a *MacPaint* To *BASIC* utility. See "Converting *MacPaint* Graphics To *M-BASIC*" and "Using *MacPaint* Images for Animation" for details on how to use it:

```
REM MacPaint to BASIC Utility
INPUT "Please name the file",filename$
OPEN "clip:picture" FOR INPUT AS 1:'reads the Clipboard
frame$=INPUT$(LOF(1),1):'converts the Clipboard contents
CLOSE 1
OPEN filename$ FOR OUTPUT AS 1:'opens disk file ready for input
PICTURE ON:PICTURE,frame$:PICTURE OFF
PICTURE,frame$:'displays image
PRINT#1,PICTURE$
PICTURE, frame$
LOCATE 12,1:PRINT "Saved under filename: ";filename$
REM saves new file to disk under given name
CLOSE 1:RUN
```

and Textsize, it allows you no obvious control over the fonts for the List and Command windows. Here is the command to change the font for those windows to 9-point Monaco:

```
POKE &H985,4:POKE &H987,9
```

In the statement above, the 4 just before the colon is Monaco's Font ID and the last 9 is the point size. By changing these two numbers to the Font ID and point size of any other font, you can make the List and Command windows display text in whatever font you want. Be forewarned, however. This command changes EVERYTHING. Window titles, menu items, and dialog boxes may look a little strange in London or other display fonts.

Converting *MacPaint* Graphics To *M–BASIC*

To convert a *MacPaint* drawing to an *M-BASIC* compatible file, lasso your *MacPaint* drawing and Copy it to the Clipboard. Now, boot *M-BASIC 2.1* (binary) and run the utility listed in "*MacPaint* To *BASIC* utility." Save the image under a filename of your own choice. You can now place the image anywhere on-screen with the command:

```
PICTURE, [string-variable],[optional
   size and position parameters].
```

An important point with the LOF (Length Of File) statement is that the numbers which follow it can be other than 1. This means that you can Open more than one file, read them into a string and subsequently Close them...so be sure to alter the LOF parameters accordingly if you plan to do animation. If making more than one such *BASIC* file at a time, arrange matters so that all the file-reading is done at the beginning of your program.

Saving and Retrieving Graphics from the Clipboard

Here is a routine to read a graphic from the Clipboard into a string variable (PIC$) and then save the string's contents as a disk file called CLIPGRAPH:

```
OPEN "CLIP:PICTURE" FOR INPUT AS #1
PIC$=INPUT$(LOF(1),1)
OPEN "CLIPGRAPH" FOR OUTPUT AS #2
PRINT #2,PIC$
CLOSE
END
```

To read in the file CLIPGRAPH and display it in the output window, use:

```
OPEN "CLIPGRAPH" FOR INPUT AS #1
PIC$=INPUT$(LOF(1),1)
PICTURE(175,75)-(270,150),PIC$
CLOSE
END
```

Using *MacPaint* Images for Animation

By refining the procedure described in "Converting *MacPaint* Graphics To *M-BASIC*," you can achieve genuine animation. To start, create a disk containing the binary version of *M-BASIC*, a *System* file, *MacPaint*, and the utility in "*MacPaint* To *BASIC*."

Now, create a drawing in *MacPaint*, Copy (do not Cut) it to the Clipboard using the lasso and Paste it into the Scrapbook. Return to your drawing and alter it in a small degree to create the next stage of the animation, and again, Copy to the Scrapbook. Repeat this procedure until you have a Scrapbook full of frames, each corresponding to a degree of movement.

Now, Open *M-BASIC*, select the last item in the Scrapbook. (Remember, the Scrapbook Pastes in like a stack—last on, first off.) Copy the image to the Clipboard and run the *MacPaint* To *BASIC* utility to create an *M-BASIC* file. Now, return to the Scrapbook and select the next to last file...and repeat the file-making process until you've saved the entire sequence of drawings.

At last, the animation can take place using the command PICTURE followed by the string(s) which stand for the individual files. Movement occurs when you rapidly superimpose one picture over another. Try it and see for yourself—and then combine the SCROLL statement for even more impressive graphics effects.

HFS

Specify Path To Open File On HFS Disk

When you want to Open a file with a command from your *BASIC* program, you'll have to specify the complete path through the folders if you're working with an HFS disk. Use the same syntax as with MFS, but between the quotes put the disk name, followed by a colon, then the outermost folder and a colon, and so on, until you've specified the complete path.

MEMORY SIZE

Using CLEAR To Maximize Work Space

If you're running out of work space in *M-BASIC*, you can free up some additional memory by using the CLEAR statement. However, when you clear space above the default work space, you will lose the use of the desk accessories. To get them back, you must exit from *M-BASIC*.

Version	Default	Maximum	Command for Max.
M-BASIC 2.0 binary math (128K)	21,000 bytes	27,454 bytes	`CLEAR,27749,1024`
M-BASIC 2.0 decimal math (128K)	21,000 bytes	27,693	`CLEAR,27993,1024`
M-BASIC 2.0 (512K)	334,170 bytes	379,706 bytes	`CLEAR,380000,1024`

Make Auxiliary Files In Folders Invisible

If your *BASIC* program needs to access files that are in folders on an HFS disk, you'll have to specify the complete path. (See "Specify Path To Open File On HFS Disk.") Once you've done that, if an innocent user moves the file you want out of the path you've specified, your program may be in trouble. Use a disk utility to make such files invisible so the user can't move them around.

FILES$ Function Doesn't Work Properly

The FILES$ function of *Microsoft BASIC* (version 2.1 or earlier) doesn't work properly with HFS. Talk to Microsoft.

INPUT

Changes In Version 2.0 and Later

M-BASIC, version 2.0 has an enhancement which permits the user to edit INPUT and LINE INPUT state-

OPTION KEYS

Statement Entry Shortcuts

Microsoft BASIC 2.0 or later allows you to enter many statements (45) with single keystrokes while holding down the OPTION key. OPTION-c, for example, will appear as DATA when you hit RETURN at the end of the line of code. Not all of the keys have hidden counterparts and the uppercase/lowercase distinction is important. The shorter statements probably are just as easy to type directly, but entering long statements like SPACE$ or USING with single strokes will save you a lot of typing.

STATEMENT	KEY	STATEMENT	KEY	STATEMENT	KEY
AND	OPTION-L	MOD	OPTION-N	SIN	OPTION-m
ASC	OPTION-A	NEXT	OPTION-g	SPACE$	OPTION-d
ATN	OPTION-C	NOT	OPTION-Y	SQR	OPTION-w
CVS	OPTION-a	ON	OPTION-2	STATIC	OPTION-W
DATA	OPTION-c	OPEN	OPTION-e	STRING$	OPTION-p
EQU	OPTION-X	OR	OPTION-:	STR$	OPTION-P
IMP	OPTION-B	PRINT	OPTION-u	TAN	OPTION-b
LOC	OPTION-*	PUT	OPTION-=	THEN	OPTION-T
LOF	OPTION-4	READ	OPTION-"	TO	OPTION-R
LOG	OPTION-3	REM	OPTION-O	USING	OPTION-E
LSET	OPTION-6	RETURN	OPTION-5	VAL	OPTION-0
MID$	OPTION-8	RIGHT$	OPTION-+	WHILE	OPTION-'
MKD$	OPTION-7	RND	OPTION-,	WRITE	OPTION-o
MKI$	OPTION-s	RSET	OPTION-.	XOR	OPTION-Z
MKS$	OPTION-r	SGN	OPTION-y		

ments with a cursor and standard mouse editing commands. However, as soon as the user enters any character, all text and screen graphics on that line to the right disappear (even in `TEXTMODE 1`). The best solution is to use `INKEY$` or edit fields for user input.

LISTINGS

File "Rewinding"

If you've read a sequential *M-BASIC* file all the way to the end, and want to start over from the beginning, Close it and then Open it again. The manual hints at this, but doesn't quite make it clear.

MENUS

Creating the Dividing Lines

Have you been using a series of dashes to print that dashed line across a menu—and suffered frustration because it was always indented from the left edge? Use a single hyphen in the `MENU` statement (`MENU 1,3,0,"-"`), and make sure the item is "disabled" so it can't be selected.

OTHER LANGUAGES

Numeric Variable Keyboard Entry Different From *Applesoft*

Microsoft BASIC and *Applesoft* have a subtle difference in the way that they handle keyboard entry of numeric variables. *Applesoft* rejects `<RETURN>` as a valid numeric input, but *M-BASIC* accepts it as a null and assigns a value of zero to the variable. You can trap for this error by requesting a string variable and then converting it back to a numeric using the `VAL(string$)` command.

Faster Printouts

Do you get frustrated while waiting for the ImageWriter to print *M-BASIC* program listings? Here's a way to get faster printouts, although they won't show keywords in bold. On page one of the *Note Pad*, enter the statement: `LPRINT CHR$(27)+"c":LPRINT DATE$,TIME$:LPRINT:LLIST`
Copy and Paste that statement to the Command window, and watch your listing print out, with date and time added in too.

PRINTING

Escape Sequence Table

The following table lists the Escape Sequence to use to change printer settings on the ImageWriter:

ESCAPE SEQUENCE	EFFECT
`CHR$(27)CHR$(88)`	Begins underline mode
`CHR$(27)CHR$(89)`	Ends underline mode
`CHR$(27)CHR$(33)`	Begins boldface mode
`CHR$(27)CHR$(34)`	Ends boldface mode
`CHR$(27)CHR$(114)`	Reverses line feed direction
`CHR$(27)CHR$(102)`	Restores normal line feed direction
`CHR$(27)CHR$(66)`	Prints 8 lines per inch
`CHR$(27)CHR$(65)`	Prints 6 lines per inch (default)
`CHR$(27)CHR$(68)`	Prints all zeros with slashes
`CHR$(27)CHR$(90)`	Cancels slashed zeros

CHARACTER PITCH COMMANDS

`CHR$(27)CHR$(110)`	Extended (9 characters per inch)
`CHR$(27)CHR$(78)`	Pica (10 cpi)
`CHR$(27)CHR$(69)`	Elite (12cpi)
`CHR$(27)CHR$(101)`	Semicondensed (13.4 cpi)
`CHR$(27)CHR$(113)`	Condensed (15cpi)
`CHR$(27)CHR$(81)`	Ultracondensed (17cpi)

Listings In Compressed Type

To get a printed listing of your program in compressed type on the ImageWriter, precede the `LLIST` command with the statement: `LPRINT CHR$(27)"Q"`

Resetting Escape Sequences

Most escape sequences have complementary commands to turn them off—which is a good thing, since you can do things like make the paper roll backwards with every line feed (see Escape Sequence Table). The two ways you can cancel printer commands are: turn the printer's power off, so it will "forget" the commands; or reset it to all the defaults by using the escape sequence: `CHR$(27)CHR$(99)`

The printer cancels some commands as soon as you issue a conflicting command. For instance, condensed mode printing will end if you send the code for ultracondensed printing. But, the printer will combine some non-conflicting commands. If you are in underline mode and send the command for boldface, you'll wind up with underlined boldface.

Resetting Line Spacing After LCOPY or Screen Dump

After you use `LCOPY` or SHIFT-COMMAND-$ to get a graphics or screen dump to the printer, the `LLIST` command prints listings in eight lines per inch mode instead of the standard six lines per inch. This makes the program lines overlap. Reset the printer to six lines per inch with: `LPRINT CHR$(27)CHR$(65)`

Sending Control Characters To the Printer with Version 2.0

Microsoft BASIC 2.0 can't send control characters to the printer unless Returns are suppressed with the statement: `WIDTH LPRINT 255`. After sending the control codes, restore Returns with: `WIDTH LPRINT 80` or any character width you desire. This was apparently not necessary with any of the 1.0x versions of *BASIC*; neither is it necessary in *BASIC 2.1*.

RAM DISKS

Microsoft BASIC Is Incompatible with RAM Disks

Do not try to use *Microsoft BASIC* with a RAM disk. For some reason, known best to the authors of the language, the combination will not allow *Microsoft BASIC* to operate properly.

WINDOWS

Double-Click To Make List Window Fill Screen

Double-click on the title bar or size box of the list window in *M-BASIC'* to "zoom" it up to fill the screen. Double-click again to revert to the previous size.

Microsoft Chart

CHART WINDOW

Always Widen Working Area To Maximum Before Starting

Always widen the window, chart area, and plot area to the maximum before starting work. Use COMMAND-L (List) to access the underlying series of windows.

HEADERS & FOOTERS

Editing Header or Footer Text Longer Than the Entry Box

You can create text in a header or footer entry box (in the Page Setup dialog) that is longer than the box. If you need to edit this text later, you can get at it by placing the cursor in the visible text near the right end of the entry box and dragging off the end. The text will scroll to the left and the extra text will appear, already selected for editing.

LABELS

Use White Background For Overlapping Labels

When using labels that overlap other parts of the chart, always select a white background—otherwise a few pixels of the overlapped lines will show through.

LEGENDS

Add Legend Before Formatting Chart

If you need a legend on your *Chart* document, add it before you do any fancy formatting, because *Chart* often will wreck all of your hard work when it rearranges everything to make room to add the legend.

FORMATTING

How To Format Headers & Footers

Although the method is a little awkward, you can embed formatting commands and other instructions in the text of the header or footer of a *Chart* document. Insert the formatting commands in the header or footer boxes in the Page Setup dialog box. The following table shows what options are available:

COMMAND	EFFECT
&L	Align the characters that follow at the left margin.
&C	Center the characters that follow.
&R	Align the characters that follow at the right margin.
&P	Print the page number.
&D	Print the current date.
&T	Print the current time.
&&	Print a single ampersand (&).

LINKING

Choose Data Type First

When linking to *Multiplan*, choose the type of data first, or each series will be out of step—categories and values will be transposed. Also, beware of changing the typeface of a linked series because sometimes that action will automatically un-link the two programs without warning.

OTHER PROGRAMS

Create A Series of Pie Charts In *MacPaint* or *MacDraw*

To achieve a sequence of pie charts (to display market shares, for example), Paste a number of pie charts you've created in *Chart* into *MacPaint* or *MacDraw*. Use the Plot Area grab handles from *Chart* to re-size each chart before exact postioning and deselecting.

MacDraw Works Well To Modify Charts "As Printed"

MacDraw is a great tool for enhancing charts created in *Microsoft Chart*. It has two distinct advantages over *MacPaint*. *MacDraw* can accept a chart in its full printed size, and after Pasting, the elements of the chart remain as individual elements that you can manipulate like any other objects in *MacDraw*.

Moving Charts To Other Applications

Be sure to choose the correct option when you're Copying charts into another application. If you are Copying the chart to *MacPaint*, choose the option to Copy the chart "As It Appears On The Screen." Otherwise, it won't fit in your drawing window after you Paste it into *MacPaint*. Most other applications will accept charts Copied "As Shown When Printed," and will display a larger chart with that option.

PATTERNS

Be Careful of Adjoining Gray Areas

The intersections of gray areas that are easy to distinguish on-screen tend to blur when the ImageWriter prints them out on paper—particularly in pie charts. Unless you're using dark outlines to emphasize the look of the figures, you should alternate light and dark colors.

Use Dark Patterns for Emphasis

Pick the patterns you use to fill the areas of your final presentation graphic very carefully. Darker patterns are much easier to perceive. As a general rule of thumb, put the most important figures in black, and the least important figures in white.

PIE CHARTS

Let *Chart* Calculate Percentages

Always let *Chart* do your arithmetic for you by entering the actual figures—not the percentages—when creating pie charts. Otherwise, you won't be able to use percentage labels on your sectors, and other statistical functions will be disabled, as well.

PRINTING

Change Margins In Page Setup To Resize Printed Chart

Chart uses the margin settings in the Page Setup dialog box to determine the size of a printed chart. To change the size of the printed chart, simply change the settings to the margins you desire.

SAVING

Save Multiple Versions of Your Chart As You Work

Working with *Microsoft Chart* is not as straightforward a process as working with some of the other graphics tools for the Mac. Don't rush. Carefully plan both the chart and (where used) the linked *Multiplan* document in advance. While developing your chart, save a number of versions along the way. The formatting commands are complex, and you can get lost.

STYLE

Best Uses For Horizontal Bar Charts

A horizontal version of the column chart is best suited to comparisons of series with fewer numbers and wider, less ordered variations. For example, an ideal data type would be how four sales regions of a particular country performed in a given month.

Best Uses For Line Charts

A line chart is best utilized for trends with time—where the relationship between the May and June figures, for example, is more important than the relationship between the target and the actual figures.

Best Uses For Pie Charts

Pie charts look great, but remember that they have limitations. The data must add up to 100 percent, and each sector must exclude all members of the others.

Don't Overdo!

Don't overdo anything in your chart—text, patterns or labels—and try to restrict each chart to a maximum of four series. If in doubt, the simple option is best.

Make Your Own Templates for Frequently Used Formats

Whenever you create a new kind of chart or graph, keep a copy in a library folder. Modifying an existing one is easier than starting from scratch. With that approach, all you need to do is use the "Open Format Only" option from the Open menu, and insert the new numbers. When setting up your *Chart* files for this purpose, avoid using non-automatic text areas because these will remain after you enter the new data.

Microsoft File

ARROW KEYS

Left and Right Arrows Change Field Position of Cursor

File takes advantage of the arrow keys on the Macintosh Plus keyboard. The right arrow (instead of TAB or RETURN) moves the cursor to the next field. The left arrow key (instead of SHIFT-TAB or SHIFT-RETURN) moves the cursor to the previous field.

Up and Down Arrows Change Record Position of Cursor

File takes advantage of the up and down arrow keys on the Macintosh Plus keyboard. The down arrow (instead of COMMAND-ENTER) moves the cursor to the same field in the next record. The up arrow key (instead of SHIFT-COMMAND-ENTER) moves the cursor to the same field in the previous record.

BUGS

New Files with *Finder 4.1*

MS-File and *Finder 4.1* can crash the system, but you really have to insist before they will. In the startup dialog box, always choose CANCEL before Opening a new document. Then you can go ahead and choose New File with no problem. To crash the system, don't choose CANCEL, but boldly press the RETURN key to bypass it and go where no mouse has gone before. Notice that the New button is dimmed, so choosing that does nothing, of course. What will you do? What WILL you do? Press RETURN and watch your system go down! For that, the Mac ought to give you a sour face, but probably will respond with its usual "Happy Mac" face, and accept whatever disks you offer.

DATA ENTRY

Shrink Data Entry Window To Speed Screen Redraw

Here's a simple method for speeding up data entry into *File*. Rather than leaving the database window open to the screen size (default setting), close it up as far as it will allow; this shows only two lines. Since *File* redraws the screen after completing an entry (when you hit the ENTER key), keeping the window small requires less redrawing, speeding things up considerably.

DATES

Date Fields Will Accept European Style for Data Entry

Microsoft File's date fields always display in American format. However, they will accept European style dates (Day/Month/Year) for data entry if you type them in with the month entered as text. For example: 8May86.

FIELDS

Accessing Parts of a Field Not Displayed

If the display box you've chosen for a field in your form design is not large enough for the data you've entered, the box displays only the first part of the data in the box, but *File* saves the rest in case you want to see it. In most cases, you can see what's in the rest of the field by clicking a few characters before the end of the box and dragging off its end. The text will scroll through the box for viewing. This works only in the horizontal direction of single line fields and not vertically with multiple line fields.

Changing Field Formats Without Losing Data

Normally, if you try to change the format of a field after you've entered data, you'll lose the data. However, here's a method for preserving your data. First, Open your form design and move the hide line so that all your fields are showing in the form. This is important if you have any hidden fields. If you don't make them show, you'll lose any data they contain. Now, return to the data entry window and use SHIFT-Click to select all the records in your database and Copy them to the Clipboard. Now, use Clear from the Edit menu to empty all your records and quit *File*. When the dialog box appears asking how to save the Clipboard, be sure to choose "Unformatted." Start up *File* again by double-clicking on your data file's icon. Choose Show Form from the Form menu and reformat your fields as you wish, clicking OK whenever *File* warns you that you'll lose data. After changing the field formats as you wish, save your changes and return to the data entry window. Select the New record and Paste in your records from the Clipboard. Choose "by Name" when the dialog box comes up.

WARNING: Do not use this technique with databases containing pictures. You'll lose them.

Use OPTION-RETURN To Insert Line Feeds

Normally, hitting RETURN while entering data into *File* will cause the insertion point to move to the next field. However, you can generate a line feed within a field by holding down the OPTION key when you hit RETURN. This is especially helpful if you have a long text field that you want to split into paragraphs for output in a report or in a word processor when you dump the report output as a text file. Be careful with this feature if you plan to transfer your datafile to another database manager. The destination database manager may not be able to tell the difference between the line feeds embedded in your fields and those that are field delineators. If it can't, it will read each one as the start of a new field and mess up your data transfer.

Use OPTION-TAB To Insert Tab Characters within Fields

Normally, hitting TAB while entering data into *File* moves the insertion point to the next field. However, you can generate a Tab character within a field by holding down the OPTION key when you hit TAB. Although the Tab character will appear only as a single space within the datafield as displayed in *File*, the Tabs will respond to the regular tab settings if you dump the records or a report containing the formatted field into a word processor for formatting. This is especially helpful for inserting tables into a field (like many examples in this book). Be careful with this feature if you plan to transfer your datafile to another database manager. The destination database manager may not be able to tell the difference the Tab characters embedded in your fields and the Tabs that are field delineators. If it can't, it will read each one as the start of a new field and ruin your data transfer.

FORMATTING

How To Format Headers & Footers

Although it's a little awkward, you can embed formatting commands and other instructions in the text of the header or footer of a *File* report document. Insert the formatting commands in the header or footer boxes in the Page Setup dialog box. The following table shows what options are available:

COMMAND	EFFECT
&L	Align the characters that follow at the left margin.
&C	Center the characters that follow.
&R	Align the characters that follow at the right margin.
&P	Print the page number.
&D	Print the current date.
&T	Print the current time.
&&	Print a single ampersand (&).

FORM

Width of Record Select Bar Varies with Number of Records

The width of the select bar on the far left of the screen in the datafile display of *File* varies to accommodate the number of digits in the record numbers. For instance, while we were compiling the items for this book in *File*, when we went over the 1,000 record mark, the bar became wide enough to push the form partially off the right side of the window and cause some strange shifting as we entered data. You can fix the problem by Opening the Form window, picking up the line and moving it back to the left. However, you may obscure some of your record numbers. You'll have to reset it every time you start a new session since *File* defaults back to the appropriate setting for the number of records in your data file.

HEADERS & FOOTERS

Editing Header or Footer Text Longer Than the Entry Box

You can enter long text into a header or footer entry box (in the Page Setup dialog). If you need to view or edit this text later, place the cursor in the visible text near the right end of the entry box and drag off the end. The text will scroll to the left and the extra text will appear selected for editing.

MEMORY

ABOUT *MICROSOFT FILE*

Keep an eye on how much memory space is left by choosing About *Microsoft File*… on the Apple menu.

OTHER PROGRAMS

Create Records for *File* In A Word Processor

If you want to enter data for use in your *File* database, but, for one reason or another, can't use *File*, you can create records in your word processor for later transfer into *File*. Do not, however, type in the names of the fields, because those will get Pasted in along with the data. Make sure that you type in the contents of the fields in the same order as the fields on your form in File. Follow each field by a Tab character and the final field in each record by a Carriage Return. If you have blank fields in your records, enter an extra Tab character for each one. If you have blank fields at the very end of your record, you don't have to enter Tabs for them because the Return character you enter to signal the end of the record will make the database manager ignore any remaining fields in the current record and start with the first field of the following record. To transfer the data into *File*, select all of the data in your word processor file. Put the cursor in front of the first character of the first record, and press SHIFT-Click while placing the cursor immediately after the last Carriage Return. Copy the records to the Clipboard, quit your word processor and start *File* by double-clicking on your datafile. Go to the end of your database and select the whole New record by clicking on the selection bar to the left of the data window. Paste your records into position, choosing the "by Name" option when the dialog box asks. If something appears wrong, you can Undo and go back to the word processor file to fix the problem.

Don't Use Embedded Tabs & Returns In Fields You Want To Transfer

If you think that you may want to transfer a database from *File* into another database manager someday, don't use embedded (OPTION-) Tabs and Carriage Returns within fields. When you try to transfer the file later, the other database manager will interpret the embedded Tabs and Returns as regular Tabs and Returns. In most cases, this will make the transfer impossible because the other database manager will interpret the Tabs as field delineators and the Returns as record delineators, messing up the order of your fields and records from *File*.

PRINTING

Use Font Substitution When Printing Reports On LaserWriter

When you are using the LaserWriter to print reports from *File*, be sure to turn on Font Substitution in the page setup dialog box. This will make sure that any of your total and subtotal fields and headers and footers are printed out in Helvetica instead of Geneva. Font Substitution will also make the rules (separating lines) in the report solid.

REPORTS

Use Save As... After Changing A Report's Page Setup

If you want to change the page setup parameters of a previously saved report design, use the Save As... option from the File menu rather than just Save after you've made the changes you want in the Page Setup dialog box. For some reason, just using Save will save any changes you've made in the report design window, but not those made to its corresponding page setup. When you use Save As..., the report's previous name will appear in the Save dialog box. Just click the Save button without changing the name and then click the Yes button when it asks you if you want to replace the existing report design of that name.

SORT

Use Save Records As... To Save In Sorted Order

This trick saves your files in a sorted order, ready for use the next time you Open the document containing your files. Normally, *Microsoft File* doesn't remember the sorted order of your records from one session to another. Although you can keep your sort criteria in the Sort window and simply sort before you start each time, that can become a tedious process with large databases (like this book). To store your records in the sorted order you want, use Save Records As... from the File menu after you've sorted them. That will save them as a new datafile in the sorted order. If you want to keep the unsorted file as a backup, Close and save it in the usual way. Otherwise, delete the old unsorted file, because it does not reflect the changes made to the sorted file while it was open. You'll get confused about which document is the current one unless you give them explicit titles.

Microsoft Word

COMMAND KEYS

Entering A New Division

You can enter a new division in *Word* by holding down the COMMAND key and hitting ENTER.

Repeat Your Last Command With COMMAND-A

You can repeat any action or command you issue in *Word*. To do so, simply hold down the COMMAND key and hit the A key.

Use COMMAND Space To Create A Non-Breakable Space

If you want two words to stay together on the same line, separate them with a non-breakable space. *Word* will treat the space as part of the words and not try to break them up at the end of the line. To create a non-breakable space, hold down the COMMAND key when you hit the spacebar.

Use SHIFT-ENTER To Enter Page Break

You can enter a page break from the keyboard. Place the cursor where you want the page break to occur, hold down the SHIFT key and hit ENTER.

Use SHIFT-RETURN To Get A New Line In the Same Paragraph

If you want to move the insertion point to the next line without generating a new paragraph, hold down the SHIFT key when you hit RETURN.

CURSOR MOVEMENT

Beginning Of Sentence

OPTION-COMMAND-QUOTE(")-J will move the cursor to the beginning of the sentence it's in.

Beginning of Sentence To the Right

OPTION-COMMAND-QUOTE(")-SEMICOLON(;) will move the cursor to the beginning of the sentence to the right.

Character Left and Right

OPTION-COMMAND-K will move the cursor one character left. To move it one character right, use OPTION-COMMAND-L.

Left and Right End of Line

OPTION-COMMAND-QUOTE(")-K will move the cursor to the left end of the line it's in. To move it to the right end of the line, use OPTION-COMMAND-QUOTE(")-L.

Line Up and Down

OPTION-COMMAND-O will move the cursor up one line. To move it down one line, use OPTION-COMMAND-COMMA(,).

Page Up and Down

OPTION-COMMAND-P will move the cursor up one page. To move it down one page, use OPTION-COMMAND-PERIOD(.).

Scroll One Line Up and Down

OPTION-COMMAND-LEFT BRACKET([) will scroll the screen up one line. To scroll it down one line, use OPTION-COMMAND-BACKSLASH(\).

Top and Bottom of Document

OPTION-COMMAND-QUOTE(")-P will move the cursor to the top of the document. To move it to the bottom of the document, use OPTION-COMMAND-QUOTE(")-PERIOD(.).

Top and Bottom of Screen

OPTION-COMMAND-QUOTE(")-O (the letter O, not the number zero) will move the cursor to the top of the screen. To move it to the bottom of the screen, use OPTION-COMMAND-QUOTE(")-COMMA(,).

Word Left and Right

OPTION-COMMAND-J will move the cursor to the beginning of the word to the left. To move it one word right, use OPTION-COMMAND-SEMICOLON(;).

DELETING FILES

Don't Delete Temporary Files While Running *Word*

If you've explored your *MS-Word* startup disk from the *Finder* installed with *Word* in *Switcher* or with a file utility desk accessory, you probably have discovered files you did not create. Resist the temptation to delete them, because *Word* creates these temporary files (such as, MW001) on your startup disk as scratchpads. Deleting them is fatal, and could crash the system, or even DESTROY your *Word* files.

DELETING TEXT

Use OPTION-BACKSPACE To Delete Previous Word

You can delete the word to the left of the insertion point by holding down the OPTION key and hitting BACKSPACE. Undo (COMMAND-Z) will reverse this operation.

DESK ACCESSORIES

Incompatibility

MS-Word has many problems with desk accessories not supplied by Apple. Early versions of *Word* are more susceptible to this problem than later ones. Evidently, *Word* doesn't have all the proper "hooks" for the DAs to grab onto. As a result, some menus and buttons don't dim when they're not functional. Also, *Word* doesn't allow control characters to pass through to the DAs, but tries to use them in your document, with unpredictable and disastrous results. A partial solution is to use a resource editor to remove some or all of the COMMAND key sequences from the menus in *Word*. However, you'll have to use the pull down menus every time, instead of the handy COMMAND key sequences. Changing them does no good. Although you can see the new COMMAND key sequences on the menus, they don't work, and the Mac will just beep at you.

DIALOG BOXES

COMMAND Key Equivalents for Buttons

The buttons in the dialog boxes of *Word* all have COMMAND-Key equivalents. Among the commands that work: COMMAND-d switches disk drives; COMMAND-e ejects a disk; and COMMAND-PERIOD cancels a command.

You can answer questions such as "Save changes before closing?" in several ways. You can click on the button displaying the answer you want, or hit RETURN to select the box with the heavier (highlighted) border. You can also press the Y key for "Yes, save it," or the N key for "No."

EDITING TEXT

BACKSPACE Variations

To select the word at the left of the insertion point, press SHIFT-BACKSPACE. Now press OPTION-BACKSPACE if you want to delete it. Hold down the BACKSPACE key and alternate pressing the SHIFT and OPTION keys if you want to continue the operation of selecting and deleting words to the left.

Don't Cut and Paste Too Many Paragraphs At A Time

Microsoft Word has a tendency to bomb if you try to Cut too many paragraphs to the Clipboard. Remember that each carriage return is considered a paragraph. To avoid problems, Cut and Paste only a few paragraphs at a time.

Use OPTION-Click To Copy A Selection of Text

To copy a selection of text from one place in your *Word* document to another, select the text you want to copy, find the place you want to insert the copy and hold down the OPTION key when you click there.

Use OPTION-SHIFT-Click To Move A Selection of Text

To move a selection of text from one place in your *Word* document to another, select the text you want to move, find the place you want to insert the selected text, and hold down the SHIFT and OPTION keys when you click there.

FIND

Finding A Circumflex

How do you search for a circumflex (^)? *MS-Word* treats the circumflex the same way as the ampersand (&). In this case, *Word* puts a circumflex at the beginning of one letter codes to search for special invisible characters (such as Tabs and Line Feeds). So, just type two circumflexes (^^) in the Find What box, and it will search for the circumflex character in the text.

Finding A Question Mark

The question mark (?) is a wild card character in *MS-Word's* search function. If you ask *Word* to search for a question mark, it will find the first character in the text, because any character meets that search criterion. To find a real question mark, used as a punctuation in the text, type a circumflex and a question mark (^?) in the "Find What" box.

FONTS

COMMAND-< or > Changes Text Size

You can change the point size of a selected block of text from the keyboard. Use COMMAND-< to decrease the font size, and COMMAND-> to increase it.

Create Unusual Sized Fonts with *MacDraw*

Do you need an unusual font size? Create your text in *MacDraw*, then Copy it into *Microsoft Word*, where you can stretch it to any size you want as a graphic image. It will print out perfectly on the LaserWriter. (Printing doesn't work as well on the ImageWriter.)

Express Font and Style Matching

To match the font and style of newly Pasted text to those in the rest of your document, keep it selected. While pressing the OPTION and COMMAND keys, move the cursor to any area that has the desired characteristics, and click the mouse. If you accidentally hit the SHIFT key, just Undo and try again.

How Small Caps Work

The "Small Caps" option in *Word* needs the upper-case letters from two font sizes. For example, if you choose 14-point Small Caps, the program uses 12-point caps for all unshifted letters; likewise 12-point Small Caps uses 10-point caps for unshifted characters. Be sure to have the size two points smaller than the Small Caps size you want to use for best results. Also, be sure to have the double-size of each of the sizes in the *System* file for high-quality printing on the ImageWriter. For example: If you want to use 12-point New York Small Caps, be sure to have 12-, 10-, 24-, and 20-point New York in your *System* file.

FOOTNOTES

An Explanation of How To Use Footnotes

A command encouragingly called Footnote appears on *Word's* Document menu. To use it, place the cursor at the point you want to footnote, and then select the Footnote command. This Opens the Footnote window —where you enter the footnote text—and a dialog box asking whether you want your footnotes numbered automatically in sequence, or whether you want to use some other mark (up to 10 characters possible), such as an asterisk (*).

To place the footnote text in the document, use the Division Layout command on the Document menu. *Word* normally places the footnotes at the bottoms of the pages containing their corresponding references, but you can also collect them at the end of a document or at breaks between other divisions specified in the document. To delete a footnote in *Word*, just delete the number or mark in the document text. The footnote numbering adjusts accordingly. If you have an early version of *Word*, try out the footnotes variations on a short, dispensable document. Early versions had tremendous problems with this feature.

FORMATTING

Erase A Paragraph's Formatting With COMMAND-SHIFT-P

You can erase all the formatting information in a paragraph by placing the insertion point anywhere in the paragraph and hitting COMMAND-SHIFT-P.

Nested Paragraphs

Make a paragraph "nested" (with an indent one-half inch greater than the previous paragraph) by placing the cursor in the text and typing N while holding down the COMMAND and SHIFT keys.

Use SHIFT-COMMAND-M To Un-Nest Paragraphs

If you want to "un-nest" a paragraph and realign its margins with the rest of your text, place the insertion point anywhere in the paragraph and hit SHIFT-COMMAND-M.

Paragraph's Formatting Information Is Stored In ¶

The formatting information for each paragraph is stored in the ¶ symbol at its end. If you delete the ¶, you also delete all of the paragraph's formatting. If you Undo the deletion, all of the formatting information will return.

Use SHIFT-COMMAND-C For Centered Paragraphs

To center the text of any paragraph in *Word*, place the insertion point anywhere in the paragraph, hold down the SHIFT and COMMAND keys and hit C.

Use SHIFT-COMMAND-F To Indent Paragraph's First Line 1/2 Inch

To indent the first line of a paragraph by 1/2 inch, place the insertion point anywhere in the paragraph and strike SHIFT-COMMAND-F.

Use SHIFT-COMMAND-J For Fully Justified Paragraphs

To justify the left and right margins for the text of any paragraph in *Word*, place the insertion point anywhere in the paragraph, hold down the SHIFT and COMMAND keys and hit J.

Use SHIFT-COMMAND-L For Left Justification

To justify the left margin of any paragraph, place the insertion point anywhere in the paragraph and hit SHIFT-COMMAND-L.

Use SHIFT-COMMAND-O To Add A Leading Line of Space

To add an open line of space before a paragraph, place the insertion point anywhere in the paragraph and hit SHIFT-COMMAND-O.

Use SHIFT-COMMAND-R for Right Justification

If you want a paragraph to be justified on the right margin, place the cursor anywhere in the paragraph and press SHIFT-COMMAND-R.

Use SHIFT-COMMAND-T To Format A Paragraph With A Hanging Indent

If you want to format a paragraph in a *Word* document to give it a hanging indent (with the first line hanging out over the left margin of the rest of the document by 1/2 inch), place the insertion point anywhere in the paragraph and hit SHIFT-COMMAND-T.

GLOSSARY

Capacity

Word stores only the names of the glossary entries in RAM. On a 512K Macintosh, you can have 1-200 entries with the lengths of their contents limited only by disk capacity. With a Mac Plus and a hard disk, you can have practically limitless glossary entries.

Making Glossary Entries

To make a glossary entry, select, then Cut or Copy some text. Now, choose Show Glossary from the Edit menu. Next, type in the abbreviation for the entry. Try to be mnemonic. If the glossary entry is your address, use "add," or maybe just "a," as the glossary entry. Type the abbreviation into the "Name in Glossary" text field. Now Paste. That completes the process. The hardest part is remembering the order—Name then Paste. Simply remember that the commands are in alphabetical order—[N]ame comes before [P]aste.

Using Glossary Entries In Your Text

To insert a Glossary entry into a document, type its abbreviation, then press COMMAND-BACKSPACE.

GRAPHICS

How To Resize A Graphic

To get the best resolution when you print a document in *Word* containing graphics, create the image in a larger size than you want the finished graphic. Then, Paste the graphic into *Word* and shrink it down. To change its size, select it and drag the little black box in the corner to make the frame the size you want the finished graphic. When you release the mouse button, the Mac redraws the graphic to fit in the new frame.

Quick Rescaling from 0 to 9

Here's a quick way to rescale a graphic in *Word*. Press COMMAND-SHIFT-Y and choose a number from 0 to 9. The graphic will rescale according to the number you choose. You'll probably need to experiment with this technique to find out how to use it to your best advantage.

HYPHENATION

Creating An Optional Hyphen

Word has an Optional Hyphen available. Optional Hyphens appear between the syllables of a word if it gets broken at the end of a line. If the complete word appears within the line, the hyphen disappears and the two parts of the word remain as one. To enter an Optional Hyphen, hold down the COMMAND key when you strike the hyphen key.

Use OPTION Hyphen For A Non-Breakable Hyphen

The word wrap routines in *Microsoft Word* will break a word at a hyphen. If you want to prevent a hypen from being broken at the end of a line, hold down the OPTION key when you type it. This is useful when you have a hyphenated word, such as Editor-in-Chief, and want the whole thing on the same line.

KEYPAD

Keypad Can't Be Used To Enter Data

Microsoft Word will not allow you to enter data from the Numerical keypad.

MAIL MERGE

Avoiding Blank Lines Generated By Missing Fields

When you use the mail merge function of *Microsoft Word*, the printer will generate a blank line if one of the fields you've specified in your word processing document is empty in a record in your database. For example, your word processing document may have two fields for two lines of an address (a company name and a street address), but some of the records in your database may have only the street address. To make the printer compress the space and print the next existing field on the next line, change the form of *Word's* IF...ELSE...ENDIF statements. Just omit the right guillemet (») after the ELSE command and *Word* won't generate a line feed if the field is missing.

OTHER PROGRAMS

Transferring *MacWrite* Documents

Microsoft Word can open a formatted *MacWrite* document. To do this, first Open a new *Word* document and Close it without typing a keystroke. Then, Open the formatted *MacWrite* document. The Mac will convert the file to a *Word* document, complete with almost all of the formatting from *MacWrite*. This process does not work in reverse, so only do this to a file after you're done working with it in *MacWrite*.

Correcting Paragraph Indents In Transferred *MacWrite* Files

When you Open a *MacWrite* file with *Word*, the paragraph indents are automatically set to a 1/8 inch indent. To change them, select the whole document by clicking in the selection bar while holding down the COMMAND key. Then, select Formats from the Paragraph menu and set the indent to whatever you desire.

PAGE NUMBERING

Conflicts With Margin Settings

The default location for page numbers in *Word* is three-quarters of an inch from the top of the page and one and one-quarter inches from the right edge of the paper. If you're not careful, the page numbers will conflict with the margin settings for your text by putting the page number too low on the page or the top margin setting too high. If the two settings conflict, *Word* won't print the page numbers.

PRINTING

High Quality 5, 6 and 7 Point Text

In *Word*, tiny type in 5, 6 and 7 point sizes will look best on the ImageWriter if you choose the high quality print option. The Mac scales the 10, 12 and 14 point fonts down to half-size when you use this technique. Be sure the larger sizes are installed in your *System* file or *Word* or this trick won't work.

Use Mail Merge Option To Chain Documents for Speedy Printing

You can create a "Master" mail merge document to chain a number of other documents for faster printing. Start with a new document and type «include DOCUMENT NAME» followed by a return. Replace DOCUMENT NAME with the filename of the first document you want printed and use OPTION-\ («) and SHIFT-OPTION-\ (») to get the special surrounding characters. Now, use SHIFT-ENTER to put in a page break. Repeat this procedure for each document you want to chain. When you're finished, choose Print Merge from the File menu and proceed as usual. This will work faster than printing the documents with the Print command in the *Finder* because the Mac will create one large print file instead of creating a separate one for each document.

RECOVERING FILES

Recovering from A Crash

If your Mac crashes while you're working with *Microsoft Word*, try this: Change all of the files beginning with MW to something else. Then change their File Type to WDBN from WTMP. Now, try to Open the files with *Word*. It doesn't always work but is worth a try. Good luck!

RULERS

Calculating True Distance From Left Edge of Paper

The zero point on the ruler shown when your cursor is in the body of your text is not the left edge of the paper. To calculate the true distance from the edge of the page, add the measurement on the ruler to the left margin you've set in the Page Setup dialog box.

Settings Only For Paragraph Where Cursor Is Located

Don't confuse the ruler settings in *Word* with those in *MacWrite*. In *Word*, the ruler displays settings only for the paragraph where the cursor is located and no more.

Two Different Types

Word rulers work two ways. When the cursor is in the body of a document, the left edge of the ruler (starting at zero) marks the beginning of the text. But, when the cursor is in a Running Head, the left edge of the ruler marks the edge of the paper.

RUNNING HEADS

Can Be At Top or Bottom of Page

Word makes little distinction between headers and footers. Instead, it classifies both as a Running Head. Just click the appropriate button for Top or Bottom in the Running Head dialog box.

Main Text May Keep Running Heads from Printing

Remember that the position of running heads is determined completely separately from the position of your body text. If you set the margins for your body text so they conflict with those of your running head, Word just ignores your running head and doesn't print it. You'll receive no error message to let you know that anything's wrong. You'll have to adjust the settings for one or both of them so*Word* doesn't try to print them in the same place on the page.

Reformatting After Deselection

After you deselect the text of a Running Head by unclicking each choice under "Occurs On" in the Running Head dialog box, the text retains the margins set when it was still a Running Head. This can be quite disconcerting if you've not changed the default Running Head margin setting of one-half inch. You must place your cursor in the text of the former Running Head, bring up the ruler, and reset the margins.

Setting the Margins

The default left margin setting for Running Heads is one-half inch from the edge of the page. To change the margin, place the cursor in the text of the Running Head and bring up the ruler. Just slide the markers around as with a regular ruler or use the Paragraph Formats dialog box. Remember, the left edge of the ruler for the Running Head is the left edge of the PAGE, not your text.

Use Running Head To Create Banner Headline In Two-Column Text

You can use the Running Head feature of *Word* to create banner headlines across two-column text. Simply select the text you want to use as the banner, specify its font, size and style, and make it a Running Head. Be sure you leave sufficient space at the top of your pages to print the banner when you specify your top margin in the Page Setup dialog box.

SAVING

Save Often To Avoid "Session Too Long"

Save your file frequently when using *Word*. If you don't, you'll get the "Session Too Long" error message and could have to wait for up to half an hour for *Word* to get itself untangled. The best way out of this nasty position is to do what the dialog box recommends: Save the file to another disk. The reason behind this is that *Word* retains information about changes so that you can Undo them several steps back. When you save the file to disk, *Word* clears all this extraneous data. But if you make a lot of changes and don't save the file frequently enough, *Word* gets clogged with all this extra information.

SELECTING

Selecting A Single Line

You can select a single line of text in *Word*. Simply move the cursor to the left of the line you want to select until it turns into an arrow and click once.

Selecting A Whole Document

To select a whole *Word* document, move the cursor to the extreme left of the window, hold down the COMMAND key and click the mouse once.

Selecting A Whole Paragraph

To select a whole paragraph of text in *Word*, move the cursor to the left of the paragraph you want to select until it turns into an arrow, and double-click.

Use COMMAND Click To Select A Whole Sentence

To select a whole sentence in *Word*, hold down the COMMAND key and click anywhere in the sentence you want to select.

Use SHIFT-BACKSPACE To Select Previous Word

You can select the word to the left of the insertion point by holding down the SHIFT key and hitting BACKSPACE.

SPACING

How To Accomplish Vertical Centering

Here's a method for vertically centering text on a page. First, type the text you want to center at the very top of a page. When finished, put the cursor after the last character of the text you want to center and insert Carriage Returns until you generate a page break. Now, select half of the space between the text and the page break and Cut it. Put the insertion point in front of the first character of the text and Paste. Remember that the psychologically perceived center of the page is slightly higher than the actual center, so you should leave a little less space above the text than below it.

Look For Spaces If Text Doesn't Center Properly

If you center a piece of text and it still doesn't appear to be centered between the margins, check for extra spaces before or after the text. The centering routines in *Word* consider the spaces as part of the text when formatting it. Simply select the space(s) and hit BACKSPACE to correct the spacing. Don't forget that centering refers to the margins, not full paper width.

WINDOWS

Zoom Window To Full Screen Size

Double-click on the title bar or size box of a *Word* window to "zoom" it up to fill the screen. Double-click again to revert to the window's previous size.

MiniFinder

DELETING FILES

Trashing from the *Finder*

Don't forget to remove a file or application from the *MiniFinder* after you've deleted it from the *Finder*. If you leave it installed in the *MiniFinder*, you won't cause any harm, but you'll get an error messsage.

DISK SPACE

OPTION-COMMAND Upon Quit Will Rebuild Desktop File

If you hold down the OPTION and COMMAND keys when you quit an application on a disk running under the *MiniFinder*, the *MiniFinder* will rebuild the invisible Desktop File. This may regain a little disk space, but all your folders will lose their names and become "Untitled #1," etc.

Throw Away The *Finder*

After you've installed the *MiniFinder* on a disk, you can delete the *Finder* and regain 47K or more of disk space. Use the *Finder* on another disk to delete the *Finder* on the *MiniFinder* disk, and then choose Set Startup to make the *MiniFinder* the startup application on its disk. Since the *MiniFinder* doesn't have provisions for copying, deleting and renaming files, you may want to install one of the desk accessories available for this purpose (like *DiskInfo* or *DiskTools*).

DRIVE BUTTON

Keyboard Equivalent

In the *MiniFinder*, and in dialog boxes with a Disk Drive selection button, you can hit TAB instead of clicking on the button.

INSTALLATION

Getting Started

When you're setting up the *MiniFinder* on a disk, don't waste time installing each file and application one at a time. Just use SHIFT-Click to select them as a group. Then, choose Use *MiniFinder* on the Special menu and Set Startup to make it the startup application on that disk.

Modifying the Files In A *MiniFinder*

The *MiniFinder* won't permit you to add or delete single applications or files. You have to start over from scratch. To change the files in a *MiniFinder*, work from a *Finder* desktop on the disk you want to change or from another disk. On the disk you want to change, use SHIFT-Click to select ALL the files and applications you want to include in your new *MiniFinder*, and select Use *MiniFinder* from the Special menu.

Multi-Level *MiniFinders* On A Hard Disk

Speed up the process of finding and Opening groups of applications and documents on a hard disk by creating a Master *MiniFinder* which contains icons for other *MiniFinders*. This method provides quick access to as many as 132 applications and documents. First, drag all the items you want to install into your Master *MiniFinder* System into a single folder. Then, select any one application and choose Use *MiniFinder* to create a *MiniFinder* icon in the System folder. This icon will act as the gateway from any of your sub-*MiniFinders* back to your Master *MiniFinder*. To create the first sub-*MiniFinder*, use SHIFT-Click to select, as a group, the 11 documents and applications you want it to contain—plus the Master *MiniFinder* icon. Then, choose Use *MiniFinder* to create the first sub-*MiniFinder*. Immediately rename the new sub-*MiniFinder* to avoid confusing the *System*. The *Finder* can't rename the icon directly, but it can change the name of a duplicate. So, duplicate the new sub-*MiniFinder* icon, give the duplicate a descriptive title, and trash its original. Be sure not to trash the Master *MiniFinder*, just the original of this duplicated pair. Repeat this procedure for each sub-*MiniFinder* you need (up to 12). When finished, select all of the sub-*MiniFinder* icons and choose Use *MiniFinder*. Leave this icon named "*MiniFinder*" and use Set Startup from the Special menu to make it your startup application. Now, your Master *MiniFinder* is the directory for all the sub-*MiniFinders*.

Remembering Files from Old *MiniFinder* to A New One

If you have a hard time remembering exactly what files were in your old *MiniFinder* when you want to reconfigure a new one, boot with the old *MiniFinder*. Use COMMAND-SHIFT-4 to dump an image of the *MiniFinder* window to the ImageWriter. Then use the procedure outlined in "Modifying the Files In a *MiniFinder*" to install your new *MiniFinder*, using the printout as a guide for the files you want to repeat or drop from your new *MiniFinder*.

OPENING FILES

Double-Click On Icon To Open It

You can double-click on an icon in the *MiniFinder* to Open it. A black outline will appear around the icon when it is selected. Although this feature works exactly like the one in the *Finder* and just as fast, it takes a little longer to change the screen, indicating that it is Opening the application. Don't worry, just wait another second for things to happen.

PROBLEMS

Can't Load the *Finder* Message

When booting a disk with a *MiniFinder*, but no *Finder* present, you may get a message from the Mac saying that it "Can't Load the *Finder*." This is usually caused by having installed the *MiniFinder* on a disk that already had another application set as the startup application. To remedy the situation, boot the Mac with a disk containing a full *Finder*. Insert the problem disk, select the *MiniFinder* icon on that disk, and choose Set Startup from the Special menu. Shut down and reboot with the *MiniFinder* disk and you should go straight to the *MiniFinder* display.

TO THE *FINDER*

Bypass the *MiniFinder* To The *Finder*

When you want to use the *Finder* instead of the *MiniFinder* (and the *Finder* is present on your startup disk), press the OPTION key while you insert the disk, or quit an application. If you forget and the *MiniFinder* appears, either hit the ENTER key (before selecting any icons), or click on the *Finder* button.

ENTER means "Go To *Finder*"

In the *MiniFinder*, the ENTER key will take you directly to the *Finder* (but only if no icons are selected).

Multiplan

APPLICATIONS

Pasting *Multiplan* Information Into Word Processors

To copy the columns and rows of a *Multiplan* spreadsheet into a word processor document is easy: Select all the cells in the spreadsheet, and Copy them to the Clipboard. Then startup your word processor and Paste the spreadsheet data into your document. However, be sure that the Tab settings in the word processor document correspond to the column widths of the spreadsheet before Pasting.

CALCULATION

My Spreadsheet Calculates Only When I Save It

If you enter new values or formulas in a spreadsheet and it doesn't recalculate the rest of the cells until you save it, you've unintentionally turned off the Automatic Calculation feature. You can simply leave the feature turned off and use Calculate Now from the Calculate menu (also COMMAND-=). Or, you can turn Automatic Calculation back on from the same menu.

Use the Round Function On Dollar Figures

If your spreadsheet contains dollar figures with decimal places less than a penny (fractional sales tax rates, millage rates, etc.), *Multiplan* will execute the calculations exactly, using those values. If that is not desirable, choose the Round function to round the figures off to two decimal places before calculation.

EDITING

Adding A Column

Add a new column to a *Multiplan* spreadsheet by holding down the SHIFT key and clicking in the head of the column to the right of the new column's intended position. *Multiplan* will shift the existing column to the right and insert a new, blank column.

FIXED

Number Displayed with FIXED Can Be Concatenated

If you display a number with the FIXED function, it acts like text. As a result, you can treat it as text for concatenation.

FONTS

Changing Fonts In *Multiplan 1.02*

As the program disk is shipped, *Multiplan 1.02* displays its spreadsheets in Seattle 10-pt. type. You can change to Geneva 9-pt. instead, and get many more rows and columns on a printed page. By far the easiest way to do this is by replacing *Multiplan's System* file with the one from *Microsoft Chart* (see "Replace *System* with *Chart's* for 9-Point Type"). However, if you don't have *Chart*, you can use Apple's *Font/DA Mover* to remove the Seattle 10- and 20-point fonts from *Multiplan's System* file. The program will default to Geneva 9-pt. type and will adjust the cell heights accordingly. However, you must reset the column widths to the size you want. If you want the program to print in Helvetica 9-pt. on the LaserWriter, make sure the *LaserWriter* files and fonts are on your disk and then use the *Font/DA Mover* to remove the Seattle fonts and Geneva 18-pt. All of this is unnecessary with versions 1.1 and later, because you can make your font choices from within *Multiplan.*

Faulty System Font On Updated *Multiplan 1.02*

If you use the *System Update* utility that was made available with *Finder 4.1* on *Microsoft Multiplan 1.02*, it does strange things to the system fonts on the disk. It makes New York 12-point a system font and

FORMATTING

How To Format Headers & Footers

Although the method is a little awkward, you can embed fomatting commands and other instructions into the text of the header or footer of a *Multiplan 1.1* document. Insert the formatting commands in the header or footer boxes in the Page Setup dialog box. Here's what options are available:

COMMAND	EFFECT
&L	Align the characters that follow at the left margin.
&C	Center the characters that follow.
&R	Align the characters that follow at the right margin.
&P	Print the page number.
&D	Print the current date.
&T	Print the current time.
&F	Print the name of the document.
&B	Print the left, center, or right part of the header or footer in bold.
&I	Print the left, center, or right part of the header or footer in italic.
&&	Print a single ampersand (&).

assigns New York 9-point as the font the *Finder* should use for its icon labels. If New York 9-pt. was not a resident of your original *System* file, the *Finder* will use New York 12-pt. and rescale it to 9-pt., making very sloppy-looking icon labels. To remedy the problem, create a new *System* file on another disk using Apple's *Font/DA Mover* to make sure that the new *System* file contains only Chicago 12, Geneva 9 and 12, Monaco 9, and Seattle 10 and 20. Then, with the Mac running under your new *System* file, trash the one on the *Multiplan* disk and replace it with your new *System* file.

HEADERS & FOOTERS

Editing Header or Footer Text Longer Than the Entry Box

In a header or footer entry box (in the Page Setup dialog), you can create text longer than the box can display. If you need to edit this text, you can view it by placing the cursor in the visible text near the right end of the entry box and dragging off the end. The text will scroll to the left and the extra text will appear, already selected for editing.

OTHER PROGRAMS

Highlighting Cells In *MacDraw* or *MacPaint*

Highlighting particular sections of a spreadsheet when you print it out is not possible within *Multiplan*. But, if you Paste it into *MacDraw* or *MacPaint*, you can put subtle tints (patterns) behind headings and important totals to make the important information in your spreadsheet stand out.

PASSWORDS

How To Remove Password Protection

If you have a legitimate reason to see a password protected spreadsheet, but don't have the password, try this. Use a disk editor (such as *MacTools*) to examine the file and find block 3, part A, position `0079`. If the flag is set (the spreadsheet is password protected) the indicator will be `01`. Change it to `00`, write the edited block to the disk, and you'll remove the password protection from the spreadsheet.

PRINTING

Set Page Breaks To Split Spreadsheet Into Printable Units

If you are printing out only certain parts of a large spreadsheet, use forced page breaks (inserted with the Set Page Break option), instead of selecting and printing each part individually. Then you can print the sections you defined with the page breaks individually or in series with the select pages option in the Print dialog box.

Simulate "Freeze Titles" On Printouts

It is possible to simulate the Freeze Titles screen option on your printouts. You can Copy and Paste an extra titles column at the left-hand side of each page (defined by the dotted lines on your screen), and then obscure it from view by dragging the column to its right back over it. You won't be able to see it on your screen, but the printer will never know you hid it and will print the titles column in its proper position.

Squeezing More Cells On Printed Page

Two methods are available for squeezing more cells onto each page of your printout. You can either choose a paper size (in Page Setup…) which is larger than the actual size of the paper you're using, or, in the same dialog box, simply set all the page margins to zero.

Very Wide Columns with Wide-Print Option

Multiplan can print out columns of up to 128 characters with the wide orientation printing option even though you can't enter numbers over 99 in the Column Width dialog box. First, Open your spreadsheet and Show Values. Then, use Column Widths to set the column width to exactly one half of the width you want on the printout (50 if you want 100, etc.). Now, select Show Formulas and the column width will double to what you want. If you choose the Column Width option again, you'll get an "Invalid Column Width" message, but it will not affect the operation of the program.

PROTECTION

Using Cell and Document Protection

Multiplan has a comprehensive protection facility, but because of the way this is explained in the manual, you might think the only reason to use the system is to stop deliberate or accidental changes to a completed model—very useful if security is a problem. However, this is by no means the only reason for getting into the protection racket.

By using Protect Document in conjunction with Remove Cell Protection, you can set up a model in which only the cells which require alteration are unprotected and highlighted. After making changes to one of these cells, press the ENTER key and you'll jump immediately to the next unprotected cell. An additional benefit is that row and column lines are suppressed on a protected sheet, which makes it look cleaner, and it's easier to read. This method is a great way to create template forms that perform a number of standard calculations on a few pieces of data that change from form to form.

SORTING

How To Sort A Series of Rows

To sort a series of rows in a *Multiplan* spreadsheet, simply select all the filled-in cells in the column containing the "field" on which you want to sort. Choose the Sort… command. In the dialog box, click your choice for sorting in ascending or descending order. All of the information in columns other than the one you sorted on will be rearranged according to the sorted column.

MusicWorks

HARD DISK 20

Convert To an .HQX File To Install

MusicWorks can't be installed in the usual fashion on Apple's Hard Disk 20. To get it to work, convert it to an .HQX file using *BinHex 4.0* and move it to the Hard Disk 20. Then, use *BinHex* again to convert it back to an application.

OverVUE

COLUMNS

Inserted Column will Require You To Reconstruct Your Template

If you insert a column into the middle of a group of columns in your data file, you'll probably confuse the report templates. The report templates specifically relate to the position of a field on the line in the data file, and the inserted column confuses the report templates. To fix the problem, choose Hide Frames, Show Frames again, and rebuild your report template to refer to the new line positions of the fields.

HYPERDRIVE

Special Version

If you're running *OverVUE* on a HyperDrive, get the Mac/XL version or you'll run out of memory.

INCOMPATIBILITIES

Disk Caching Programs

OverVUE can Bomb when used with memory cache software such as *TurboCharger* or *PowerCache*. If you have trouble, try a smaller cache size, or delete the cache application entirely. It doesn't appear to have any problems with the automatic disk caching on the Mac Plus.

OTHER PROGRAMS

Creating Tabs Between Fields for Export

OverVUE is one of those exceptions to the rule: It doesn't use Tab characters to separate fields. This can be a problem when you want to Paste information from *OverVUE* into a database manager or spreadsheet that uses Tab characters as separators. Fortunately, the solution is easy: Place a tilde character (~) between fields in the Report Generator.

PageMaker

BUGS

Deleting Large Number of Pages

The early versions of *PageMaker* sometimes crash when you try to delete several pages in succession. To avoid this, delete only one or two pages and then Save the file. Because each page contains a large amount of data, the Save process is slow. Versions 1.2 and later should not exhibit this problem.

COMMAND KEYS

COMMAND-Click Will Toggle Between Full Page and Fit In Window

If you hold down the COMMAND key when you click in the page window, the display will alternate back and forth between the Full Page view of your page and the Fit In Window view.

LASERWRITER

LaserWriter Must Be Named "LASERWRITER" with Version 1.1

For some strange reason, version 1.1 of *PageMaker* will recognize the LaserWriter on AppleTalk only if you have named it "LASERWRITER." If *PageMaker* can't find the LaserWriter, look in the *Chooser* desk accessory and check to be sure its name is "LASERWRITER." Use the *Namer* utility on the *Printer Installer* disk to change it back to "LASERWRITER" if necessary.

LASERWRITER PLUS

PageMaker 1.2 Is First To Support LaserWriter Plus Fonts

If you are running *PageMaker* on the LaserWriter Plus, you should get the free upgrade to version 1.2 so you can use the additional fonts. Otherwise, the printer will continue to treat the new ROM-based fonts (and other Adobe fonts that you download into it) as bit-mapped images.

PAGE SETUP

Make Permanent Page Setup Changes On Desktop

Tired of having to alter your Page Setup settings every time you start a new publication? If you choose Page Setup from the File menu while you have no document open and only *PageMaker's* gray desktop is showing, the changes you make will be remembered by *PageMaker* every time you start a new publication.

PLACEMENT

Actual Size Is More Accurate Than 200%

PageMaker's 200% size has the largest number of fractional markings on the rulers, and ought to be the most accurate. However, in many cases items that appear to be placed correctly in 200% are slightly off in Actual Size. The screen display is often inaccurate to some degree, but the printed version best matches the Actual Size screen.

PRINTING

Reset the LaserWriter If It's Been Initialized with Laser Prep

When you want to print a *PageMaker* file on the LaserWriter after using it to print from other applications, turn the LaserWriter's power switch off and back on again to reset it. The reason is that *PageMaker* will initialize the LaserWriter with *Aldus Prep*, but won't replace the old *Laser Prep* file. Since both are large files, they occupy memory the Laser-Writer could use for other purposes, and this slows down the page composition process. In reverse, if you want to print on the LaserWriter with another application after using *PageMaker*, reset it and let your Mac reinitialize it with *Laser Prep* after it's printed out the test page. If your Mac is a part of a network and your *PageMaker* printouts are especially slow, someone on the network may have initialized the LaserWriter with *Laser Prep*. Try resetting it to speed your printing.

SAVING

Save and Save Again

PageMaker is a very complex program and demands a great deal of the Macintosh. As a result, it confuses the machine and crashes more often than other programs. (Most of the page makeup programs on the market suffer from the same problem.) The only way to work around this problem is to save your files very often and keep up-to-date backups. The capability and flexibility of the software is worth this extra effort and the software publishers are working as fast as they can to make their programs more crash-proof.

SCROLLING

OPTION-Click Gives You *MacPaint* Style Hand

You can get a *MacPaint* style hand on a *PageMaker* screen by holding down the OPTION key and clicking on your document (anywhere other than on a column guide). The hand works almost exactly like the one in *MacPaint*. It drags your image around the window and redraws any portions that were not on the screen before you started the drag after you've dropped the image.

SNAP TO GUIDES

Position of Pointer Determines If Snap to Guides Is Active

You can turn off Snap to Guides in the Tools menu if you don't want it active. However, if you only want to make one move that is not affected by the guides, you simply need to be careful where you place the pointer. If the pointer is close to one of the guides and Snap to Guides is turned on, the item you're moving will be affected by the guides. If your pointer is positioned away from the guides when you start the move (regardless of the position of the object you're moving) your move won't be affected by the guides.

Paradise Hard Disks

DESKTOP

Close Volume By Dragging To the Trash To Update Desktop File

When you Close a volume on a Paradise Hard Disk with the volume mounting desk accessory, it does not update the volume's desktop file. This usually results in loss of position information for your icons. However, if you drag the volume's icon to the trashcan to Close it, that action will update its desktop file and your icons will be where you left them the next time you Open the volume.

INTERFERENCE

Paradise Hard Disks May Cause Excessive RF Interference

Some Paradise Hard Disk owners have complained about interference in radio and television reception. If you've had no problems, don't worry about it. However, if you're having problems, contact the manufacturer. To minimize the problem, try placing the Paradise drive close to the Mac and coil up the cable that connects the two units.

MANAGER

Don't Use Disk Caching with Paradise Manager

Don't use any disk caching (from Mac Plus *Control Panel* or with a disk cache utility) when working with the Paradise Manager program. You could cause problems with your hard disk. Get in contact with Paradise for the software patch to solve this problem.

MODEMS

Modem Compatibility

Although Paradise hard disks give you a replacement serial port for the one they take away in the back of the Mac, the extra port will not support a modem. You can leave your modem connected to the modem port on the back of the Mac and connect the Paradise to the printer port and the ImageWriter to the Paradise's serial port. You can then use the ImageWriter by using the *Chooser* desk accessory.

SPOOLER

Don't Set Spooler Size To Zero

If you set the Paradise print spooler size to zero, you won't be able to print at all. If you don't want to use it, set it to the smallest size you can, greater than zero.

High Quality Printing Is Faster without the Spooler

If you're printing your document out on the ImageWriter in High (Best) quality, set the Paradise spooler size as small as possible without setting it to zero. Printing will be faster than if you used the spooler.

PowerCache

BUGS

Switching System Disks

If you use *PowerCache*, avoid switching disks that contain *System* files or the cache software may cause your Mac to hang. Starting up an application from another disk when it contains a *System* file is a frequent cause of this problem. So, keep a copy of that application on a disk without a *System* file if you use it frequently with a *PowerCache* equipped startup disk for another application.

INCOMPATIBILITIES

Dangerous To Mac/XL *System* Files

Don't try to run *PowerCache* on a Mac/XL. A damaged *System* file will be your reward if you try.

Don't Run On HyperDrive 20

Don't try to run *PowerCache* on a HyperDrive 20. You'll get a bomb.

Rags to Riches

CHART OF ACCOUNTS

Accounts Cannot Be Deleted

When you make up your Chart of Accounts in *Rags to Riches*, think before you post. You cannot delete an account once you have added it to the chart. You can redefine it completely for use elsewhere, but you can't simply get rid of it.

COMMAND Key Codes Cannot Be Erased

Once you assign a key code to an account, you cannot decide later to use that account without a key code. You can change it to any other key code you want, but you must have something in the key code field. Unused and unwanted key codes don't interfere with the operation of the program. They are just excess baggage on the screen and in reports.

Hidden Capital Account In *General Ledger*

A conventional set of books has a Capital account that reflects the accumulated net profit or loss of the business. However, the *Rags to Riches G/L* does not keep this account as a regular account in the chart, but calculates it when you print an Income Summary and Balance Sheet report. It appears on the Balance Sheet as "Computed Retained Earnings" just beneath the owner's Capital account.

DISK CONFIGURATION

Put G/L, A/R, and A/P All On One 800K Disk

Although *Rags to Riches* provides its programs on individual 400K disks, you can combine them on an 800K disk. First, make a startup disk with the fonts and printers you want to use with *Rags to Riches*. Copy the program files to this disk. The files you want have "RR" logo icons and are named *Ledger*, *Payables* and *Receivables*. The disk should still have room for the Templates folder as well, unless you have a monster font collection and the *LaserWriter* files on the disk. Second, make up a data disk with no *System* files. When you create the data files for each program, make sure you save them to this disk. Be sure to keep a backup copy of the data disk. A backup copy of the startup disk isn't really necessary, since you can reconstruct it from the original disks, but it can save you time when your startup disk runs into trouble. If you have two drives, you may want to Close the directory window for the startup disk and keep only the window for the data disk showing on the desktop.

RAM Disks

CONFIGURING

Put the System Folder In the RamDisk

Here's a configuration that minimizes disk swapping and allows you to have several applications on a disk. Configure your RAM Disk to contain the *System* file, *Finder* and *ImageWriter* driver. After booting the RAM Disk, remove the *System* disk and you'll have two free drives (internal and external). In one of the drives, put a disk containing the applications you want to use. The extra disk space gained by having no *System* or *Finder* will allow several medium-sized applications on a disk. You can use the second drive for your data disks and almost never suffer from the "disk shuffle."

MODIFYING APPLICATIONS

Use A Phantom Copy of Your Application For Complex Modification

If you are going to make some tricky changes to your application program (like using *ResEdit* to alter its resources), load a phantom copy of the application into your RAM disk and make the modifications there. That way, you won't risk any damage to your disk copy of the application, and if you mess things up, you can start over easily by flipping the power switch.

SAVING

Save Data Files from RAM Disk to Floppy Often

If you can, avoid storing data files on your RAM disk. The best use for the RAM disk is for more static files (like applications and *System* files). However, if you find it necessary to store your data files on a RAM disk, be sure to save them often to a floppy (using Save As...) so you don't risk losing data in a system crash or power failure. After you've used Save As..., most applications will work with the copy on the floppy and ignore the RAM disk copy, slowing down operations. To avoid this, immediately use Save As... again after saving the copy to the floppy, to save back to your RAM disk. The operation is quick and you'll then be working from your RAM disk copy again.

RamStart

HFS

Keep Files To Be Copied To RAM Disk At Root Level

With version 1.0 of Tony Nelson's *RamStart* program, you can avoid problems on an HFS system by keeping all the programs you want to copy to the RAM disk at the root level. However, the best remedy is to get the upgraded version 1.21 or 1.22.

Red Ryder

INCOMPATIBILITIES

Red Ryder 7.0 and HD20/HFS Are Incompatible

Some users have reported a sporadic bug when using *Red Ryder 7.0* on an Apple Hard Disk 20 running under the Hierarchical File System. If you put *Red Ryder* in a folder, the folder can take up as much as 15 megabytes of disk space and prevent it from being available to other programs until the folder is deleted. Version 9.2 fixes this bug.

Versions 8 and Later Don't Support 128K Macs

128K Macs are quickly becoming non-standard in the Mac world. Versions 8 and on of *Red Ryder* no longer support the 128K configuration.

Version 8 Crashes On Quit with Some Configurations

Red Ryder version 8 may crash when you quit if you're working with the old 64K ROMs and a hard disk. Version 9.2 should work fine in that combination.

Version 8 Doesn't Support CompuServe "B" Protocol

Version 8 of *Red Ryder* has problems when you try to use CompuServe's B protocol. Get version 9.2 or later to fix this problem.

ResEdit

COMMAND KEYS

OPTION-SHIFT Allows You to Open Resource as Another Type

When you Open a resource, if you hold down the OPTION and SHIFT keys, you'll get a dialog box that will allow you to Open the resource as though it were another type. On newer versions of the program, you can do this with the Open As... option on the File menu. This feature is particularly useful for examining version resources. Open them as STR resources and instead of seeing hex data, you'll usually see an English language string. That string typically contains version numbers and other similar data, but it may contain anything. Just type in the box to add to or change the text that's already there.

CUTTING

Don't Forget That Cutting Puts Data On the Clipboard

If you're having trouble Cutting in *ResEdit*, the problem may be that the Clipboard is filling up. Remember that whenever you Cut something, it goes to the Clipboard, replacing anything that was there previously. However, when you Clear, the data is simply removed. Cuts can be undone, Clears can't.

HFS

Keep Files You Want To Open At the Root Level

When you're working with *ResEdit* on an HFS system, keep any files you want to Open with *ResEdit* at the root level on the disk. If you try to Open a file from inside a folder, *ResEdit* may create a new resource instead of Opening the file you wanted.

ICONS

Making Redesigned Icons Appear On the Desktop

After you use *ResEdit* or a similar utility to modify an icon, your new design won't necessarily appear on the desktop when you return to the *Finder*. This happens because the *Finder* is still working with a copy of the old icon in its desktop file. To get your new design into the desktop file, you'll have to make the *Finder* rebuild it either by removing the desktop file with a disk utility or by ejecting the disk, trashing its icon, and reinserting it while holding down the OPTION and COMMAND keys. After either of these procedures, your new icon should appear on the desktop.

PRECAUTIONS

Be Safe Not Sorry

Hacking around with the innards of a Macintosh application with *ResEdit* is not something to take lightly; *ResEdit* has the power to mess up your files totally. (Read that last sentence again!) Make sure that you are working on backups, not on originals. Don't take the chance of trashing a file (or disk) for which you have no backup.

RESOURCES

Newer Versions of *ResEdit* Can Create Resources

If you've ever struggled with some of the utilities for creating resources, you'll be glad to hear that later versions of *ResEdit* can create resources. Just use the New option on the File menu.

VERSION RESOURCE

Inside the Version

What's actually in a version resource? It could be nothing at all, but usually inspection will show a lot of hex numbers, and a text string detailing the version number. Since *ResEdit* doesn't know what a MACA (or any other version) resource is, the data is presented as a jumble of hex numbers (or data). If you suspect that the resource holds a *Pascal* format, length-delimited string (That's what these things are called), then *ResEdit* can read the string. Tell *ResEdit* to Open a resource and display it as if it were a different type. Do this by Opening the resource while holding down the SHIFT and OPTION keys as you double-click. You will get a special window that allows you to select how you want the resource displayed. Scroll down to STR and double-click on it. You can now read this string and change it at will.

Role-Playing Games

PLAYING TIPS

A Weapon In Hand Is Worth Two In the Bag

All the fancy weapons and armor in the known world won't help you in battle if you forgot to equip the item (that is, put it in your hand). Also, if your game requires that characters eat, stock up on supplies before making any long journeys or you might starve before you find another McDonnall's.

Be Prepared

At times you'll enter a situation that requires a special item (armor, weapon or perhaps a coordinate). For example, blasting off into space without the proper protection can be rather messy. And, it can be frustrating if you don't already know where you're going.

Becoming A Better Fighter

The life of your party ultimately rests on its skill as a fighting unit. Making good use of all your characters, and of the combat area, can swing the battle's outcome to your favor.

First, know your opponent. If you're fighting a group of relative weaklings like kobolds and orcs, throwing a seventh-level "nuke" spell just might be overkill. Let your fighters pick them off one by one, and save your strength for bigger fish. On the flip side, don't feel obligated to fight to the finish against whatever huge creature is thrown your way. Many games give players the option of running away during combat. The option is there for a reason!

If a creature is poisonous and the game allows for it, let your archers or wizards fight from a safe distance. Just remember that you must already have your missile weapon in hand if you want to use it.

In conventional battles, the wisest move is to maneuver the opponents to an area most favorable for you. Don't rush up to a crew of ten orcs, letting three of them swing at Ralph the fighter for every swipe he takes at them. If you can't bait the monsters into attacking three of your characters with one of theirs, at least keep the odds even.

Finally, keep an eye on the relative health of your characters, and pull those near death out of harm's way when possible. A quick healing spell in the heat of battle can keep a critically injured fighter from becoming a dead one.

Keep Accurate Maps

Any game which involves dungeons will require players to keep accurate maps if they hope to find their way back to terra firma. Only by keeping reasonably accurate records of where you've been will you be able to figure out how to get back there in a hurry—or where to explore new territory.

Large-grid graph paper is the dungeon explorer's best friend. Count each step you take as a single square, noting on the map turns to the right or left and any doors or hallways you see. Use a fresh sheet of paper if you go up or down any elevators or stairs. Be sure to make note of any objects you leave behind, or landmarks you might want to get back to.

Nothing Is Permanent

Nothing is permanent, not even what happens to characters. While most role-playing games allow for resurrection of the dead, this is just a time- and money-consuming process. Simply removing the disk from the drive before you enter a dangerous situation is a perfect failsafe against whatever horror befalls the party. Be warned though—in at least one game we know of, characters must go through a false death before finding a crucial area in the game.

There's Always a Way!

If you can't enter a specific area, you need an object that will unlock the path. This could be a boat (and you may need something in hand just to board), or a key or a statue, or it could just be a piece of information you may have missed along the way. Don't despair. Just redouble your efforts to find the missing puzzle piece. At times, one word will do the job. Just make sure it's the right one.

Sargon III

SETUP

How To Handicap

Sargon III is a very good chess player—better than about 85% of the tournament players in the US. Therefore, you must handicap the program to make play more enjoyable for a less experienced player. Likewise, if you are using the program as a "board" for two unequal players, your play will be more enjoyable if you handicap the better player. To handicap, take pieces away from the better player's setup before play begins. The wider the gap between the abilities of the players, the more pieces you remove. To handicap *Sargon III*, pull down the Options menu and select Change Board. Then, you can drag the pieces you want off the board. When you're ready to play, click OK.

Smartcom II

DATA CAPTURE

Be Careful How You Save Data

If you elect to capture data to your disk after it has been received, be sure to highlight the text you want to save. The capture routine saves ONLY selected text. If you save a file (no matter how much text it contains) with nothing selected, the result is an empty file. *Smartcom II* does not check to see if any text is selected before saving, but goes blindly forward with the operation. However, if you inadvertently Close your current communications document without Saving the contents of the capture buffer, don't panic. Just re-Open any communications document. It doesn't even have to be the one you last used. If you didn't use the Clear command from the Edit menu to purge the buffer before you Closed, the text will still be in the capture buffer and will magically appear in the document window. This won't save you if you quit *Smartcom*, but only works if you Close your communications document.

Save and Save As... Save Only Your Settings

The Save and Save as... commands in the File menu save only the settings, not the data in the capture buffer. The manual explains this fact plainly enough, but it's very easy to forget since it's contrary to the way most Mac programs work.

HFS

Smartcom 2.1a Doesn't Know How To Deal with Folders

Earlier versions of *Smartcom* can't recognize documents or applications residing in folders on an HFS system. The program will work, but all of the applications and documents must reside at the root level. Version 2.2b corrects this problem.

SIDEKICK

Modified *System* File May Cause Problems With *Sidekick*

Hayes has removed some resources from the *System* file on the distribution disk for *Smartcom II*. This may cause you some problems if you try to use the *Sidekick* desk accessories. You can fix the problem by replacing the *System* file with a standard one.

SoundCap

BUGS

Open Command Causes Problems With Versions 3.4/3.5

When you choose the Open command from the edit menu in *SoundCap 3.4/3.5*, a Toolbox channel is left open every time you Open an uncompressed sound. This may have some bad effects if all the channels are used up when you try to save a file. Also, it will make the *Finder* prevent you from deleting the file until you reboot the Mac.

Spreadsheets

TEXT FORMATTING

Multiple Columns of Text

Spreadsheets on the Mac are useful for creating multiple columns of text, because you can insert them easily into other applications as pre-formatted lists or tables. Just select the fonts, sizes, and styles you want when you get it into the word processor. One advantage is that you can add, change, or delete the information in any cell without affecting the position of entries in the following columns and rows (as would happen with a word processor). Other kinds of manipulations are easier too—like interchanging, inserting, or deleting a column or a row. The spreadsheet will perform calculations for you, and update the results when you change entries. Why spend time entering the numbers from your expense report into the *Calculator*? If that part of the expense report originates in a spreadsheet template, the spreadsheet can figure it all out for you before you Paste the entire thing into a word procesing document.

Switcher

CLIPBOARD

Don't Always Convert Clipboard

Don't automatically choose the Always Convert Clipboard option when working with *Switcher*. It slows down the operation of the program. Hold down the OPTION key while switching to convert the Clipboard easily and comparatively quickly.

CONFIGURATION

Attach Document

An application in a *Switcher* set can Open a specific document when launched from a saved *Switcher* set. To attach a document, select an active or nonactive application's slot in the *Switcher* screen. Choose Attach Document from the File menu. A box will appear with a list of all the documents the application can Open. Select the document and click Open. The document's name now appears in the application's slot in the *Switcher* screen. If the application is active, it doesn't open the document you just selected because the document currently Opened in the application might be destroyed before you save your changes. However, if the application is nonactive, the document will Open when you start the application. If you save the *Switcher* set, the document will be attached to the application every time you load the set until you change the configuration.

Back After Launch May Confuse Disk Swapping Sequence

If you have the Back After Launch option checked in your *Switcher* configuration dialog box, it may confuse the disk swapping sequence when you're launching applications that are copy protected and require you to insert a "master disk." When the application is launched from its *Switcher* slot, it will eject the disk containing the copy and ask for the master disk. However, *Switcher* will take over at that point and return you to its screen, asking you to insert its own disk. The workaround for this is to continue launching applications until you have the complete set that you want. Then, rotate to the screen of the application that requested the master disk—the request should still be on the screen. Use COMMAND-SHIFT-1 or 2 to eject the *Switcher* disk and insert the master disk. The Mac should verify from the master disk, eject it, and ask you to reinsert the *Switcher* disk.

Put *Finder*, *System* and DAs On Only One Disk

To avoid confusing you or the *Switcher*, put your *System* files (*Finder*, *System*, and desk accessory files) on one disk only.

Save Screen

You can save 22K of memory per application in a *Switcher* set by turning off the Save Screen option. Your switching time will increase slightly because the Mac must redraw each application's screen when you switch to it. Some applications (especially graphics programs) may not be able to redraw the screen properly. You can turn off the Save Screen option ("On" is the default setting) before you launch an application, by choosing Configure Then Install, from the *Switcher* menu—or after you launch, by double-clicking on the Mac icon in the slot of the application you want to reconfigure. Just click in the box beside Save Screen. A circle with a slash will appear in the screen of the Mac icon when you click OK, indicating that the application's screen will not be saved between switches. Each of the applications in a *Switcher* set can have a different configuration. For example, you may want *Switcher* to save *MacPaint* and *MacDraw* screens, but not *MacWrite*.

Caution: After you've turned Save Screen off, you may not always have enough memory to turn it back on, depending on what you've done in the interim. *Switcher* beeps in that case.

DISK SPACE

Make *Switcher* the Startup and Throw Away *Finder*

If you make *Switcher* the startup application using the *Finder's* Set Startup command from the Special menu, you can then remove the *Finder* from the disk (although you'll have to do it from a *Finder* other than the one you want to throw away) and regain another 47K or more of spare room.

Use Applications On More Than One Disk

You don't have to have all the applications you want to use with *Switcher* on the same disk. When you install programs in *Switcher*, it doesn't care which drive the programs are on—as long as the applications are present somewhere, *Switcher* will find them to install. It will even put up a polite message—without an unpleasant crash—if the program you want to install is not currently present in one of the drives.

FINDER

Getting Out Quickly

To exit the *Finder* and return to the *Switcher* screen, double-click on the *Switcher* icon on the desktop.

Include the *Finder* In Your Applications Set — If You Can

If you can afford the disk space, always include the *Finder* in a *Switcher* set. When someone walks into your office and wants a copy of a file, or when you need to throw away some documents to retrieve disk space, you'll know why. If you use the *Finder*, be sure it is the first application that you install in your set and that you allocate enough memory for the appropriate version of the *Finder*. If you can't afford the memory, a desk accessory that provides the file manipulation capabilities of the *Finder* (like *Disk-Tools* from Batteries Included) may serve your needs.

With *Finder* Installed, You Can Launch Other Applications

Installing the *Finder* as one of your applications in the *Switcher* not only lets you shift files around between disks, but it also allows you to launch applications not already in *Switcher*. For example, using a typical *MacWrite/MacPaint/Finder* combination in *Switcher*, you may want to bring in a *MacProject* chart or a *BASIC* listing. Simply move to the *Finder*, launch the new application, Cut or Copy the material required, then switch back to the application you were in before. The *Switcher's* double arrow will appear in the new application's window. You many need to reinstall the *Finder* after quitting the new application, but it's much faster than having to reinstall the whole *Switcher* set.

HARD DISKS

Rename *Switcher* If You Have To Boot from A Floppy

Strange though it may seem, you can get *Switcher* to run automatically on a hard disk booted from a floppy by renaming it "*MiniFinder*." The only way to get back to the *Finder* is to start it from within *Switcher* and then quit *Switcher*. It's roundabout, but it works.

INCOMPATIBILITIES

Don't Try To Run *Microsoft Word/Finder* Combo In *Switcher*

You may run into serious problems if you run *Microsoft Word* and the *Finder* at the same time in a *Switcher* set. Both programs can get confused and *Word's* temporary files may be damaged by the *Finder*.

System 3.1.1b Won't Allow *MacWrite* & *Excel* To Run On *Switcher 4.8*

Version 3.1.1b of the *System* software has a few bugs. One of them is that you won't be able to run *MacWrite* with *Excel* in *Switcher 4.8*. They're "working on it."

MACWRITE

Don't Use Two Copies of *MacWrite* At Once

If you Open two copies of *MacWrite* under *Switcher* with different documents in each, you are courting disaster for one or both of your documents. *MacWrite* creates temporary work files for its own use as it works, and both copies of *MacWrite* are busy creating temporary files with the same names—or at least trying to. If the copy of *MacWrite* you're working with gets confused, it could trash your document. This is also true for *MacPaint*. You'll probably be safe if the two copies of either application you want to use are on two different disks, or in two different volumes of your hard disk.

MacWrite May Truncate Text Files In Too Small A Partition

If you allocate too small a partition to *MacWrite* under *Switcher*, it may truncate (without warning) any text-only files you try to load. For instance, if you try to load a 17K datafile containing 1200 lines with *MacWrite* running in a 144K partition, not all of the file will get loaded and *MacWrite* will give you no indication that it's truncated the file. However, the same file will load without any problems if you run *MacWrite* with a 196K partition.

MEMORY SIZE

Setting Preferred and Minimum Memory Sizes

Although some recent releases of applications have a size resource that automatically tells *Switcher* their preferred and minimum memory sizes, you have to set these options for most applications if you want them set at other than 128K. You can change these settings only before launching an application. To do so, choose Configure then Install from the *Switcher* menu and input the settings you want in the dialog box that appears. *Switcher* will first attempt to allocate the Preferred Memory Size when you launch the application. If the Mac doesn't have enough memory, it will attempt to allocate the Minimum Memory Size. If it doesn't have enough memory to do that, it will give you an error message. It will not allow you to allocate less than 64K.

The dialog box has two buttons in the lower left corner—Permanent and Temporary. Clicking on the Permanent button after changing your memory size settings will make *Switcher* remember these settings for all future uses of the application. Clicking on the Temporary button will make the settings in the box apply only to the current session.

Insufficient Memory Message On 512K Mac With RAM Disk

If you get the message: "Sorry, but you don't have enough memory to run the *Switcher*. Go get a 512K Macintosh." when you try to run *Switcher* on a 512K Mac, don't assume you've got a serious problem. Most likely, you tried to run the *Switcher* after using a startup disk with a RAM Disk installed. This will not work. To resolve the problem, replace the offending *System* file (not the whole System folder) with a virgin copy.

Interpreting the *Switcher* Information Window

The *Switcher* Information window in earlier versions doesn't offer an explanation of what the different shades mean in the horizontal bar chart to the right of the application list. The darker shade indicates the percentage of the memory allocated to the current application. The lighter shade indicates the currently unused portion of the application's allocated memory. The Free Memory shown is only an estimate and is usually understated. If the free memory shown is close to, but slightly less than, what you need, you can still attempt to install another application. *Switcher* will tell you if the Mac doesn't have enough memory.

The miniature screen shown below the application list is for the application currently checked above. If Save Screen is turned off for the application, no screen image will appear.

MacDraw Limitations

MacDraw works well with a 128K memory allocation in *Switcher*, and works with the Same One Twice option. But, it has a design flaw which limits the amount of memory you can use. Never create a document which uses more than 80% of *MacDraw*'s available memory and never Cut or Paste within the program when doing so would consume more than 80% of the memory. (You can check the amount of memory used in the window that appears when you choose About *MacDraw*... from the Apple menu.) The design flaw causes *MacDraw* to crash under *Switcher* if more than 80% of the 128K allocated is used.

MacWrite Requires More than 128K To Work with LaserWriter

If you are going to use *MacWrite* with the LaserWriter, the default *Switcher* memory allocation of 128K is not sufficient. For best results, configure *Switcher* to allow 144K for *MacWrite*.

Preferred Memory Size for *Jazz*

Jazz requires an allocation of 304K to operate properly with *Switcher*.

Preferred Memory Size for *Laserbase*

The 512K version of *Laserbase* does not really need the full 512K to work. It works—a bit slower—in 235K.

Preferred Memory Size for *MacPaint*

MacPaint will operate best in *Switcher* with a memory allocation of 179K. Also, be sure to make *Switcher* save *MacPaint*'s screen to avoid problems.

Preferred Memory Size For *MegaForm*

MegaForm will work with *Switcher*. 180K works well, but experiment with slightly less to find the optimum memory setting.

Preferred Memory Size for Odesta's *Helix*

Helix requires a memory configuration of 310K to operate properly with *Switcher*.

Preferred Memory Sizes For Microsoft Products

According to Microsoft's *Excel* manual, these are the optimum memory sizes for each of their products in a *Switcher* set: *Chart* – 192K; *Excel* – 304-512K; *File* – 288K; *Multiplan* – 160K; *Word* – 160K.

Use At Least 192K Partition For *Finder 5.2* and Later

Finder, versions 5.2 and later, requires more memory to operate properly. Allow at least 192K in *Switcher*.

QUITTING

Always Quit All Applications Before *Switcher*

Switcher can not check to make sure that you have saved all of your files and have quit each application properly before allowing you to quit *Switcher* itself. Always switch to each application, save your changes (if you want to), and quit. If the *Finder* is one of your applications, you can quit by switching to it and double-clicking on the *Switcher* icon. That removes the *Finder* and returns you to the *Switcher* screen. You can quit *Switcher* if only one application is still installed. The *Switcher* screen disappears and the remaining application appears in the screen. However, the application will be able to use only the amount of memory set for it in *Switcher*. If you want the application to utilize all your Mac's RAM, quit the *Switcher* set and start up the application from the *Finder*.

Emergency Exit In Case of System Hang or Crash

If one of the applications you're running under *Switcher* "hangs" or "crashes," don't hit the restart button or turn your Mac off and back on. First, try holding down the OPTION-COMMAND-SHIFT-Period key combination. If your problem is only within the application you crashed, you should return to the *Switcher* screen. If this works, go to each of the application windows that didn't crash, save and quit immediately, quit *Switcher*, and restart the system. The crash may have done damage to the *System* files shared by the applications, so if you don't quit immediately, further work could destroy your applications and their files.

SAME ONE TWICE

Using Same One Twice with Apple Applications

The Same One Twice option in *Switcher's* configuration dialog box is a risky option. Some applications generate temporary files as they run and may be confused by two copies of the application trying to work from duplicate filenames. The following applications from Apple Computer will not operate with the Same One Twice option: *Finder*, *Font/DA Mover*, *MacWrite* and *MacPaint*. *MacDraw* and *MacProject* will work with Same One Twice.

SAFETY

Safest Settings

The *Switcher* manual recommends the following settings as the safest for most applications. If a setting isn't listed, it has no effect on the safety of using *Switcher*. Also, regardless of your settings, save your work frequently to avoid possible problems:

Preferred Memory Size	128
Minimum Memory Size	128
Save Screen	On
Always Convert Clipboard	Off
Same One Twice	Off
Maximum Number of 128K Applications (Mac 512K)	3
Maximum Number of 128K Applications (Mac XL, 512K)	2
Maximum Number of 128K Applications (Mac XL, 1 megabyte)	6

SHORTCUTS

Keyboard Shortcuts For Switching Applications

Three keyboard shortcuts are available for switching among applications when running a system configured with *Switcher*. Typing COMMAND-[switches you to the left. Typing COMMAND-] switches you to the right. Typing COMMAND-\ returns you to the *Switcher* screen.

Disable Keyboard Switching If Applications Conflict

Some applications (such as *Microsoft Word*) use the same COMMAND key sequences (COMMAND in combination with [,], and \) as *Switcher*. You can use the applications' key sequences by choosing the Disable Keyboard Switching option in the configuration dialog box in the *Switcher* screen.

Returning To the *Switcher* Screen

Four ways to return to the *Switcher* screen are available within an application which is running in a *Switcher* set: 1) If you have chosen the "*Switcher* In Rotation" option in configuring the set, simply click on one of the arrow ends on each application screen until *Switcher* rolls into view. 2) If you click on the center bar of the *Switcher* arrow, the *Switcher* screen will pop up. 3) *Switcher* adds a Desk Accessory to the Apple menu in an application you're running with it—"*Switcher*." Choose the menu item and you'll be right back at the *Switcher* screen. 4) Use the keyboard shortcut of COMMAND-\ to do the same thing.

SLOTS

Don't Forget *Switcher* Has More Than Four Slots

Switcher can handle more than the four slots that it shows on its screen—something that's easy to forget if you're used to a system without enough memory or disk space to configure more than three or four applications. However, *Switcher* actually has eight available slots if you have enough memory and disk space. Just use the scroll bar on the right side of *Switcher's* screen to get at the other slots for configuration.

STARTUP

Create A Turnkey Startup Set of Applications

You can create a turnkey *Switcher* system for each set of applications you use. Make *Switcher* the startup application on your diskette and name the *Switcher* document that you want to use "Switcher.StartUp". Then, you can simply insert the disk you want to work with, turn on your Macintosh, get a cup of coffee, and return to find all your applications and documents ready and waiting for you.

Hold OPTION Key Down To Bypass Startup Document

If you've designated a startup set of applications in a file called "Switcher.Startup," you can bypass the loading of this document by holding down the OPTION key when you start *Switcher*.

Telecommunications

BANKING SERVICES

Use TTY Mode for Banking Services If They Don't Support Macintosh

If your on-line banking service doesn't support the Macintosh, use the TTY mode on your terminal software. TTY is the simplest kind of "dumb" terminal and almost any on-line service can support that mode of operation.

CABLES

Make Sure You Use the Right Cable

Make certain that you are using a cable specifically designed for modem communications between your Mac and modem. The most common error made—by dealers as well as everyone else—is to mix up an ImageWriter cable with the modem cable and then try to use it with a modem. An ImageWriter cable may look the same as a modem cable, but it will not work.

CHARGES

Tips For Reducing On-Line Charges For Investors or Researchers

1. Always plan ahead for each session. Make a list of the specific databases you plan to utilize, and of the stock issues or subject key words you wish to research.
2. Look up ticker symbols, database reference codes, and other shortcuts you can use and write them down.
3. When accessing one of the services, always have the printed documentation handy. All of them have some sort of small reference card that is invaluable for finding your way through the systems.
4. Make use of your software's text capture or record capabilities to save each session to a disk file. Later, while you're off-line, you can review information at your leisure without incurring on-line charges.
5. Learn how to use your communication software's automation facilities if it has any. Macros may seem difficult at first, but they certainly save time in the long run.

PHONE LINES

Failed Transmissions

If you are using a protocol transmission and it keeps failing midway through the process, suspect a noisy phone line. This can be caused by anything from faulty equipment at your end to electrical storms and other interference. If a transfer keeps failing midway, try to get a cleaner connection by hanging up and redialing.

Turning Off *Call Waiting™*

As you probably know, if the phone line you're using with your modem is equipped with *Call Waiting* from your telephone company, the tone for an incoming call will interrupt your session and do all sorts of strange and annoying things. In most areas of the country, telephone companies have modified their equipment with *Selective Call Waiting™*, so you can turn it off. To do so, have your software enter *70 on Touch-Tone™ lines or 1170 on pulse lines BEFORE the telephone number. Hanging up the modem automatically reactivates *Call Waiting*.

SETTINGS

If You Can't See What You're Typing

One of the most common problems in Mac-to-Mac communications is that one person doesn't see what he is typing, but only what the other person is typing. To fix the problem, set the "local echo" or "local character echo" choice on your terminal software to "on."

XMODEM

Aborting A File Transfer with XModem Protocol

If you want to abort a file transfer that you're receiving, type Control-X followed by a number of Returns. If you're the one sending the file, use Control-D.

Tempo

BUGS

Holding Down the COMMAND Key Can Suppress Upper Case Characters

When you invoke a macro in *Tempo*, be sure not to hold down the COMMAND key too long. *Tempo* has a technical quirk that causes upper case characters to come out in lower case if you linger on the COMMAND key. If you have problems with this, use the OPTION key instead of the COMMAND key when you are creating macros.

COMMAND KEYS

Be Sure You Don't Duplicate Application's COMMAND Keys

When you are creating a macro that you plan to use in a number of applications, be sure to look at the COMMAND keys already used in each application. If you don't, you could create duplicates and cause problems. Be sure to stay away from the most standard ones, such as X for Cut, C for Copy, and V for Paste.

CONSTRUCTION MACROS

Keep Your Macros Modular

When you are building *Tempo* macros, use the program's branching capabilities and build large macros in modular sections which branch to one another. Not only does this make editing your macros easier, but it allows you to build a library of basic macro modules that you can link in different ways to form much more complex macros.

Locate Macro Combo Keys Near COMMAND or OPTION Key

When possible, try to locate the key you want to use in combination with the COMMAND or OPTION key to launch a macro as close to the control key as possible. If you have a large number of macros, try to place the most frequently used ones nearer the COMMAND (or OPTION) key.

INCOMPATIBILITIES

Problems With Mac 512/HD 20/ AppleTalk Combination

Do not try to use *Tempo* with a combination of the Mac 512, Hard Disk 20, and AppleTalk. Although the program works fine with any of them individually or in any pairing, the three together do not work. The Mac Plus in combination with the HD 20 and AppleTalk seems to work fine.

Problems With Microsoft Products

Tempo has problems working with some Microsoft products. You may have to use real-time with some of their dialog boxes.

Problems With Other Programs

Tempo has problems with *ThinkTank 512* and *Ready-SetGo* version 2.0. It also sometimes has problems converting the Clipboard when used with *Switcher*.

STARTUP MACROS

Use *Tempo* To Install Itself Upon Startup

A handy use for *Tempo's* ability to run a macro when you startup the Mac is to make it install itself in the menu bar (by selecting *Tempo* from the Apple menu). Then you won't have to remember to install *Tempo* before using Command key combinations to run macros. This feature doesn't work with the Mac Plus *System 3.1*, *Finder 1.1*, and Tempo 1.1, but should be corrected in later versions.

ThinkTank

APPLICATIONS

Organizing and Archiving Scrapbooks with *ThinkTank 512*

If you store a lot of graphics in various Scrapbooks, you can organize and archive them with *ThinkTank*. You can Paste an entire Scrapbook into *ThinkTank* with one command. By returning to the *Finder* to activate different Scrapbook Files (see "Multiple Scrapbooks On the Same Disk"), you can load them all into *ThinkTank* graphic windows. Browse through your pictures and label them; print out the graphics, or just the titles, from different Scrapbooks. You can rearrange your pages and put them all back into the Scrapbook with a single command; the sorted pages can replace the current Scrapbook, or be added to it.

Personal Calendar in *ThinkTank 512*

Creating and maintaining a personal calendar is a less obvious application for *ThinkTank*, but an extremely useful one. Make the first level months, the next weeks, and then days; or, divide the months directly into dates. You can divide the subheadings under the days into time slots, or use them as a general Things-To-Do List (or both). If something doesn't get done on Monday, drag it down to Tuesday. You can assign a priority number to each to-do item as you type it in, and let *ThinkTank* arrange them in order—it sorts any sublevel or headlines without disturbing the rest of the outline. (Since it sorts alphabetically, use the same number of digits in numeric headings (001, for example, if other numbers need three digits.) You can then print out your daily or weekly schedule; Open a text window to make notes about things you want to bring up at the 3 o'clock meeting; and Cut items that you've taken care of.

COPIES

Running *ThinkTank 128* from A Copy

ThinkTank 128 can run from a copy in the external drive if you follow these instructions. First, copy *ThinkTank* and *Tankops* to a disk with a *System* file from the original *ThinkTank* disk. Then, boot the Mac with no disk in the internal drive, but with your copy in the external drive so it becomes the startup disk. Then, insert your original disk in the internal drive and double-click on the *ThinkTank* or *ThinkTank* document file on the copy. *ThinkTank* will look for the original in the internal drive and then run the program from the copy. You can use COMMAND-SHIFT-1 to eject the original, but don't put any other disk in the internal drive or the system will crash when you exit the program.

INCOMPATIBILITIES

Disk Caching Programs

Don't try to use *ThinkTank* with disk cache programs, such as *PowerCache* or *TurboCharger*. *ThinkTank* uses memory in different ways than most applications, and may have problems when it encounters a cache area.

Using *Microsoft BASIC* To Convert *ThinkTank* Files

This short routine in *Microsoft BASIC* converts your *ThinkTank* files into text documents, removing the Header text and preserving the indentations:

```
OPEN FILES$(1,"TEXT") FOR INPUT AS #1
OPEN FILES$(0,"Name for converted file?") FOR OUTPUT AS #2
WHILE NOT EOF(1)
  LINE INPUT#1,D$
  S=VAL(MID$(D$,7,1))
  PRINT#2,SPC(5*S);MID$(D$,12)
WEND
CLOSE#1
CLOSE#2
CLS:PRINT "Conversion Complete"
PRINT
END
```

OTHER PROGRAMS

Opening A *ThinkTank* Outline with *MacWrite*

When you transfer a *ThinkTank* outline into *MacWrite* via the Clipboard, it loses the indentations. But, you can Open your outline with *MacWrite*, and then use Search and Replace to restore your indents. First, Open your *ThinkTank* document from within *MacWrite*. Then, set Tabs at half-inch intervals on the top ruler. Delete the prefix ".HEAD 0 +" from your summit headline and reformat the headline as you want it to appear. Then, choose Change from the Search menu and enter ".HEAD 1 ?" (be sure to use the space characters) in the Find What box and replace it with nothing using Change All. Then, search for ".HEAD 2 ?" and replace it with a Tab character (see "Search and Replace Tabs and Returns Using *Note Pad*"). Then, search for ".HEAD 3 ?" and replace it with two Tab characters). Follow this procedure for whatever number of levels of headings are in your document, adding one more Tab character for each level. You may need to make some manual adjustments to headings that are longer that the width you allow on the page to make them wrap to the left margin of the heading instead of the left margin of the page. You'll still have to transfer any pictures via the Clipboard because *MacWrite* Opens them as gibberish. Text windows will transfer, but will be flush to the left margin with a Return character at the end of each line. Delete the Returns to make them format properly.

Opening A *ThinkTank* Outline with *Microsoft Word*

When you transfer a *ThinkTank* outline into *Microsoft Word* via the Clipboard, it loses the indentations. But, you can Open your outline with *Word* and use Search and Replace to preserve your indents. First, Open your *ThinkTank* document from within *Word*. Then, select the whole document by pressing COMMAND and clicking in the left margin and set Tabs at half-inch intervals. Then, delete the prefix ".HEAD 0 +" from your summit headline and reformat the headline as you want it to appear. Then, choose Change from the Search menu and search for ".HEAD 1 ?" (be sure to use the space characters). Choose Show ¶ to show the number of spaces between headings and replace with nothing. Then, search for ".HEAD 2 ?" and replace it with ^t (a Tab character). Then, search for ".HEAD 3 ?" and replace it with ^t^t (two Tab characters). Follow this procedure for whatever number of levels of headings are in your document, adding one more ^t for each level. You may need to make some manual adjustments to headings that are longer that the width you allow on the page to make them wrap to the left margin of the heading instead of the left margin of the page. You'll still have to transfer any pictures via the Clipboard because *Word* Opens them as gibberish. Text windows will transfer, but will be flush to the left margin with a Return character after each line. Delete the Returns to make them format properly.

Through The Looking Glass

GOODIES

Many Concealed Features

Through The Looking Glass has many concealed features that are not mentioned in the game's rather terse documentation. Some of them are listed below. For a sample, try clicking on the score and then on the resulting Cheshire Cat's eyes, nose and mouth.

SPECIAL EFFECTS

Cheshire Cat's Left Eye Changes Opposing Pieces

If you click on the Cheshire Cat's left eye, you'll find that the opposing pieces change at random.

Cat's Mouth Turns Board Upside Down

If you click on the Cheshire Cat's mouth, the playing board will turn upside down to give you a different view of the world.

Cat's Nose Reverses Mouse Movements

Clicking on the Cheshire Cat's nose reverses all of your mouse movements on the screen. Move the mouse left and the cursor will go right, move up and it will go down. Thrills!

Cat's Right Eye Disintegrates Board

If you click on the Cheshire Cat's right eye, the black hole on the playing board will multiply until the whole board is eaten away.

ThunderScan

MAC PLUS

You Need an Adapter for *ThunderScan* to Run On A Mac Plus

The original *ThunderScan* derived its power from the serial ports on the Mac. However, when Apple changed the port configuration for the Mac Plus, they removed the power supply pins from the serial ports. As a result, *ThunderScan* won't run on a Mac Plus without a special power adapter you can order from Thunderware, Inc., 21 Orinda Way, Orinda, CA 94563, or call (415) 254-6581.

SCANNING

Scan Originals with Vertical Lines Sideways

If the original image you are going to scan has a lot of vertical lines, you'll get a clearer scan if you put the image on its side in the ImageWriter. Use the software to rotate the image back to a vertical position. If you scan such an image in the normal manner, the vertical lines will have a tendency to be quite ragged.

TROUBLE SHOOTING

Check the Tape On the ImageWriter If You're Getting Bad Lines

If you suddenly start to get just a couple of bad lines in your scans, check the tape on the platen of the ImageWriter. If it's frayed, the scanner may lose track of the edge of your image. If you've used all of the tapes that came with the *ThunderScan*, more are available from ThunderWare, Inc. (See earlier hint for their address and phone.)

TurboCharger

CACHE SIZE

Preferred Cache Sizes For Microsoft Products

These are the preferred cache sizes for Microsoft software used with *TurboCharger: Chart*—256K; *Excel*— (*TurboCharger* not practical); *File*—192K; *Multiplan*—256K; *Word*—256K.

DISK SPACE

Throw Away *TurboControl* After Setting Cache Size

You can regain 14K of disk space on a disk you have "Turbocharged" by throwing away the *TurboControl* utility. Be sure you have set the cache size to what you want for that disk by running *TurboControl* before throwing it away. If you ever need to change the size of the cache, be sure you have a little more than 14K available on the disk and copy *TurboControl* back in from another disk. Change the size of the cache and then throw it away again.

Ultima II

BUGS

Myra Breckenridge's Revenge

Any female character in *Ultima II* has to undergo an involuntary sex change operation if she wants to raise any of her attributes. Sad, but true. If you trot your female player character into Hotel California (wouldn't you know it??) and let her loose on the desk clerk, the next thing you know, she's a he. It looks particularly silly when 'his' name is Gwendolyn. There's no way to switch her back.

VideoWorks

MEMORY SPACE

Be Conservative In the Number Of Objects You Animate

Each individual object (sprite) you animate takes up memory space and slows down *VideoWorks*. Be economical in choosing how many objects you're going to animate during each sequence.

PLAYER

Making A Self-Running Animation

When you have completed your animation, you can put it on a disk with the *VideoWorks Player* and set it up to run as soon as the disk is inserted. First, copy the System folder and the *VideoWorks Player* from the *MacroMind Utilities Disk* (*M.U.D.*) to a blank disk. Then, copy the Demo List document from your *VideoWorks* disk and your animation documents to the new disk. Select the *VideoWorks Player* icon on your new disk and select Set Startup from the Special menu. Now, when you insert the new disk, your animation will run automatically.

TECHNIQUE

Study the Animation Masters

Although *VideoWorks* is a wonderful animation tool and its manual covers the most basic animation techniques, don't neglect to study the basics before you try to construct a complex animation. Go to the library and get several of the animation primers and study the masters' techniques to find out how to give your animations polish. Also, the old technique of making hand-drawn "flip-books" helps by giving you a feeling for how the animation sequence works before you try to take on the power of *VideoWorks*. Other helpful sources of information for animation are Edward Mybridge's studies in movement. The subtleties of how a ball bounces and how a man moves his arm have to be studied in the real world in order to make animations of these and similar movements believable.

MAJOR CATEGORY INDEX

Category Index

Category Index

Category Index

Category Index

Category Index

Category Index

SUBJECT INDEX

Subject Index

RANDAL L KOTTWITZ

Born in Blue Hill, Nebraska, Randy Kottwitz has accumulated experience in many fields. While at Western Michigan University in Kalamazoo, Michigan, he supervised crews for over fifty stage productions, taught courses in makeup design and application, and served as musical director for several stage musicals. He was the founding director of the Hartford Community Theatre in Hartford, Michigan. In a major shift in careers, Randy was named Editor-in-Chief of *SoftSide* magazine in 1981 and served in that capacity and as the magazine's Publisher until late 1983. He was one of the very first users of the Apple Lisa computer, the 128K Macintosh, and of the Macintosh Plus. He runs his life on the Mac and has considered a permanent mouse implant. Currently, Randy is president of the consulting firm Kottwitz & Associates in Merrimack, New Hampshire. He and his associates provide a full range of publishing, marketing, trade show, and computer services to high tech publishing and consumer electronics firms around the world. Kottwitz & Associates acts as the Research & Development firm for *MacUser* Publications, Inc.

TRADEMARK INFORMATION

This book comments on many hardware and software products. Many of those products are identified by their trade names. In most cases, these designations are claimed as legally protected trademarks by the companies which make the products. We have made every attempt to credit the appropriate manufacturer or publisher in the following list. It is not our intent to use any of these names generically, and the reader is cautioned to investigate a claimed trademark before using it for any purpose except to refer to the product to which it is attached.

Airborne!™ and Paint Cutter™ are trademarks of Silicon Beach Software, Incorporated; Apple® is a registered trademark, and AMAZing™, AppleTalk™, Finder™, Font/DA Mover™, Hard Disk 20™, HFS™, ImageWriter™, LaserWriter™, LaserWriter Plus™, Localizer™, MacDraw™, MacPaint™, MacPascal™, MacProject™, MacTerminal™, MacWrite™, Mac/XL™, MiniFinder™, ResEdit™, Switcher™, and Through The Looking Glass™ are trademarks of, and Macintosh® is a registered trademark licensed to Apple Computer, Incorporated; BatteryPak™ and DiskTools™ are trademarks of Batteries Included; Bernoulli Box™ is a trademark of IOMEGA Corporation; ClickOn™ is a trademark of T/Maker Company; ColorPrint™ is a trademark of Esoft Enterprises; CompuServe® is a registered trademark of CompuServe Information Service; ConcertWare™ is a trademark of the ConcertWare Group; Copy II Hard Disk™ and MacTools™ are trademarks of Central Point Software, Incorporated; Courier 2400™ is a trademark of USRobotics; Crunch® is a registered trademark of Crunch Software Corporation licensed to Paladin Software Corporation; Deja Vu™ and Dinner At Eight™ are trademarks of Rubicon Publishing; Deluxe Music Construction Set™ is a trademark of Electronic Arts, Incorporated; DiskInfo™ is a trademark of Maltreya Design; Dollars and $ense™ is a trademark of Tronix Publishing, Incorporated; ExperLisp™ is a trademark of ExperTelligence; Fedit™ is a trademark of MacMaster Software; Filevision™ is a trademark of Telos Software Products; 1st Base™ and 1st Merge™ are trademarks of Template Systems, Incorporated; FONTastic™ is a trademark of Altsys Corporation; Hayden Speller™ and Sargon III™ are trademarks of Hayden Software Company, Incorporated; Helix™ is a trademark of Odesta Corporation; HFS Backup™ is a trademark of Personal Computer Peripherals Corporation; HyperDrive™ is a trademark of General Computer Company; IBM® is a registered trademark and PC-DOS™ is a trademark of International Business Machines Corporation; Jazz™ is a trademark of Lotus Development Corporation; Just Text™ is a trademark of Knowledge Engineering; Mac240™ is a trademark of White Pine Software, Incorporated; MacAdvantage UCSD Pascal™ is a trademark of SofTech Microsystems, Incorporated; MacAttack™ is a trademark of Miles Computing; MACBACK™ is a trademark of Peripheral Land; MacCharlie™ is a trademark of Dayna Communications; MacDraft™ is a trademark of Innovative Data Design, Incorporated; MacFortran™ is a trademark of Absoft Corporation; MacNifties™ is a trademark of the Kette Group, Incorporated; MacServe™ and XL/Serve™ are trademarks of Infosphere, Incorporated; MacSpell+™ is a trademark of Creighton Development, Incorporated; MacTablet™ is a trademark of Summagraphics Corporation; MacType™ is a trademark of Palantir Software; MacUser™ is a trademark of MacUser Publications, Incorporated; MegaForm™ is a trademark of Megahaus Corporation; Microsoft®, MS-DOS® and Multiplan® are registered trademarks of Microsoft Corporation; MusicWorks™ and VideoWorks™ are trademarks of MacroMind; NEON™ is a trademark of Kriya Systems, Incorporated; OverVUE™ is a trademark of ProVUE Development Corporation; PageMaker™ is a trademark of Aldus Corporation; Paradise MAC 10 & 20™ are trademarks of Paradise Systems, Incorporated; PostScript™ is a trademark of Adobe Systems, Incorporated; Rags to Riches™ is a trademark of Chang Labs; RamStart™ is a trademark of George Nelson; Red Ryder™ is a trademark of The FreeSoft Company; SideKick® is a registered trademark of Borland International, Incorporated; Smartcom II™ is a trademark of Hayes Microcomputer Products, Incorporated; SoundCap™ is a trademark of Fratal Software; Straight Talk™ is a trademark of Dow Jones & Company, Incorporated; Tempo™ is a trademark of Affinity Microsystems, Limited; ThinkTank™ is a trademark of Living Videotext, Incorporated; ThunderScan™ is a trademark of Thunderware, Incorporated; TML Pascal™ is a trademark of TML Systems; TurboCharger™ is a trademark of Nevins Microsystems, Incorporated; Ultima II™ is a trademark of Sierra On-Line, Incorporated; VAX® is a registered trademark, and ReGIS Graphics Editor™, and VMS™ are trademarks of Digital Equipment Corporation; VersaTerm™ is a trademark of Peripherals, Supplies & Computers; WordStar® is a registered trademark of MicroPro International Corporation;